CATCHING THE NE

The Misadventures of Online Dating

MÓNICA FERNANDES

Published in the United States of America by Evolution Essentials, LLC and Mónica Fernandes

Catching the One: The Misadventures of Online Dating Copyright © 2024 by Mónica Fernandes

For privacy reasons, names, locations, and dates may have been changed.

Book Cover by Mónica Fernandes

FIRST EDITION

ISBN 979-8-9912835-0-2

This book is dedicated to all the women brave enough to dip their feet in the online dating world while looking for a long-lasting relationship.

INTRODUCTION

As I sat in business class returning from the magical Azores Islands, I never thought I'd end up here, a survivor of online dating. Five years flashed in my memory like one of those sped-up movies, part Charlie Chaplin, part Twilight Zone.

The whole dating concept was still somehow foreign to me. I didn't do much of it as a younger person, perhaps because I was brought up relatively sheltered in Lisbon, Portugal. Back then, I was too scared of life or making any social imprint—God forbid someone would notice me! No one ever spoke to me about dating or relationships, and whatever expectations my parents had, they didn't voice to me.

At eighteen, I had a burst of courage and took off for college across the big Atlantic Pond, landing not by parachute but close. Naïve and innocent, with a dreamy filter of reality, I tried to discover my identity. Sure, I had platonic crushes throughout the years, but never anything that would catapult me out of my timidity cocoon. After my first and only long-term relationship, I found myself married and then divorced. Alone at thirty-six, I felt emotionally wounded and fragile, not knowing what to expect from the daunting world of dating, let alone online dating.

I had friends who found their partners that way, and I was hoping to do the same, the never-ending Hopeful looking for the Holy Grail.

As I slowly dabbled in the online dating scene, two imaginary angels emerged on my shoulders, each coming to life out of the craziness and the sarcasm required to navigate the choppy waters of online dating.

The Jokester embodied my disorganized sarcastic ego, who, in many ways, didn't give a crap about outcomes. He was all about gluttony and sloth. Careless about his appearance and nutrition, he loved beer and fast food, none of which I consumed.

Ms. Diva was the brunette European version of Jessica Rabbit, who merged an Amazon warrior princess with the sex kitten within most women. She was a girly girl, oozing sex appeal with a naughty side while maintaining a strong ethical conscience. Romance and lust, two things missing from most of my past, were at the forefront of Ms. Diva's world.

As I went through each adventure, these two extreme sidekicks became my writing companions. Above all, they had my best interest at heart and did an excellent job representing different facets of my mental and emotional universes.

I didn't set out to write a guide of any kind. These stories stemmed from the beginning entries of a log of my dates. Initially, I kept these on my iPad mini due to my fleeting memory. Then, they blossomed into chapters, relaying my stories chronologically and changing people's names, websites, and apps.

In writing this book, I aim to entertain you and provide tips to mid-life online daters to help them avoid great calamities.

As you sift through my dating adventures, you might notice I took some breaks, sometimes months at a time, either because I still split my life between two continents or needed an emotional time-out.

I don't want to disclose the ending or even tell you what my life is like now, but I can certainly share that it was all worth it. Anything is possible, and limits are only real if you make them real.

People often say that things happen for a reason. That statement has always made me uncomfortable. I can't imagine what plausible explanations could exist for some of the things I endured, but I can tell you that harmony can come when you least expect it or, better yet, when you have given up and think the whole world is against you.

These dating adventures taught me many life lessons, where I could dig deeper within myself and discover some shocking albeit alarming things.

Five years later, I went to visit a psychic. I don't think everyone can read energy, but the woman I saw had the gift. She didn't ask me one question and was right about everything past and present. She did mention the future, and I became hopeful that the abundance she spoke about would manifest. I am a believer. The Holy Grail exists within me and is within all of us. In my case, I am living proof that happiness is possible.
1

---

1. Please note: When I used these websites and apps, certain features were limited and set up differently. There are more sites and apps now.

CHAPTER 1

FLAVIUS

Brazilian Let-down

Setting up the profile on Catch.com was hard work: you don't want to give your life away, but you don't want to be vague, either. I had to become familiar with the winking—yes, you could electronically wink at someone, which meant, "Hey, what's up?" or "How' you doin'?" Then Catch would send you potential Catches every day, and you could sift through those after reading the profiles, then click on "Interested," "Not Interested," or "Maybe." Now that has all changed, and when I wrote this, you could pick from "I'm intrigued" or "No way." The writers on Catch.com were working hard to come up with these clarifying buttons.

I was passive during the first few months and more like an observer. I was shy about contacting anyone. Most people who contacted me were left waiting for a reply. I was not interested.

One night, I was at my friend Sharon's house with our friend Nina, and after a couple of glasses of wine, I confessed I signed up for Catch. They were flabbergasted. Probably, they did not expect it from me, but they found themselves curious. A laptop came out of nowhere, and they wanted to see what was on the market, even though neither was looking. Curiosity is a strange animal indeed. So, under the influence of bold, delicious Malbec and girlfriends, I winked away and winked back. This whole thing was preposterous—I knew I would regret it in the morning.

The truth was that I needed to start somewhere. I was paying for the service too, so I had to at least wink. So, one of the winks led to a couple of emails. His name was Flavius. I thought about the name for a second—my nose twitched in judgment. Yes, it's an Italian name. It's not a name I particularly liked. It reminded me of Roman times and gladiators. Of merciless deaths in the coliseum and dictating emperors with head wreaths, thinking they were all that and a pocketful of gold coins.

I should have lightened up—something my ex-husband had repeatedly reminded me to do.

Flavius's picture wasn't bad. Dark brown hair, dark eyes, robust features. According to the profile, there was a picture with a shoulder-length-haired kid I assumed was his son. He was divorced and worked in Cambridge, MA, and I forgot the rest of the details, but I remembered him saying that to contact him, one had to be emotionally stable and secure. Well, I was not emotionally unstable and not insecure. So, through our various emails, I learned Flavius was Brazilian. One side of his family was Italian, and the other was Portuguese. It intrigued me. Brazilians are very passionate. The Italian and Portuguese combination promised to be quite lethal. I was intensely "intrigued."

But Christmas came around, and I returned to Europe to see family. I emailed him, saying I would contact him in mid-January upon my return.

I did. We exchanged phone numbers after I got back, and he called me. We talked a couple of times, and he sounded nice. Brazilians ooze charm, and as much as that excited me, it scared me because they can be players. My friend Lucy, who is Brazilian, had told me as much. Well, I needed to take a risk.

He wanted to have drinks. I was okay with that. As we tried to figure out where to meet, I didn't want to pick somewhere I usually went to, so I told him I would travel to him. He lived in the Taunton area. He chose Benjamin's, which coincidentally was the restaurant I visited with my family when I graduated with my bachelor's. I texted the location, the time, his name, and phone number to my friend Lara as a backup procedure in case I got kidnapped or killed.

I was the first one to arrive. Flavius texted me, saying that he was running a few minutes late. Everything went through my head. I was not dressed too businesslike or looked like a party girl. It was a happy medium because this could have turned out to be a disaster, and I needed to be prepared to adjourn if that happened. The restaurant was surprisingly bare of people on a Wednesday evening, and I felt a little isolated. But the bartender was close by.

Then Flavius came in. He was handsome. He approached me and took the lead, moving us from the table to the bar. Now that I think about it, I'm unsure why, but it was not a bad idea. The place was practically deserted. And the bar was closer to the door.

We ended up ordering drinks. I ordered a glass of red wine. I don't recall what he ordered. And we put in for an appetizer.

The conversation was exciting. Not disappointing to his heritage, this man was undoubtedly a charmer. We alternated between English and Portuguese, a breath of fresh air. He worked in upper management at a construction firm in Boston. He bragged about his management skills and that he had a secretary. I asked questions about his upbringing and found out he went through military service in Brazil, and after that, he moved to the United States for college. I had moved to the US for college, too. He was doing a master's program while working full-time. He was also divorced and had an 11-year-old son who lived with his mother. He was into martial arts. I took seven years of karate in the past. He was still doing it. He was obviously in great shape. Me, not so much anymore. Curvy is the description I stuck with, and it was accurate. I had a few extra pounds, but I was well-proportioned. I had lost sixty pounds and needed to lose a few more, but I was happy with my appearance. I thought he was too. You know right away when a man wants you, especially a Brazilian.

One thing I found odd was that he never asked me what I did for a living. I volunteered my academic background, which satisfied his curiosity.

He walked me to my car and casually mentioned that he lived a few blocks from where we were. He kissed me good night and asked me if we could go out the following night because he enjoyed himself and thought we had made a connection. I agreed. It was an excellent first date, but I needed to become more expert on first dates or dating. Details would have to be determined during the next day.

As I drove home, I didn't think online dating was so bad. After all, I had a lovely evening.

The following day, though, I had one nagging thought. During our conversation, he mentioned religion. He was a newborn Christian and had gone on and on about it. I was not that religious. I had been spiritual but not religious for many years, and before that, I considered myself agnostic. That thought kept creeping up the following day, like an annoying headache you can't get rid of. We texted the location for our second date at Stone Forge in Raynham. I had never been to that location. I was happy that it was another place I was not a regular.

So, as I applied my make-up and got ready to go out, I decided to mention the religion thing. I had always heard that one should never discuss religion or politics because there are bound to be disagreements. I was thirty-six, and he was thirty-eight. We had developed opinions on both ends and beginning a head-to-head argument on either of those subjects would be like a Presidential debate, where no one would convince the other party.

I needed to say something, or the second date wouldn't end well.

This place was bustling with people. I was a little nervous that I might bump into someone I knew from my business networking circles. After all, I was recently separated, and few people knew about that, and I hadn't even started the paperwork on getting divorced. How was I going to explain this man?

He was a gentleman who brought on the charm in full swing. He flattered me left and right. He told me he wanted to feel my lips on his again. And the color of my face transmuted into a scarlet hue because I was not used to receiving compliments. I was not used to hearing how beautiful I was or how a man wanted me. That was all new territory for me. I needed to get the religion topic out of the way. And sometimes, I can be a little too blunt and a little too brutal with my honesty, so I needed to make sure I would do it smoothly and not offend him. I didn't want to do that when this man devoured me with his eyes.

Again, we had drinks and appetizers. He was very masculine, just from the way he ordered our drinks. He asked for whisky, and he was very knowledgeable about it. I knew nothing of the brown spirits. I took a huge breath and cautiously approached the subject of religion. I told him I needed to get something off my chest. I told him I respected his beliefs and how he felt about his faith, but I would not be converted, just like I expected him not to convert to my religion. We needed to keep the subjects of religion and politics off the table, and if that was an issue for him now, I needed to know because that can be a deal breaker.

He seemed very supportive and understanding, and he said he wouldn't mention those topics again and was comfortable leaving those subject matters out of our conversations. I was pleased. We had a lovely time. He was flirting, and I was flirting right back. By the end of the night, he hinted at prolonging the night. He wanted me to either go over to his house or for him to go over to mine.

After two dates? I was unfamiliar with dating protocols, but even I thought that was too soon, regardless of your chemistry with one person. I kept thinking about knives and serial killers and being bound, gagged, raped, and asphyxiated with a plastic bag. Being cut into little, tiny pieces or acid poured over me. Screams, desperation, craziness, total and utter insanity. I have watched way too many episodes of Law and Order, Criminal Minds, and Dexter. And my answer was a definite "no." I was very flattered, but it was too soon.

I went home. I was indeed a victim of sexual attraction. There was no denying it. But I was not going to dive into that pool of desire yet. I didn't know him. In my imaginary code of dating ethics, two dates did not amount to jumping into the sack.

When I got home, he texted me a picture. You could tell he had taken it in his bathroom. It was a picture in the mirror. He was wearing his expensive Brazilian black trunks and his 6-pack naked abs. Holy crap! That wasn't my response, of course, but I probably said something along the lines of "impressive."

Then came the first disappointment. I didn't hear from Flavius for over a week.

Then I got a text: "What are you doing?" as in, "What are you up to?"

Are you kidding me? I was appalled. I gave him a short comeback and didn't get a reply.

My father became ill and needed surgery, so I left for Europe. I didn't have time to think about Gladiator man. I returned to the States, and then he called me again. I told him I didn't understand his sporadic text messages and lack of communication. He apologized and insisted on a third date. I reluctantly agreed. He called me on the day of the date and said he needed to take a rain check: he was in the hospital with a family member who had just passed. He seemed legitimately sad, so I showed him moral support and said it wouldn't be a problem. I didn't hear back from him until a couple of months later. I had another trip overseas in May, and my cell phone's text gong went off, and it was Flavius with the same question, "What are you doing?" I sighed and didn't respond. I wasn't about to waste international texting charges on him. He texted me again: "No more talking?" No response. I was already paying for the incoming charges. He winked at me several more times through Catch and didn't get a response. I was done.

If someone couldn't give me his time and consideration, I would do the same.

I did hear from him almost a year later during the Boston Marathon bombings, inquiring about a booty call. I declined.

And that was my first online dating experience.

CHAPTER 2

JAMES
Ivy League Crash

One month later, I still wasn't very active on Catch. Suddenly, a chat screen popped up, and James started talking to me. I usually ignored those pop-up things; they reminded me of annoying ads, and I tended to x-off of all that. As a rule of thumb, I typically watched recorded TV because I had no patience for commercials, and that fast-forward button was my best friend. Like I didn't want religion shoved down my throat, I had a similar thought process regarding advertising. It seemed ironic since I had a marketing background.

I didn't respond to James right away. I checked out his profile. James was another divorced man, father of one—a professional, 45 years old, seeking women 36 to 50. I decided to respond. Our conversation was surprisingly intellectual. He could spell, which was a huge relief. Most people can't spell anything nowadays with this electronic age and the dumbing-down of society. I thought my parents talked about that back then, and I still thought it was happening now. Maybe civilization was in permanent decline after all.

He was quick and witty, and I was intrigued. His picture wasn't super clear, but he seemed average-looking on my taste scale, whatever that meant. I wanted a clearer picture and figured there could be no harm in asking. Why not? He could say no, and that was fine. So, I gave him my generic Gmail address, and he emailed me a photo. Inadvertently or not, he used his work email, so I could see where it was coming from. He worked for a sports medicine equipment company as a high-level executive. It showed his last name and cell phone number. Deliberate?

The picture was quite clear. He was on a trip somewhere amidst a lush green background. It could have been Costa Rica or some other tropical jungle destination. I secretly wondered who took the picture. Again, my taste meter said: "Hey, he's not bad. I can work with that."

I found Google to be extremely useful at times. Especially if you had someone's full name, job title, and company, you could find out a lot. He was not on Facebook, but he popped up on LinkedIn. And I didn't have to link to him to view his profile. He had worked for the same parent company (a very well-known one), which owned the company he currently worked at, for the past eighteen years. Job security could be an excellent tell-tale sign of a man's character. It showed me loyalty and dedication and that he must be valued or probably too expensive to get rid of. His education was Ivy League. For once, I felt intimidated: a bachelor's from Cornell and an MBA from Georgetown. This man was most likely brilliant. According to my calculations, he had been the Director of Business Development for the past eight years, which made him number two in his company.

A couple of days later, we chatted some more and exchanged numbers. I felt like I could give him mine because even though he had no idea who I was, what my last name was, or anything more than what I disclosed on my profile, I knew the major points of his résumé. I was becoming the female version of Sherlock Holmes, but much cuter, and without leaving the computer screen, so in a sense, more efficient as well. I was not terribly concerned about giving out my cell number as it was not directly linked to my home. I didn't realize at this stage that one could find your home address with your first name and cell phone number.

We started texting for hours. Texting can be pretty addictive. It involved words, you see. And I liked words. If someone were a proficient writer, texting could become a stimulating and creative process. Imagination could run wild; if you were good at it, there was potential for many innuendos without ever seeing that person or knowing their facial expressions.

In essence, you could develop an emotional attachment through text. When AOL chat rooms were trendy in the late nineties, I had my first experience with this, and I knew that one could fall in love that way. At least, if one were like me, inclined to be utterly smitten with words. That had happened a couple of times back then.

James was genuinely reeling me in with his proper grammar and correct spelling. He was turning out to be quite interesting indeed. Then, something unexpected happened. One night, he joked that he would pay me $500 for one night of sex. I was very offended and about to delete his number. He apologized profusely and said that he was only joking.

Imagine Ms. Diva, my fabulous little mini conscience on my shoulder, dressed in red lace from head to toe. Even though she was offended, as much as she got excited with the prospect of sex in general, she was not selling herself, even if it was for a billion dollars. She had her standards.

I was genuinely skeptical. Was he joking? Was it some test? Why would you say that to someone? Maybe this was some Ivy League humor I did not comprehend. It felt dirty. It never crossed my mind to accept money for sex. I knew that's allegedly the oldest profession in the world, but I never went to school for that. My background was in marketing communications, which I was pretty sure was legal worldwide. Ms. Diva concurred.

On that occasion, and maybe blind-sided by his impressive background, I didn't take that as a total red flag, and perhaps I should have. Who knows?

James dropped the subject, and reluctantly, I continued texting him. Sometimes, the texting got quite spicy, and I was surprised when I received a photo of his private member in an eager salutation. Ms. Diva was horrified, and her buddy, the Jokester, started laughing his tush off. Why would you send anyone photos like that? I told James that I was not looking for a booty call. I had no interest in going that route. I was looking to connect with someone, and sex was not my top priority. Don't get me wrong, it was on my list. I believed that chemistry needed to be present, and as much as I felt that the whole process started in the brain for women—maybe that was generalizing things a great deal—meeting in person was a requirement to establish the chemical reaction that can happen between two people. And even though I had the habit of saying that I was always right—yes, I know, it's a terrible thing to say—it's arrogant and obnoxious; unfortunately, I had a fantastic track record of being right, so it was a realistic statement.

James traveled a great deal, so our texting continued for over a month without meeting. Then, he asked me out on a dinner date. Finally, we were going to meet!

He told me that if you're really into someone, dinner is adequate because you can spend more than an hour or two getting to know them instead of an hour of coffee or a drink. Of course, I was not sure which dating protocol book that was in, as I had not read any, but I was sure such a thing existed.

There was a massive storm, and James got stuck at the Chicago airport and could not fly back. He apologized and promised we would get together another time. After his return, the texting continued, a little too spicy for someone who had never met me. With challenging conflicting schedules, we set up another date. The day before, he casually mentioned he had a work meeting the same night as our date, which told me he either forgot about it or it wasn't a priority.

Then he told me he would be busy for most of the summer, and I got the hint that he either didn't want to meet me or had something or someone else in the works. Either way, it would have been nice to know upfront. He mentioned he was tired of me not following through on the naughty talk, which meant he just wanted to come over. Another one bit the dust.

Why did men think that was perfectly normal? It was okay for us women to open our doors, hearts, and legs to them as if it were the most casual thing on the planet. Well, that was different from how I rolled. I intended to establish a mental and emotional connection to see if personalities were compatible—yes, on the physical level as well.

In recent years, I learned that just because you have a physical connection with someone, it doesn't logically follow that you match on other levels. Here I was, coming out of a twelve-year relationship, where I didn't even remember what chemistry was, and my experience with these two potential matches was all about physical pleasure. This subject still confused me, and I felt it was worth exploring further—but not here and not now.

Needless to say, James disappeared. I was beginning to doubt that even if you had a fantastic résumé, it all boiled down to men's genitalia. I was turned off in my quest to meet new people. So, I canceled my Catch membership and thought I needed to focus on other things.

Over a year later, he found me on Plenty of Sharks and contacted me again, but I didn't bite.

CHAPTER 3

GARY
Blast from the Past

I focused on work, family, and friends, and part of me was still mourning the death of my marriage. The more I thought about it, the more I concluded that I did everything possible to fix things. I sought outside support with professional counseling, individual and couples; I relied heavily on my sacred support system and my friends, and the more time passed, the more I felt disconnected.

Even though I momentarily shut off the online dating journey, I still wanted someone in my life.

There is something about things happening in your life that feel uncomfortable, and you wish they didn't happen, but in a way, they are necessary to create perspective within your soul.

Grocery shopping was a weekly endeavor, and even though I shopped at different places, there was one grocery store I always gravitated toward because it was the closest to me. As I was strolling inside with my cart, my heart came to a completely sudden stop. In front of me was someone I hadn't seen in sixteen years—Gary, the first man I had ever slept with (there was not a long list of those either, so don't think you're going to get a pornographic account Fifty-Shades-of-Grey-style, 'cause that ain't happening). He was on the phone, his eyes locked with mine, and I felt I would fall over.

This was the last person I ever expected to see again in my entire life. I was naïve back then. I was a late bloomer in that department. My heart fell hard for this massively intimidating State Trooper with a beautiful brown complexion and dark expressive eyes, and I was smitten then. He, of course, broke my heart, and the last time I saw him, I was in tears, begging him not to leave me. He said he had to because he loved me so much that the best thing for me was for him to let me go. I deserved better. I wondered if he meant those words. It was an emotionally violent goodbye at the ripe age of twenty-two, worthy of a dramatic movie on Lifetime. I thought it would scar me for the rest of my life, and it did, in more ways than one.

But here he was in front of me. He didn't look any different. The only change was that he was not in his blue Massachusetts State Police uniform, and I had to admit that it had always turned me on. Maybe it was the concept of defying authority buried somewhere in the deepest part of my being. Here he was in civilian clothes with a shopping cart in the grocery store I had frequented for the past three years. It seemed impossible. It had to be a hallucination. We both stopped, and I figured I'd wait for him to finish his call, which provoked a weird pause, excruciatingly uncomfortable.

I always vowed that if I ever saw him again, I would call him every name in the book, screaming, kicking, and cursing for the world to hear. Now, at thirty-seven, I was doing no such thing. I just stood there and thought about what I was wearing and didn't feel insecure. I looked good. I probably looked better than when he had seen me last. I was more mature and more confident, and I was sure that no one could ever walk all over me again. Of course, I could greatly debate that last part and write a Ph.D. thesis on the subject.

He ended the call and said hello. I think he was as surprised as I was. Still stunned, it felt like an out-of-space encounter. We didn't touch or hug, even though it had been sixteen years. And even though I was talking calmly, I realized I had forgiven him. I had forgiven him and didn't feel the need to express it. I was being myself.

Coincidentally, he was living a couple of towns over. He had been divorced for seven years and hesitated when I asked his status. He said he was dating, but I was under the impression that he must have been living with someone. And I was not going to go under that tree again. I will admit to you, though, it did cross my mind. He flattered me twice, telling me I was beautiful. I politely thanked him, paid for my groceries, and left without looking back.

Then, out of thin air, my cynical alter ego, Ms. Diva, perched on my shoulder like a supermodel cockatiel and, with semi-closed sultry eyes, whispered in my ear: "Honey, don't even think about it! Been there, done that. Remember the consequences of him leaving you."

I nodded in silent response and walked to my car.

Dumbfounded, I looked at the sky and mumbled, "What are you trying to tell me?" Why was a blast from the past making an unexpected entrance at this stage of my life? Was it a coincidence? I no longer believed in coincidences, but I would not analyze them to death or lose any sleep over them. I needed to focus on other stuff.

And I did, and put the online dating journey on hold. Ms. Diva wasn't necessarily happy about this, as she was looking forward to some playtime. But she shrugged and exhaled instead.

CHAPTER 4
BARELY BARRY

I had a very busy December with a work trip overseas with a hundred travel agents. I spent a week at home. And then I went to see my parents for the holidays. By then, I had been separated for a year and two months. I started the divorce paperwork with my attorney but needed to be more active with the process. It didn't help that I saw my future ex-husband occasionally. He never changed his mailing address, so he either picked up the mail or dropped me a check, as the car insurance bill still covered our cars under the same policy. The more I saw him, the more I felt terrible about dragging out the whole thing, and I didn't want him to be under the impression that there was a chance we would reconcile, even though my love for him had not changed and probably never would.

I was in avoidance mode about lots of things. I procrastinated about putting the final dot on the marriage. I needed to work on making decisions about my job. I needed to work on making more money. For God's sake, my salary wasn't enough to support my household. I was volunteering too much and felt unappreciated by many. I lost the motivation to get back in shape and lose more weight. These were my issues. I didn't want to deal with any of them. Don't get me wrong: I liked myself. Could I be more proactive about stuff? Absolutely. But I knew that I missed an emotional connection. I craved it.

My mother's side of the family was fighting. It was a double-edged sword to have a family business with a gigantic family. I had opinions that I only revealed to my brother, who shared the same views. My brother and I were close. It was not always that way, but now we had each other's back. He also had a rough patch in the last few years, and it wasn't very pleasant to see our cousins not getting along. We only wanted harmony for the family.

During one of our conversations, he mentioned that his friend had had good luck with a free site called Cherub's Arrow. I was surprised. All the successes I heard about were on Catch.com, which, to have full access to everything, you needed to pay for a membership.

I decided that it was time to give the online thing another shot. Let's face it: I was still not going to do the bar scene. I created a profile. I liked that they had many questions one could answer, so the statistical matchmaking could theoretically be more efficient. And you could answer as many questions as you wanted, which increased your profile's completion.

Then, I got locked out of it. These things must now pinpoint where you are on the globe, and since it's an American site, it shut me out. I got frustrated but saw it as a sign that it wasn't the right time.

January 1st came, and we got devastating news. Our twenty-five-year-old cousin was the victim of a hit and run and was barely hanging on to life in the hospital. It didn't look good. We found out a thirty-year-old drunk woman hit him while he was walking with a friend downtown because the police found the side mirror of her BMW at the scene. She was caught not long after, sleeping in her car, and allegedly didn't recall hitting anyone. But she obviously recalled drinking as she refused a Breathalyzer test.

My cousin passed away not even twenty-four hours later. Our family was broken. I changed my flight to depart later than scheduled, and my brother, who was spending New Year's in Miami, made arrangements to return the morning of the funeral. It was hard. My heart bled more for those left behind. God had another angel in the skies, watching over us. I imagined my cousin was with my grandmother, watching over all of us. There was no sense one could make from such tragedies. Besides the pain, the rawness of emotions brought people together, and love blossomed and filled our hearts. It was overwhelming. I tried to be there, I tried to alleviate the pain in others, and I always tended to want to fix things, and sometimes things were not fixable. Sometimes, you were the one that needed to be fixed, allowing the time to mourn. You could not be strong for everyone.

On the day of the funeral, my uncle, the boy's grandfather, who did not know about the death due to his flailing health, had a major stroke, and my brother, my cousin, my aunt, and I stayed at the hospital until the wee hours of the morning. He ended up being transferred to the city and was recovering slowly. But, at the time, it was another roller-coaster no one anticipated.

The day I left Europe, I also found out a close family friend had passed from a cancerous brain tumor. Zombie-like, I returned to the States.

I felt defeated the next couple of weeks, besides some scheduled commitments. I felt deflated and lost. Not just because I was allowing myself to mourn in my own way but because I needed to be alone.

I contacted Cherub's Arrow, explaining my situation and why they should unblock my account, and so after a couple of weeks, they did. While I waited, I also started up a profile on POS (Plenty of Sharks), which was also free. The name Plenty of Sharks is a little weird. I understood the concept but heard mixed reviews about it.

At this point, I didn't care. I just wanted to meet new people who weren't women. I knew plenty of good women in my life. I seemed to get along famously with women. Between belonging to women's networking groups and developing great relationships over the years, I fostered many friendships with amazing women. I felt blessed in that department.

I casually started browsing Cherub's Arrow. I received a ton of emails, the majority of which I deleted.

Then, I got a message from Barry. "And when can we curl up in front of that fireplace of yours to have an intense conversation?" He was quoting my profile, of course. I thought it was a bold move on his part but amusing, so I responded that we needed to start with a conversation first and asked what his name was. A bunch of messages followed, and he gave me his cell number. I wanted to ask questions, and he said he preferred I contact him through his phone so he could answer all of them.

We exchanged some texts back and forth, and he asked me out at the end of January. I spent the entire week with my "goils"—my two best friends from college, Taylor, and Emma. So, I explained the situation. I told him I would love to meet him another time. He said we would figure something out. I agreed. My goils thought he was cute. They even helped me coordinate an outfit together to prepare when we'd go out.

We didn't. I never heard back from Barry.

CHAPTER 5

GARY

Another Blast from the Past

How could it be that I had another encounter with Gary in the same grocery store less than six months apart?

I wore black, and everything was fresh and raw in the grief department. I hadn't seen the man in sixteen years, and here we were!

I thought we'd just say hello. Nope, no such luck. This time, it was outside the store, and he had a couple of bags of groceries in his hands. I shook my head and said hello as if not caring what he thought, and I was yet again perplexed.

We must have talked for half an hour. Suddenly, I told Gary about my grief, and he told me about his. I had lost my twenty-five-year-old cousin to a drunk driver on New Year's. He had lost his mother in August. And that day would have been her birthday had she been alive. I wondered about synchronicity and the atomic order of the world.

Next, I knew, the eye faucets opened, and here I was in the parking lot of Stop & Shop with tears streaming down my face, and him apologizing for talking about this subject and me telling him not to worry, that there was nothing that could be done. He took the opportunity to say that I was too pretty to cry, and I thanked him. It was a very bizarre experience. Ms.

Diva hadn't forgotten the past and scolded me. She reminded me that my past self was probably rolling in her grave, kicking and screaming in fury, wanting to punch him out, tackle him to the ground, and murder him on the spot. My present self just stood there in mourning garb, looking like a wounded angel, vulnerable and pathetic, with emotions raw on the skin's surface. Ms. Diva just shook her head in disbelief. My other sidekick, the Jokester, was watching Netflix and drinking beer. He couldn't be bothered with parking lot drama, but he did glance my way a couple of times.

I cut the conversation short, as I needed to go to my writers' group half an hour away. He didn't ask for my number, and I didn't ask for his. I was numb. And it sucked.

One never expects to bump into blasts from the past, and there is a reason they are called blasts: if you drag your past into the present, it's wired to blow up in your face.

The past certainly programs you, and if you have an experience, in this case, a rapport of a romantic nature with someone, it shapes you. Sometimes, it creates good memories, sets the bar high for the next one, or creates some wounds you may never recover from. Even the Jokester knew what I was talking about. Despite his demeanor and Netflix binging, he saw firsthand what emotional scars could do. They shape you to have behaviors that are not normal. One behaves in self-defense to avoid getting hurt again, and that can, in turn, hurt someone else.

If you don't do any self-analysis along the way, you miss out on the opportunity to recognize these behaviors and habits, acknowledge they are not innate to you, and do something about them. Maybe you can monitor your reactions. This is tricky because human nature can be volatile, and not every situation is controllable, and indeed, not every behavior is either.

The Jokester yawned. He was officially bored. He wanted to turn the page, but there was no remote button for that.

CHAPTER 6

JOSH
Mr. Right Aid

Cherub's Arrow proved to be quite active. I got lots of emails. Some I responded to, just out of courtesy and politeness, most likely second-guessing myself that there should be some sort of protocol in manners when people got in touch with you, even if nothing appealed to me about their conversation.

I never brushed up on protocols. I never purchased a manual of dating, let alone online dating: total randomness and a total lack of preparation on my part. I was emerging as a mediocre student of dating protocols.

I had a clear picture of what I did not want. But I needed a clearer vision of what I wanted. However, one of my big turn-offs was the human inability to spell. That was one of my pet peeves. I knew I was good at languages, partly due to talent and education. My English was probably better than most native speakers because of my overachieving, obsessive compulsion for correct spelling and grammar. Punctuation was not my forte, probably due to a different meter of my native language. However, if English was your first (and sometimes only) language and you went to high school, it was unbelievable to me that someone would murder their native language regularly. I didn't understand making mistakes with "their," "there," and "they're." Or "its" and "it's," misspelling "recieve" and "beleive." And a never-ending list of similar shenanigans that made me sift through endless messages on these dating sites.

I got an email message from Josh. Well written. I didn't respond immediately, and then I thought, why not A string of emails ensued. No spelling errors. He was the manager of a Rite Aid pharmacy in Rhode Island. He wanted my cell number, but I didn't oblige. He started emailing me at all times of the day, checking on me as if I was in some unstable situation needing constant monitoring. It was a total turnoff. That was the end of Mr. Right Aid.

Ms. Diva made another appearance. Sipping on Moët & Chandon, she told me, "Darling, you should be living this life—lounging on a white-sanded beach, being wined and dined and jeweled by a hot, smart, and hard body of a man."

I couldn't agree more. Whatever she envisioned for me wasn't Mr. Right Aid, Mr. Right Now, Mr. Almost Right from the Past, or Mr. Controlling. Mr. Right was, however, MIA.

CHAPTER 7

DAVID
Mr. Not Really Here

Another one who emailed me on Cherub's Arrow was a musician whose picture didn't spike my interest. I decided to respond because he was persistent. I wasn't sure why he wanted to establish any type of relationship when he was in Collegeville, Pennsylvania. I looked it up on a map. My radius was small. I didn't want to drive hundreds of miles to meet people.

I wasn't looking for pen pals either. I corresponded with many people worldwide, but less frequently now due to social media. Facebook changed the lives of so many. You became the star of your page, and your profile was a gateway to the rest of the world, making you a virtual hero or heroine on-screen where your "friends" witnessed whatever you wanted to share with the virtual globe. But if your friends were across the big pond, it was the next step above email because your friend was more present in your mind than if you just emailed them or wrote to them, which, unfortunately, had been getting out of style.

David had a beard and glasses and looked older than he claimed to be. He always asked me how I was doing and what the weather was like. That was the extent of him wanting to get to know me. The weather wasn't great, as a matter of fact. This winter in New England was a harsh one. The Blizzard of 2013 had been affectionately dubbed Nemo, which was ridiculous. Everyone made jokes about the white and orange-red fish cartoon. No one thought about the noun Nemo, Latin for 'no man' or 'no one,' which probably didn't bode well and unfortunately had nothing to do with a cute, animated character. When I heard the name Nemo, I thought about Jules Verne's captain of the Nautilus submarine. It didn't even dawn on me that Nemo could refer to anything else. I imagined we'd be trapped in a submarine, and no one came to the rescue. Lots of people lost power, and the coast was flooded.

I was supposed to work the entire weekend at the Boston Globe Travel Show. Still, meteorology, a science with much amplitude for error, seemed pretty sound, and the State of Massachusetts was on high alert, with the Governor issuing a driving ban. Had I gone up to the city, I would have been stuck there for at least three days. Most of the show ended up being canceled—a nightmarish fluke for the industry, as I knew vendors had come from all over the world and paid thousands of dollars to be there, expecting tens of thousands in foot traffic.

So, I opted to stay home. Sometimes, I would give David short answers or not answer him at all. I didn't want to hurt anyone's feelings: I didn't set out to do that when I started this journey. And I probably didn't measure its effect on my feelings either. I faked that I was always cool about everything, but the people who truly knew me could read me like a cheap Harlequin romance novel—raw, real, emotional, and imperfect.

He used the chat feature once, and feeling bad, I replied. Anyone could see you were on chat, so there'd be nowhere to hide unless you blocked that user.

We chatted a little, and then I told him I had to go work out, which I did, but not right that second. Occasionally, he emailed me, and I replied with one-liners. That was it. Not sure if there was a tragic or fateful dénouement here. But Ms. Diva turned to my Jokester, fat-bellied, impatient, and demanding to be entertained. She was bored, and he just wanted to eat junk food and watch my life adventures as if they were the year's blockbuster. As much as both my little devils were rooting for me, I suspected nothing of interest was going on. There were no fireworks, no red carpet events, and I knew I was boring them to death.

CHAPTER 8

SAM

Picture Perfect

So, as a paying member of Catch, I decided that I needed to become more proactive. My friend Sarah came over. You see, Nemo showed me a little mercy. I never lost power. Thank God and the Angels above because, before the storm, I suspected something was amiss with my thermostat. I had oil, so I was confident about the power source. I pushed the buttons on the thermostat during the blizzard, nervously eyeing all the candles in my house. It didn't matter if I raised it to 80 degrees Fahrenheit (approximately 27 degrees Celsius). My two oil-filled electric heaters saved me from being engulfed by Nemo's cold wind and massive snow and prevented me from having my house turn into an igloo.

Sarah had a lot of connections. And she knew a couple of heating oil men. After a few phone calls and some experiments in my basement trying to flush out the pipes and after dangling buckets of scalding water, two out of the three zones in the house were working. Except for the zone of the main house, my furnace and the rest of the heating system were fine. So, her friend was nice enough to come. He was a little late because he was very busy with people who had no heat in the aftermath of Mad Nemo.

While we waited for him, Sarah advised me about online dating, as she had often used online sites and apps. She told me I needed to be more proactive. I should comment and click the "Like" button to show interest in their photos. So, we sifted through some people, and I hit the "Like" button countless times.

Suddenly, one guy responded with a chat window. He was very hand-some. There were only two pictures on his profile, but they caught my eye. Sarah coached me a little on what to say on the chat. He worked for a medical insurance company in Boston. Divorced, two kids. No spelling errors in the profile.

I should have seen it was too good to be true. Less than 24 hours later, after lots of texting—yes, he had given me his number, a red flag cautiously took flight inside my mind. Call it intuition or gut feeling, whatever you like. The following day, Sarah and I met up at the gym, and in the middle of my workout, I told her about this. She gave me a great idea. Why not ask him to send me a face shot of himself taken at that precise moment?

When I asked him that, there was a long pause. He tried to deflect and asked me for a picture. And I replied, "No, no, I am asking you." A few minutes later, he sent me a photo. The sky was blue. The type of blue in spring or summer, not at present in the dead of winter. His face glared with sunglasses, a little far away, and you could tell it was a completely different guy from the profile pictures. I was appalled. I pointed out to him right away that the image he had just sent me did not match the photos on his profile. He admitted it: "Yes, you're right." I was more appalled. I showed Sarah my phone, and she was just as surprised as me, but she told me that people always use fake photos.

What would be the point of this? If you tried to meet someone on-line and lied about the most basic fact by using someone else's photos, wouldn't that backfire? I texted Sam back and asked who the guy in the online images was. The response I got was surprisingly honest. "Some actor." I couldn't believe it. I was unsure if I was angrier for being duped or that he dared to admit it. He probably thought he would have a 50% chance of me wanting to continue talking to him or dropping him like a fly.

"Please delete my number. This is a deal breaker for me. I wish you luck with your search." I thought my text was adequate. The response I got was a mean-spirited one: "Picky, I understand. Your curvy anyway." Yes, he misspelled "You're." That pissed me off.

I found a second profile with his real picture. I glanced at it disgustedly and saw that he even lied about where he lived. The whole thing was a charade. I was disappointed and wondered if I should continue online dating to find a Catch. I persevered.

The Jokester had BBQ sauce dripping from his stubble chin and threw a greasy French fry at my one-woman TV show.

CHAPTER 9

DON

Hip Attachment in Town

Navigating between Catch, Cherub's Arrow, and Plenty of Sharks, I found that the latter was where men were the most aggressive about approaching a woman. My inbox was flooded with requests and hellos. I deleted most of the messages from the guys who emailed me. I found they had nothing in common with me from reading their profiles, or I was not physically attracted to them.

Chat windows popped up if I was logged in, and I x-ed out of most of them. I got an initial email from Don with just his name. I didn't respond right away. A couple of emails later, I opted to use the chat.

One of the scary things about Don was that he lived in my town. That was a little too close for comfort. He wasn't bad-looking. Not really my type—not that I had a particular type, but he had a nice body. Ms. Diva concurred. We chatted for a bit, and it was entertaining. The next day, he was on chat, and he told me about a program on MTV, a channel I never watched. Catfish Show was a documentary about two guys who helped people who had online relationships but never met each other. However, they had some suspicions about the identity of that person.

The show was on when I was chatting with Don. I decided to watch, and I was hypnotized. I could not believe that Nev, the leading investigator of the show, had been a victim of a fraudulent online relationship with someone he had corresponded with for nine months. And the stories got worse. Some people texted or emailed each other for years and had yet to meet. That was unfathomable to me. How could you not be more proactive and meet someone you had an online relationship with? What possible excuse could be in the way? Usually, there was always some underlying big lie, such as a fake identity or a different gender behind those stories. It was bad. It was terrible. As I chatted with Don, I started feeling sorry for the victims of those scams.

I didn't want that to happen to me. However, Nev and Max (co-host cameraman—later replaced by Kamie) taught me a big lesson that would have probably prevented my experience with Sam, the fake profile photo guy. The giant lesson was a simple one: to use Google Images. According to them, you can drag and drop a photo on Google Images, and Google will search for that image online. I experimented with this, and it worked. I could obtain full names, job information, and sometimes resumes. It was a fantastic tool; I wished I had known about it earlier.

I even dragged my own photo, and I could come up with my own full name. I had a book launch in November 2012 in Massachusetts. It also listed me on a website directory. But that was it, at least for the moment.

I was secretly grateful to Don for letting me know about the show. We had fun commenting back and forth about the victims and perpetrators of the online dating mystery relationships. At some point, he gave me his cell number, and we texted back and forth.

And that was all we did for the next few days. He usually sent me a "good morning" message, which I thought was sweet. I was not completely satisfied with some of his spelling, but I let it slide. I shouldn't expect the rest of the world to spell perfectly, but part of me cringed.

One night, Don called me, and we talked for over an hour. I felt a little excited about the progress. I didn't think he was Prince Charming, but the worst that could happen between us was friendship. We obviously could entertain each other while watching Catfish. There was something remarkable about the whole process.

We texted back and forth, and he said we should meet. He wanted to take me to dinner in Federal Hill, the Italian quarter of Providence, Rhode Island. A friend of his owned a Mexican restaurant there. It's interesting how neighborhoods transitioned over time. The last time I was in Federal Hill, I noticed other ethnic restaurants moving in, which couldn't be further from Italian. And I loved Italian food, so that was unsettling to me. As a creature of habits, I resisted change with some things. Just some things.

He wanted to pick me up at my house. I refused. I mean, I hadn't even met the guy; I did not know him from Adam, although he lived less than a mile from my house, according to his comments. He was very insulted and, via text, was very determined to let me know that and questioned me why I was being so paranoid. I explained to him that it was nothing against him per se, but I was not about to give my address to someone I had never met. I was a woman living by myself and still had some sanity in my brain. He was offended and called off the date. I was shocked. How could someone be unsympathetic to the fact that I wasn't willing to make my sacred space available to potential crazies? If he canceled because of something like that, he would not have been worth meeting anyway, but deep down, I was perplexed. Before we met, he wanted to "friend" me on Facebook, and I refused.

Then he started texting again. I called him, and I was a little animated in my defense. "Sweetie, calm down, you're really upset." He had no experience with Southern European charm and how we expressed ourselves. Sometimes, we were loud, but that didn't necessarily mean we were mad—well, most of the time, anyway. He calmed down and suggested we meet for coffee instead.

Now, things were going to become real. We decided to meet at Panera Bread at 6 p.m. one night, not far from us.

The night before our first date, I slept poorly. And I beat myself up for that. I usually slept soundly and straight through the night. The following day, I was tired. I decided to do something about my puffy eyes. I made some green tea using two bags and then used them under my eyelids for a few minutes, hoping to see a cosmetic metamorphosis. Such was not the case. The eyes were still puffy, and my dark circles were a second pair of eyes. I decided I had to load up on makeup. What would a girl like me do without makeup? Makeup was one of those necessary inventions that had survived for millennia, and thank the heavens for that. I patted myself on the back once I applied my second face. It looked like I almost had a facelift without looking like a porcelain doll. Ms. Diva approved.

My nerves were getting on edge as 6 p.m. approached, not only because of the date with Don but because he had picked that Panera Bread. I had multiple business meetings there and wanted to avoid bumping into anyone I knew. God forbid I would have to introduce him. What would I say? "Hey, this is Don, and I have never met him before?" It would be so awkward. Writing about this made me queasy as if my stomach was churning something greasier than butter or lard.

I wore the outfit Taylor had picked for my eventual date with Barry, which never happened: black pants, royal blue short booties (yes, it sounds crazy, but they looked stylish and trendy), a fuchsia knit tunic hugging my curves, a long black cotton cardigan, and an extra-wide belt. As fashionable as I looked, I was conservative in many ways. I was not revealing much, but wasn't hiding who I was.

I got to Panera five minutes earlier, thinking I might see him walk in. But it was a futile effort as it was raining, and the winter night was darker than black.

I texted my friend Lara, who was my partner in crime, with all of this. I always texted her to let her know where I was. Let me rephrase the "always" part. The only other time it had happened was when I had gone out with Flavius the year before.

I asked her if I should go in or wait for six o'clock. She suggested I go in so I could pick my seat, which was quite clever as I would be in control of my position. Everyone knew how much I loved to be in control, slightly type A. The Jokester snorted, and some beer came out of his nose.

I ensured I had everything—keys and purse—and walked quickly to the door as the rain furiously came down. I was not sure if that was a good or bad omen. I tended to adopt silly superstitions with no factual or scientific basis whatsoever.

I was the first one there. I strategically chose a booth where I could sit facing the door but at a distance. He texted me that he'd arrived, and I told him I was already inside. He walked in, and I got up and waved.

He was better looking in person. Perhaps a little shorter than I thought, but that might be due to my royal blue high heels. He bought me a cup of coffee. My stomach growled for food, but coffee was the plan anyway.

We sat and talked for almost three hours. He was holding my hands on the table at one point, and they got sweaty. I could tell he was into me. My stomach did summersaults even if he wasn't my type, whatever that meant. Type was such a generalizing concept that I decided that at least we could perhaps have some fun and see where it went. He mentioned he had hurt his foot and refused to see a doctor. I asked him about icing the foot and if he had some arnica. He had no idea what I was talking about.

Later that night, after we parted, he called me, and we talked a little more about how nervous I was and how nervous he was. He told me I was more attractive in person than in my photos. I was not sure what kind of Kool-Aid he was drinking, but I thanked him anyway.

A couple of days later, we went out for a drink. I brought him a reusable chiropractic soft pack that could be heated or iced and an arnica cream.

He was very touched by it. But that was me, wanting to make everyone feel better. He was holding my hands again. This time, we were in a local hip restaurant I usually frequented, and I hoped not to bump into anyone I knew again.

I recall having a couple of dirty martinis. I was not nervous, but I decided that Don was not "the right one" for me. For no reason whatsoever, he had no relationship with his family. Both his parents were alive, and he had three siblings. He had not had any fallouts with them. Nothing major happened, but in his words, he was "not interested in having any type of relationship with them." This was strange to me, and I didn't understand. My family was an ocean away. I talked to my parents every day, even if we had nothing interesting to relate to one another. I spoke to my brother more sporadically, but I knew he was available to me. I missed my cousins too. How could this guy not want to have a relationship with his family? And not have a plausible reason for that either? It didn't sit right with me.

As I was talking to him, I also noticed I was doing most of the talking, and he was doing most of the staring. He blurted something out about hoping I was not talking to any other guys on Plenty of Sharks. I said no, which was accurate then, but I was talking to other guys on the other two sites. I omitted that fact because he was getting too attached and possessive fast. He spoke about the future, and I was not sure there would be any with us.

He didn't have many interests other than going to the gym. I didn't think he was very educated; he probably finished high school. I was not a snob, but I tended to get a little intellectual at times, borderline philosophical, and I didn't know if we would have much to talk about, which was not a good omen. He laughed a lot at my jokes, though. I often used humor to relax.

He mentioned the future, and I told him I had a few busy weeks ahead, including a night with girlfriends the next day. It wasn't that I was playing hard to get, but I was swamped between work commitments and friends.

We walked to my car when we left the restaurant, and he kissed me. He was not a good kisser, and I was not used to that—another not-so-great omen. So, I kind of broke the kiss apart and left. He texted me later that he could have kissed me all night long. I bet he did. I was glad it was over!

The next night, I was out with Kris and Dina, my girlfriends. We went to a restaurant to kill time before getting pedicures at a fancy spa and then planned to go out to eat and drink some more – yes, the spa had already given us two glasses of wine. So, while at the restaurant, Don texted me. I didn't respond. He knew I was out with my girls. He texted me again, a little ticked off I hadn't responded. This was definitely not going to work. I confided in my friends.

They gave me great advice, and the consensus was that I needed to stop dating him. I agreed, naturally, but I didn't want to hurt anyone's feelings. I texted him. "I'm out with my girlfriends. I'll talk to you tomorrow." He replied with some "ok" response.

I didn't want to see him again but knew a phone call was looming the next day to put an end to all of this. I was independent. There was no way I would start having to justify all my moves to someone. I knew his wife of seventeen years had cheated on him, but that "paranoia" he accused me of could not be thrown my way. I didn't need it, didn't want it, and didn't deserve it. No, this had to stop. Plus, he was a terrible kisser. The more I thought about the whole thing, the more determined I became. It was better to break things off immediately than to give this any more fuel.

The next day, I had a major hangover. I drank a lot of water but felt the weight of the fun and drinks. My head throbbed, and I postponed the call. My hearing was not the best, so I didn't hear the first text, only the second. The first one was "hey." The second one was, "Hey, this is not going to work out. We are looking for two different things. Take care and good luck." I felt a big smile on my face. I was being broken up with, and I couldn't feel happier. I texted back. "Thank you, and take care." That saved me a phone call. I understood he did not want to remain friends. He unfriended me on Facebook, which was a little harsh, but now, looking back, I guess it made sense. Case closed.

The kicker was that a few days later, he saw that I was online on Plenty of Sharks and initiated a chat, which I didn't respond to. Later, I received a message in my inbox stating that he just wanted to say hello. My response was hello back, and good luck with your search. The case was definitely closed.

Ms. Diva lounged on a red velvet chaise longue, wearing nothing but sexy black lace lingerie. "Honey, when will you be wearing this outfit? At this rate, we'll need to buy some mothballs."

Chapter 10
DANIEL
Cuff Me Now

Back to the drawing board. I was browsing Cherub's Arrow and saw this photo of a man with a crew cut, a little gray on the sides, with the face of an angel. Well, maybe an angel is too religious and ethereal. But he was exceedingly attractive. I clicked on his profile and read that he was divorced, a father of two, finishing his Master's in Public Administration, and serving in the National Guard for the past twenty years. That made him smart and a hero. His priority was to be the best father and person he could be. And he could spell, which was a plus. I was intrigued. I did something strange. I added him as a favorite. I figured if he was ever online at the same time I was and if he had the chat option available, I was going to be notified and would make a move.

I felt like a huntress. And that was a strange concept. Ms. Diva whispered, "Watch out: woman on the prowl, hungry female predator." The Jokester mumbled, "I could come up with nastier headlines by the second." But this was the reality of online dating. If you wanted to be the chooser of people, you needed to be proactive and kind of attack. The more time passed, the more I realized this game had no rules.

One day, he was online, and with the chat option on, I made the first move. The worst that could happen was someone not responding, and I guess there was a 50/50 chance of it happening. He replied. I quickly realized that the chat window was sometimes not perfectly accurate. We chatted for a little, and then he stopped replying, so it could either be the window's sluggishness, he didn't want to talk to me, or he was talking to someone else. The possibilities were endless as to why that was happening, and I couldn't take it personally. I eventually closed it off and shrugged my shoulders.

A handful of days later, I noticed he was on again. I took my Angel Oracle cards out and was determined that the cards would decide for me. Was I going to start a chat window or just leave it alone? The answer was a resounding yes.

So, I did. We chatted for three hours. I was mesmerized. Now, thinking about it, I was unsure if it was because he was intelligent and ambitious or because he wore two uniforms. He was a cop, aside from being in the National Guard.

I had to leave the conversation. I saved the chat. He told me he would be on later, and I did something I hadn't done before. I volunteered my cell number and told him he could text me.

Then I remembered the Catfish Show tip about Googling a photo. I saved his profile photo onto my desktop and dragged it onto Google Images. I got a hit on LinkedIn, of all places. I clicked on it. It prompted me to sign in, and I read his entire resume. This man was a go-getter. It was impressive, and I was proud of myself for discovering more about him, the town, one of the main ones in Rhode Island. From his conversation, he was probably going to be chief. Who was the detective now?

That night, I had scheduled an intense P90X workout with my friend Lara, and I later texted her. "Oh, this guy is awesome... Scared of fucking it up." When I got home, I had a request from him to connect on LinkedIn. I screwed up. I should not have signed in under my account—he obviously could tell who was looking at his profile. I didn't use LinkedIn so much, as I was not job-hunting. And the more I thought about it, the more I realized I shouldn't have jumped at giving him my number because he never texted or called me.

I emailed him through Cherub's Arrow to let him know I enjoyed our chat and that if he wanted to connect again, he could let me know. He never does. His face kept popping into my head, and I felt this slight rejection affect my ego. If only I could have met him. It was not in the cards.

CHAPTER 11

TOM

In Between Jobs

I reached out to Tom, and we chatted. I enjoyed reading his profile, and he gave me his Skype username. I thought that was cool, and we chatted briefly a couple more times through Skype, omitting the audio or video options.

Shortly after that, we decided we should meet. He volunteered his phone number, which was visible on his Skype profile. I never really looked at that stuff since I had only used Skype in the past to talk with my family and friends abroad. I saved his number on my phone and texted him a few days later.

We texted back and forth for almost two weeks. Surprisingly, neither of us picked up the phone to hear each other's voice. "What a shocker!" Ms. Diva chimed in. We then decided on a day to meet. He was very busy with job interviews between Providence and Boston. He could spell, which was a great thing that I always found to be a rarity. Out of the corner of my eye, I saw the Jokester roll his eyes while chewing tobacco.

Our conversations seemed intelligent. Tom was originally from Pennsylvania and was close to his family, which was a breath of fresh air from my last date with Don, who wanted nothing to do with his family for no reason.

He rescheduled our get-together as his goddaughter was being confirmed in Pennsylvania, and he had to drive down. This was the beginning of March, and we had another snowstorm that weekend. This time, the weather people were deadly wrong. They predicted one to three inches, and we got two feet. I was back at shoveling like a grizzly bear, regretting every second of not forking over the dough to hire someone to plow my two driveways. I thought about Tom, who had to drive in that Godforsaken snow.

We rescheduled to meet the following week on a Friday night—time and place to be determined.

I got a text on Wednesday asking to take a rain check because his former co-workers wanted to go out, and the next day, he had a St. Patrick's Day party in Waltham. I was not happy but told him I would give this "one more try." He seemed appreciative, and I told him he would have to make it up to me. We rescheduled for the following Friday. He said it would be better because he was preparing for a critical interview and would not be "quality first-date material." His words, not mine. Ms. Diva yawned at this point.

One day later, he texted me that his friends were total idiots and they fell through, and he wondered if I was still free but that I probably already made other plans. I told him I hadn't—"pathetic," according to the Jokester because he hadn't given me that much notice. I agreed to meet him that Friday night. He picked a fancy sushi restaurant in Providence. I guess he felt like he owed me big time. Part of me felt a little guilty that I would be wined and dined as Tom was between jobs, but the other part was curious about him. I felt like he understood my humor, and if you didn't appreciate my humor, it would have been a big problem for me. I could be witty and sarcastic; I needed someone to comprehend that.

I concluded that one was expected to get nervous before a first date. Ms. Diva yawned again. I secretly wondered how often I would have to go through this process. Two of my friends who did the online dating thing and met their husbands that way went through this process for about two years, off and on. I felt like I was just getting started. One of them said she must have met fifty men that way. The mere thought of a high number like that was daunting enough. How was I going to make any sense of this?

I was finding out that there were no rules to this game. I forced myself to view this as a game. A game of life, and it was hard work. It took patience and perseverance, and I imagined I could go through a plethora of situations I was not looking forward to, with the hope of some carrot dangling at the end of the tunnel. One could only hope there would be light, but there were no guarantees.

I sort of agreed with my friend who went out with fifty men. It had to be a numbers game. You had to have luck at some point. I wished it to be so. I refused to do the bar hunting, and I was too old for the club scene, even if, in my head and my house, I danced my big tush off.

I sprayed Bach Flowers Rescue Remedy in my mouth several times, hoping it would relieve my nerves. It surprisingly did. I looked up the restaurant online and instantly realized it would be a fancier Asian restaurant. They even had Valet Parking. The Jokester snorted as he couldn't care less about those details.

Because I was counting calories with myFitnessPal, I decided that sushi was a great splurge, and I estimated that I would drink at least two glasses of wine. I saved 940 calories of my daily allotment just for dinner.

I talked to Lara, my go-to BFF, about these things. She suggested I dress "conservative-sexy." I was not sure what that meant. For me, it was either one or the other. She said to wear black pants and a colorful top. So, I tried a bunch of outfits on, took my iPad out, and snapped some shots straight to her iPhone.

I was not feeling any of the outfits—one could get self-conscious with these things. After all, you were being judged for your appearance first. The mind would come later, if at all.

So, we decided on black pants, a black top with an attractive collar, and a dark purple, yes purple, blazer I had just bought. It matched my hair perfectly, as I had two streaks of purple semi-hidden on both sides of my head. Even though it was unconventional, I had them for a few years at that point. I loved purple, and it took me a long time to have the guts to do it. I finally did, and now, for some bizarre reason, I could not think of my hair without those two strands. I knew it was a little out there, and I didn't care what people thought. It was my hair, and I could do whatever I wanted. Some of my friends had commented I could pull it off. Whether that was true or not, it was now part of me. And I could change my mind and get rid of them one day. Who knew?

Lara told me not to do dramatic eyes, but you couldn't take makeup away from me. I loved makeup. I told her that I would take a picture, too. So, I meticulously applied purple and black eye shadow with a smoky effect and neutral lips. Ms. Diva lounged on my bed in a black satin robe with feathered high heels and approved of my reflection in the mirror.

I decided to take advantage of the complimentary valet parking.

I got there first. The place was beautiful: on the water, impeccable decoration, great ambiance, and superb lighting. I was excited. I looked around the bar area to see if Tom had arrived. He had not. I knew he made reservations, so I asked, and they said they didn't have them. Plus, I didn't know his last name. Not a minute later, he walked in, wearing a long dark grey wool coat. We hugged. He looked stressed out. My first impression was that his online photos were better than reality. They took our coats, and we followed the waitress to our table overlooking the water.

He was on edge. He excused himself to use the restrooms. Once he got back, it took him a while to relax. He kept looking at the menu, which was extensively overwhelming. We finally ordered.

We had a good conversation, but I did not sense any spark, which was a huge problem. He had also removed his profile from the site because he realized he didn't have time to date.

He started yawning. He must just be beaten by the stress. It was time to go. I knew the bill wasn't cheap, but it was time to go.

We hugged goodbye and didn't make plans for another date. We left it up in the air, but we probably wouldn't see each other again. I texted him. "Thank you for dinner. Get some rest." And he texted me back much later. "You're welcome. Sleep well."

I couldn't believe that my gut was so wrong about our connection. I thought he had gotten my humor over the texts. Looking back, I realized that I wasn't even flirting a little, which was a sign of a lack of spark. And you have got to have a spark. As the Millionaire Matchmaker, Patti Stanger, bluntly says, "You got to have the juices flowing." Crass but true. Chemistry was just as important as intellectual connection, and I was unsure if I was a proponent of developing chemistry over time. That's what happened with my marriage, and I guess I wanted to experience chemistry first as a sign of your body launching the pheromone brigade. Mine was MIA.

Ms. Diva was still on my bed and exhaled a nice big breath as if saying in French, "tant pis" (too damn bad).

CHAPTER 12

JUAN
Latin Hunk

I was very disappointed with Catch.com. I paid a 6-month membership, which wasn't cheap, and I was not connecting with anyone. The free Cherub's Arrow and Plenty of Sharks bred more fruit than the paid, most popular online dating website, which always bragged about millions of members on countless television commercials.

The sites differed, and I saw that a few people were on both free ones, just like me. I thought, why not give this a real shot and cover all the bases?

I got messages almost daily, and when I looked at the guys' profiles, I got discouraged. The highlight of Plenty of Sharks at that time was that if someone emailed you and you didn't respond, every time you checked your inbox, it showed you if that person was online and available to chat. Sometimes, chat windows opened and I just x-ed them off. With one look at their profile, I'd belt out a sound of utter disgust or sometimes a foul-mouthed sailor-like exclamation.

Suddenly, Ms. Diva saw this handsome olive-skinned man with a gorgeous smile. "This one," she ordered. I clicked on his profile and sent him a message. The next couple of days were filled with back-and-forth messages. Then, he gave me his phone number.

We texted a bit, and then we talked on the phone. He had a Spanish accent, even though he was born in New York City. When he was two years old, his parents moved to Atlanta, Georgia, and they still lived there, along with his brother, who was getting married in June. His mother was from Peru, and his father was from Puerto Rico.

We talked a few times and made plans to meet for coffee on a Sunday night.

I was nervous again. I couldn't help but think it was natural to be nervous before a first date. I wondered if all women were nervous before their first dates. I also wondered if men were nervous, too, or if their skin was thicker than ours. The Jokester shrugged while eating a burrito.

We made plans to meet at Panera Bread. I arrived a few minutes earlier, and the person walking ahead of me informed me that it was closed for a staff meeting. Great!

I texted Juan the news from my car. He was surprised. I noticed a white vehicle entering the parking lot, and he got out while on the phone. We hugged. "He's cute," Ms. Diva purred. We tried to figure out a place that was open for coffee.

I followed him. His car had New Hampshire plates, which made no sense as he told me he lived in Rhode Island. He pulled into the IHOP parking lot. Lovely! I couldn't remember the last time I went into one. Ms. Diva wore latex gloves, and the Jokester drooled at the idea. Not the most glamorous place in the world, especially past 8 p.m. on a Sunday—the place was empty but still open. We were only there for coffee anyway, even though I hadn't had dinner. But I settled for coffee.

The more I talked to him, the more I was interested in what he had to say. He had been married for twelve years and claimed he treated his wife like a queen and gave her everything. Then, when she reached success in her professional career, she cheated on him, and they got divorced. The two children, a boy and a girl, lived with her, but he was involved in their lives.

What I found fascinating about Juan was that he appeared to be one of those hip and hot Latino guys with a laser focus. He was finishing a master's in systems engineering, which, in my mind, signified something along the lines of a computer geek with coding and stuff, but he was not your stereotypical geek.

The conversation was so great that I noticed I was flirting a bit, even though it wasn't something that happened easily to me with just coffee—I needed a couple of drinks in me to let loose like that. But there I was, in the extreme, unromantic ambiance of IHOP, flirting like a schoolgirl.

We said goodbye with a hug. He didn't try to kiss me. It was always one of those awkward old-fashioned protocols of having a first kiss on a first date, but I thought maybe the chemistry was one-sided.

But it wasn't, because we went out a few more times and dated for several months. The kissing left much to be desired at first. He started sucking on my mouth as if he was a slimy leech, and bad kissers were the worst. The good thing was that I trained him on that, and as the weeks went by, he got better and better. Progress was part of evolution most of the time.

The Jokester and Ms. Diva sat on my couch, observing the unfolding of two months with Juan. The Jokester ate lollipops, and Ms. Diva sipped Sauvignon Blanc with a pink feathered boa around her neck and a see-through negligée.

I thought the honeymoon phase lasted three months, but technology was now moving at the speed of light, and so was dating. And now the honeymoon phase was shorter, like Daylight Savings time, except it wasn't that time of year.

Juan came over a lot but then realized we were in a full-fledged relationship. He became comfortable showing his true colors. I am unsure what product he used on his hair, but it left a strange stain on my pillowcase that I could never remove. He cooked for me and made my kitchen a mess, but we laughed about it. I was on the fence with him because he became a bit erratic.

I had my suspicions he had bipolar disorder, even though he claimed his ex-wife did. I didn't intend to demean any mental illness. Still, until then, I had never experienced the whole walking-on-eggshells modus operandi: one minute, he was happy, wanted us to buy a house on a beach in Brazil, and sent me real estate links to my email. The other minute, he aggressively asked me why I liked him and told me he'd already budgeted his move to Tibet for two years and that the plane ticket would cost two thousand dollars. I reminded him he had two little kids, and he told me he wanted to escape responsibility.

The Jokester and Ms. Diva straightened their backs on the couch while popping popcorn like bullets from a machine gun.

I made reservations for dinner at a nice restaurant. I dressed up and looked forward to not cooking. My glassful of patience was spilled when he called from Boston as he was getting out of work and told me that he would be an hour late because he'd rather go to the gym with his co-worker. Well, I'd rather move on.

CHAPTER 13
PROFESSOR JOHN
Looking for a Dictionary

On Cherub's Arrow, a professor with a far-away profile photo starts emailing me. I got a little intimidated right away because his highest level of education was a PhD. Academia tended to do that to me. Not that I considered myself a dummy, but this whole stereotype was attached to academia about being too intellectual, not very down-to-earth, borderline pompous, and conceited. I had two friends who were professors, and they were far from any of those generalizations.

Professor John complimented me on my choice of movies, as that was part of my profile—favorite books and other categories, and said he was also a fan of Gary Oldman and familiar with The Fifth Element, one of my favorite movies. Then, he told me about all the quizzes he was correcting. He liked that I was picky with spelling and joked about how I would be horrified by some of the stuff his students wrote. Several emails went back and forth, and I realized I needed a dictionary with some of the words he used. He told me his theory on why women of a certain age (30s and above) had online dating profiles. He didn't think they should be so picky because they didn't look as good as they did in their 20s. That remark naturally ensued in a defensive email on behalf of all women above age thirty, and he then told me that I was taking his email way too seriously.

No, seriously, Professor? If there was to be humor in your email, you needed to give me a clue because I couldn't read between the lines without comedic breadcrumbs. Another red flag to me was his aversion to the word iPad. Don't be a hater because I had an iPad, dude. Seriously.

Ms. Diva's boa almost choked her in anger. As careless as he was, the Jokester was a feminist and was already not fond of the Professor.

I agreed to meet for coffee a few days later, even though he wanted to meet that day. Something I wrote must have sparked an interest.

We decided to meet on Tuesday at 6 p.m. at a Panera Bread between our locations. That chain was profiting greatly from my dates.

I arrived first. Again.

I saw him come in. He was so-so at first glance. I'm not sure why he had bragged about his looks so much. That may have explained why his profile photo was at a distance. His fashion left much to be desired as well. Even the Jokester, who was not a fashionista like Ms. Diva, could see the eighties motif a mile away.

We sat for coffee and got into the wonderful delight of a first date, trying to get to know each other. The professor was not as intimidating as he thought, and I noticed he had some sort of eye condition where one of his tear ducts kept leaking. Even my fat-bellied Jokester was grossed out and desperately reached for a tissue to give to him.

Then I asked him what his problem was with iPads and technology in general. He was a college professor. Whether you liked it or not, technology was part of his students' lives, and if you taught management, it wouldn't be a bad idea to incorporate some semblance of that in your classes. Just a thought! But I was not preaching, just opinionating.

Then, I listened to his marriage story. His wife cheated on him with someone from work. He was pursuing his doctorate, but the divorce set him back, and he halted his degree. Didn't people put their level of education as a PhD after they had completed it? But I kept my mouth shut. He didn't want to bother me with his thesis because it would probably be boring, and I wouldn't be interested in it. "Try me." He explained it—in a boring way—but it sounded interesting, nonetheless. Something about comparing union and non-union companies' management styles, performance, and overall employee satisfaction. It sounded like he should continue it, and it could be helpful for companies, but he didn't sound inclined to.

Ms. Diva yawned and changed into unsexy pajamas. She was officially turned off.

I sensed no spark whatsoever, and it was evident that the feeling was mutual. It was time to adjourn. He said goodbye, barely looking at me. I'm not sure what his deal was—or maybe he had several issues—and we went our separate ways.

Chapter 14
STEWART
The Freemason

I must admit this process can be pretty frustrating. One had to go through messages, winks, and people choosing you (which meant exactly squat), and after a while, you start wondering if the time spent reading and sifting through information is worth it. Maybe one is better off being safe and single without any homework or research on the male species around your geographic area.

I got a very long email in my Plenty of Sharks inbox, which was unusual. There were no spelling mistakes, a lengthy explanation of good character, his passion for writing, and the fact that he was the father of a little girl who lived with his ex.

As a writer, I found lengthy messages in my online dating inboxes suspicious. They could come across as "copy and paste" emails.

I let it simmer for a while. But then I started feeling guilty that someone would invest the time to write me such a long email, so I replied. Two weeks later, which was probably not appropriate email etiquette.

I got a response, and we started emailing back and forth.

I tried to be open-minded and not too judgmental about these things, but let's face it, this stuff was damn important. If I was going to open my life to someone, that was a vulnerable spot, and I needed to be picky and judgmental.

Even though he started telling me that he might not be able to afford a date with me right off the bat, I agreed to meet. Let me back up for a second. I was still trying to get my mind wrapped around this. He told me he was a writer and spent much time writing. He even told me what his books were all about: a fantasy series of nine books. I asked him if he had started writing it, as his detailed description over the phone was very intense. He said he was working on outlines. Hmm, okay. I was the anti-outline queen. Scattered in life, scattered in writing, and not exceptionally organized in that sphere, but that was me. Hence, that is probably why I had so many long-term projects or ongoing novels with no end in sight. So, this guy worked seasonally as a lawn specialist, and the rest of the year, let me see if I got this right, he was writing—or working on outlines, and working—ready for this, at a Freemason Lodge.

Now, pardon my judgment and skepticism. I didn't know much about Freemasonry, but I knew it was open only to men, and it made me think of the Knights Templar, Order of Christ, and secret societies, Da Vinci Code-style. I decided to do a little research even though I planned on asking Stewart about all of this.

After reading about hierarchy and Masonic history, I was still not sure about any of it. Stewart talked about his "brothers," and I realized he referred to the other masons.

My Jokester popped open a can of beer and snorted. Ms. Diva was not very impressed thus far, mainly because he might not be financially stable.

We met at Ruby Tuesday's. He had lovely blue eyes, and the conversation flowed. He was slightly more overweight than in his pictures, but I was not concerned with that; I was merely observant. The Jokester snorted again. Stewart gave me a goodnight kiss, and I was pleasantly surprised. The following days gave rise to lots of calls, and the sex talk started coming up. I told him he could talk all he wanted, but I was far from ready for anything.

He said he realized that and was just into talking about it. I didn't have a problem talking about sex. I was astounded at how stimulating it could be to hear someone else talk about it more than me voicing anything about it.

We talked a lot on the phone, and I felt we connected on different levels. The only thing that worried me was that he often brought up the subject of money or lack thereof, and I was in no position to help or be anyone's sugar mamma. Money was a subject that could ruin the mood of everything as it was our exchange method of value. But the conversations were fruitful nonetheless, so I brushed it off.

We talked about getting together for another date. I scheduled a trip to Cancun in April and told him I would contact him after. He said the following weekend would work beautifully as he didn't have his daughter over, which he usually did every weekend. When I got back, I reached out. He asked me via text how my trip was, and I told him I had a blast. That was the last time I heard from him. I also noticed that he took down his profile from Plenty of Sharks. I left him a voice mail but never heard back, but I doubted it had anything to do with me. It was legitimate to think he met someone else, but I wished he had the decency to let me know. My quest was far from over. Another one bit the dust.

Chapter 15

AARON
Long Island Ice-T

L ong Island Ice-T was the nickname given to Aaron, a county cop from Long Island. Lara, my emergency BFF, said it was a cross between the drink and Ice-T from Law and Order, SVU. It was indeed an appropriate nickname.

Aaron contacted me through Cherub's Arrow. I questioned why he would be contacting anyone in Massachusetts. He explained I showed up in his search—whatever that meant. Just because I was almost four hours away and he hadn't set a geographic parameter didn't make it a good idea, but I had a thing for law enforcement. He seemed very nice, except for his height. I know, I know—I sounded so discriminating.

He was 5'9. I was 5'7, which meant Ms. Diva longingly stared at my high heels' museum in the closet. She wore my open-toe fuchsia suede six-inch heels and waved her long-nailed index finger. "You won't be wearing these without him looking like a little person."

We texted and talked on the phone for a couple of weeks. Aaron was obsessed with his newly obtained German Shepard puppy and unable to leave her alone for long. He would make frequent runs home to check on her during work hours. County police officers worked overtime, much like other police officers. These overtime sessions included standing around doing nothing, doing much the bare minimum in construction details, sitting in their cars, and not even directing traffic. They made at least three times as much as I did and were not using their brain most of the time. Maybe I could have done that job. This was my assessment after having dated two police officers.

And Aaron had time to text me. Your tax dollars at work, ladies and gentlemen of New York State. He suggested we meet but wanted me to pick him up in Bridgeport, Connecticut, two and a half hours away, as he was taking the ferry from the very convenient Long Island location mere minutes from his house. He had the excuse of his dog. He must not have heard of doggy daycare. Why would you buy a dog in the first place, especially when so many needed homes at shelters? We all know that a man's best friend needs more attention than their feline counterpart. Or maybe he shouldn't have selected women more than fifteen minutes away from his house!

I agreed to meet him even if I was the one doing most of the driving. I was trying to be more flexible, make more concessions, and be more diplomatic. I wasn't great at that.

The day before our first meeting and my drive down, he told me he needed to cancel as his neighbor and friend had passed away. Our texting relationship dwindled after that as he insisted I drive to his house in Long Island, and I refused.

Long Island Ice-T bit the dust, and I was still thirsty.

The Jokester opened another can of beer. Not my drink of choice. Ms. Diva toasted me with a glass of bold Cabernet Sauvignon. She downed a big gulp—un-ladylike for her but necessary. Otherwise, she'd have to get up and prance on those pink open-toe heels to make herself an extra dirty vodka martini with three olives. She didn't feel like getting up.

CHAPTER 16

ANDREW

Chance Encounter

After a week at Ocean Park, Maine, running down and tired, where I poured of myself at a Writers Conference, I looked forward to spending a few hours at the beach before my two-hour ride home. At the end of the conference, the conference organizers and friends of mine invited me to lunch, but knowing my propensity for the beach, they gave me the option of lunch or an early dinner. I opted for lunch so I could go straight home from the beach.

We went to Clam Bake, a restaurant about ten minutes away. I was there the year before with them, and I had forgotten it was also close to the ocean. I could go to the beach after lunch, but between my poor sense of direction and not feeling like plugging in the GPS, I followed their silver Jeep back to Porter Hall at Ocean Park as they still had to do some conference cleanup. We said goodbye. I saw my friend's hand wave from the driver's side window. I beeped the horn a couple of times, and we went our separate ways. I found a parking spot ahead not far from the beach near the tennis courts. I dreaded the thought of yellow balls shattering my car windows but dismissed it. I grabbed my beach bag, containing my towel and sunscreen; that's all I needed.

I walked by the Soda Fountain and the library and climbed the small dune with the muted wooden path to the beach. It was high tide, and this was a more civilized beach compared to Old Orchard Beach. Even though it was the same stretch of sand, Old Orchard had the pier, the amusement park, and a stampede of French Canadians plopping their gear inches from your towel.

I found a spot closer to the water, slightly slanted. The beach was not overly crowded, and I was happy with the location. I laid out my pink and purple printed towel and removed my shorts and shirt. I had no business wearing a bikini due to extra weight, but I was under the impression I was proportionate enough, and my belly needed some sun to make up for all those lost years of darkness. Ms. Diva approved. I sprayed SPF 30 Australian Gold with Bronzer with its pineapple fragrance, transporting my olfactory brain to some white sanded beach in the Caribbean. I wore new bottoms—black boy shorts which held everything in place. My top matched my towel, pinks, and blacks in leopard print, my wild side peeking at the sun. There was not as much seaweed as the previous day. I lay down and noticed the sun warming my skin with the cool breeze, providing some relief. I didn't feel like reading or writing. My mind wanted to soak up the last hours of sun before I went back to reality in Massachusetts. My shoulders inched into the sand beneath me, and I sighed in relief. Both Ms. Diva and the Jokester were thrilled.

I sensed peace approaching. Muscles began to relax, my skin smooth and brown, rejoicing. I heard voices approaching, and to my surprise, an entire family parked their stuff less than two feet from my growing serenity. I shook my head in annoyance but said nothing while my eyes threw daggers in their direction. It wasn't the kids who were bothering me but the father and grandfather close to me. They were so loud. They could have picked countless different spots on the beach. I told myself I should lighten up. The Jokester told me not to allow them to ruin my last precious vacation moments. Then, the father rotated his chair to be parallel with my towel. Hell no!

I decided to relocate my stuff toward the back of the beach. I found a nice clearing and decided that if it happened again, it would be time for me to call it a day. I repeated the process of getting settled. I sat down again, slid my bra straps under my arms to avoid unnecessary tan lines, and lay back down, removing my sunglasses to prevent raccoon eyes. I had enough dark circles as it was. I was ready. Ready to lounge and let these sunrays do their job. Ms. Diva told me this was as close to heaven as possible. Her beach body was way better than mine, without cellulite nor a middle "situation," and her bikini was out of a Sports Illustrated cover.

"Excuse me." The man's voice above me made me practically jump off my towel. He was handsome, I thought. "I hope I'm not bothering you. I was just on my way out of the beach. I live a couple of streets down from here. I'm Andrew."

He reached down and shook my hand. I told him my name and tried to compute what was happening.

"Are you from this area?" He seemed so tall to me. "I come to this beach every day but have never seen you."

"I live in Massachusetts. I just finished a Writers' conference in town and am just spending the last moments here before I have to drive down."

"Do you write for a living?"

"Kind of," I smirked.

"I also write, but about existentialism."

I was dumbfounded. I hadn't heard that word since my intense philosophy classes at the French Lycée back home over twenty years earlier.

He continued. "I'm a professor with a Ph.D. in psychology, and have my psychotherapy private practice, specializing in men."

"I don't specialize in men." We both laughed.

He loved the arts and reading but didn't watch the news or read newspapers. "Neither do I," I responded. Maybe I was being punked. I looked around to see if cameras were going to pop out of the sand.

He asked me if I would like to have coffee in the Boston area. He talked about museums. I said, "Sure." He told me he had nothing in his pockets and asked if I texted. My phone was resting on my towel, probably as stunned as I was, but as if nodding its head. "Yeah, I text." My chest was being held by the bra straps underneath my arms. If I tried to sit up, I'd give him a show, so I just remained there, talking to him, thinking how messy my hair must have been in my imperfect ponytail with wild, frizzy wisps around my face. And my face, God forbid, had no makeup! I didn't even have sunglasses on; I was squinting like an idiot. Yeah, real attractive.

I grabbed my phone and took down his information, realizing that the story would end there if I didn't initiate communication with him. And he left.

I felt the breeze across my face and wondered if this was all a dream. Where were the cameras? My brother called me right away after I texted him. I relayed the story, and he asked me the same question. Was this a joke? Even the Jokester thought it was a joke, as he lathered some oil on his body and soaked up the sun.

I hung up the phone and checked in with my intuition while my mind still yelled in disbelief.

I realized Andrew had taken a considerable risk. I had the control. I could start communication or just go about my life wondering about this man. My grandmother came to the forefront of my thoughts. She'd been gone for twenty years. The anniversary of her death was the following day. I didn't typically feel her presence, but maybe she had sent him to me. He appeared out of the sky above me. He later told me that something had been preventing him from exiting the beach without trying to talk to me. Perhaps the forces that be. He also told me he wasn't supposed to be at "our beach" that day, but his afternoon clients had canceled, allowing him to come for his daily swim.

Ms. Diva sighed, waiting for the credits to roll, "...and they lived happily ever after," along with "The End."

CHAPTER 17
NO HAPPY ENDING YET

I, indeed, texted Andrew. In less than twenty-four hours, I shivered and relished in what I now realized was magic. He called it fate and destiny. He said he had dreamed about me, and there I was. I was under the impression that such stories were works of fiction in the fairytale category. The more we talked later, the more I realized the serendipitous nature of destiny: the moon, the stars, and the sun lining up on purpose just for us. My grandmother must have waived her magic wand of love and sprinkled it on us, on two people who probably would have never met, or maybe we would have eventually found each other.

This story had all the ingredients for a happy ending. Even the Jokester got a little teary-eyed, and Ms. Diva sighed at the possibility of lots of sex and babies.

Andrew and I dated for a couple of months. Some might think that his being in Maine was the relationship's demise. I didn't believe in long-distance relationships —that was true. However, that was not the reason why it failed.

One gets to know another, and as I said before, the honeymoon phase was no longer three months but less.

Andrew lived on the upstairs floor of a house on campus, home to deeply psychologically disturbed children ages five to eighteen. He was one of the psychotherapists on call and a professor at an online university. He was the thesis advisor to students pursuing their graduate degrees in psychology and had a private counseling practice.

Naturally, I was intellectually turned on because there was someone who had more degrees than me and kept texting me Neruda love quotes. Our physical chemistry was off the charts. I was smitten. I saw an ecstatic Jokester dry-humping a pillow on the couch and Ms. Diva stretched like a cat in heat on my bed, wearing nothing. Both my little devils were happy, and so was I.

He certainly liked to text. Whenever I tried to call him up, he never picked up. Later, I discovered he had a phone call aversion: he associated voice phone calls with conflict. I could see my psychologist friends' heads spin like a poltergeist.

Andrew came from an academic family; his dad was also a psychotherapist at the campus where Andrew lived. With a journalistic background, his mom had been a public relations director for a hospital and was now retired. His sister was married to a minister and had two boys. He explained that, for whatever reason, the four of them lived with his parents in Portland. That was unusual, especially after learning that the sister's marriage wasn't great.

Andrew was divorced and had sixteen-year-old twins, a boy and a girl. He claimed to get along well with his ex-wife, who had a boyfriend of her own and was very happy. I thought that was nice, even if it seemed like a lot to take in.

He mentioned something about me meeting his kids. It had been a month, and I told him I was not ready. He asked if he could introduce me to his parents, and I agreed to meet them, which meant meeting his sister and brother-in-law as well, as they all lived under the same roof.

Before then, he came down to Massachusetts to visit me and cut his trip short, having to leave early as his dad had to go to the hospital with suspicions of a heart attack, which ended up being a panic attack.

That's what he told me anyway. Before I left for Maine to meet the parents, he asked me not to mention the hospital incident. I wondered why. I asked him about it, and he said it concerned his dad's pride. His father wouldn't feel at ease. Okay. The Jokester was scratching his head.

On the drive up, I felt nervous about meeting the parents. I hadn't met any significant other's parents in over a decade. I felt like I would be placed on a slab of judgment with a lynching potential—never a good feeling.

I had bought a Pier One candle for his parents as a thank-you-for-having-me gift because I had always been taught not to show up empty-handed at anyone's house.

I parked at the campus where he lived, and Andrew drove us into Portland. He casually asked if I wanted to stop by his office and see it beforehand. I agreed. He turned into a residential street and parked his car in front of a house. He pointed to it. "That's my parents' house." Then he pointed to the house next door and added, "That's where my ex-wife lives with our kids, and it's where my office is."

Ms. Diva clutched her hand to her heart as if having a heart attack.

Huh? I told him I didn't understand. Was he planning on walking into his ex-wife's house, where his office was, trailing me behind him? Partially frozen in the passenger seat of his car, I was not in the mood to get out.

"Where is this dinner happening?" I asked him.

He pointed to his ex-wife's house.

You had to be fucking kidding me! Then he said that it was their homecoming dance, and all the kids were getting ready for it, and he had been slow cooking something in his ex-wife's house since that morning.

I didn't think my mind could handle all this. Andrew got out of the car. Like a robot, I followed him, baffled and shaking. What was I doing?

"How could you do this to me?"

He didn't respond. Ms. Diva transformed into sleek ninja gear made of black leather, ready to obliterate Andrew.

We walked into the house, and not even a minute later, someone was coming up from the basement. It was his ex-wife. In the next half hour, I met his kids, his nephews, the kids' friends, his parents, his sister, and his brother-in-law. Everyone knew I was coming except me. And this dinner had nothing to do with me meeting the parents. It was all about the homecoming dance and the kids. I had told him I wasn't ready to meet his kids. That was ignored.

It took me a while to digest all this information. Of course, I was polite and didn't even think of ruining the evening. I enjoyed talking to his family, especially his mom, who asked me to friend her on Facebook. She seemed normal.

All in all, I behaved like a lady. Ms. Diva threw her undulating Lauren Bacall dark waves over her shoulder, still dressed as a ninja. Looking back, I felt betrayed and lied to, and I didn't know why I should continue the relationship.

He convinced his ex-wife to turn her sunroom into his private psychotherapy office to save money. I concluded the whole clan mentality was worrisome: the parents, sister, brother-in-law, and nephews lived next door to the ex-wife and children. How in the world was I going to fit into this scenario?

The next time he came to Massachusetts was the last time I saw him. He cut our weekend short again, making me doubt if his father had gone to the hospital a few weeks earlier. This time, his kids had been caught drinking at a Halloween party, and his ex-wife and sister couldn't stop texting him, and he proclaimed himself to be the core of this family. That made perfect sense, as Andrew, the Core, was falling apart right before me. I ended up canceling the reservations I had made that weekend. Again.

I concluded that Andrew was emotionally immature with his obsession with texting me and not dealing with things over the phone or in person like an adult. It was ironic for a psychotherapist, but it didn't surprise me.

In addition, I realized he was so selfish that things had to revolve around his world. A good example was when we were relaxing at my house once, and out of the blue, he asked me if I could go outside to his car to pick up the trash from the passenger seat—just because he didn't feel like doing it. I was even more alarmed when I did it. The Jokester hit me over the head with a baseball bat, screaming at me, "What the hell are you doing? What's wrong with his legs? He's a selfish asshole, and you should use the bag full of trash and beat the shit out of him." I was appalled at my obedience.

I never saw him again. He tried for the next few months to get me back, but the big news I was dealing with was that I loved myself. I was not okay with being treated poorly and expected others to treat me like I deserved—with respect, thoughtfulness, and kindness.

One of the times on the phone—yes, he did pick up the phone numerous times to try and convince me that he was going to step up and be the man he knew he could be (yeah, right, the Jokester was rolling in a mud bath, and would not stop laughing), I channeled my Jokester during the call. "I'm not picking up your fucking trash."

CHAPTER 18
A PAUSE

I took a hiatus of over three months after investing time in Andrew. So, back to the drawing board. I reactivated Cherub's Arrow and Plenty of Sharks. I didn't bother with Catch—too much money and no return. I decided to upgrade my Cherub's Arrow membership because out of the three, I liked that one the best at the time. I was not a math person, but the endless questions boded well statistically, as it could match you more efficiently.

I had a house guest who was temporarily living with me, and she laughed quite a bit at my expense when I showed her the caliber of men who emailed me through those two sites. Now, it was time to be picky, so if looking at a picture caused repulsion or reading a profile left me nauseous, it was time to keep searching for the Holy Grail of the One, if there was such a thing. Men of all colors and sizes, practically illiterate candidates who didn't bother to read my profile and only looked at photos. Then I got the twenty-one to twenty-five-year-olds who claimed to like older women. I didn't know if I should laugh or cry.

A very handsome twenty-five-year-old emailed me, and I, incredulously and in a moment of sheer stupidity, gave him my phone number. I shouldn't have been surprised to learn that this young male specimen had a very kinky side, a foot fetish, and an obsession with opaque pantyhose. My shock continued when he divulged he was a habitual porn watcher. I should have called his mother if I ever bothered to give continuity to this charade. I got the impression that all he wanted was sex, but I may have been wrong. I stopped texting him because it was around Thanksgiving, and I was too busy and stressed. In addition, my divorce was final, with lawyer meetings and court rulings. Even though the thought of being seduced by a hot twenty-five-year-old independent man enticed part of me, it screamed trouble and was too much of a headache for my current reality.

I moved on.

And here started a series of short-lived online scenarios amounting to nothing but more frustration and more desperation.

The holidays were around the corner. I flew home. I bought myself an upgrade at the airport, even though I shouldn't have. Ms. Diva loved luxury and being catered to, and the Jokester sipped on free alcohol the whole time.

The ex-boyfriend from Maine kept texting me every couple of days like clockwork. I decided that having a long-term relationship via text was not what I was looking for. As much as on paper or a digital screen, he looked good, his incapacity to act on his words spoke louder than anything while triggering memories of my marriage. This girl had learned. Or at least she thought she had. Sometimes, I wondered if I needed to be slapped upside the head so I didn't repeat mistakes or make poor choices. In this online dating world, it would be considered giving fuel to the fire by nurturing communications I knew could be hazardous to my health or knew they were dead ends right away.

One of the guys I talked to commented that I must receive many messages, that every man must want me, and that I must have men pursuing me at all times of the day. He was perplexed about why I was on a dating site. Yeah, okay, Planet Earth was calling. But it made me realize that I was surrounded mainly by women, and the men in my life were either married, gay, or unavailable. I had passed the clubbing age and didn't go to bars to meet or hunt men.

I asked myself if I was being too picky about looks, the content of their profile, and spelling mistakes. Was I too wrapped up in my pet peeves and overlooking someone I shouldn't? Should I follow my mind or my heart?

I didn't want to fall into the trap of settling for someone I knew from the get-go would break my heart or not treat me right. I was working on my flexibility. Yes, Tauruses tended to have inflexible tendencies. But with this growing flexibility came the risk of compromising oneself and tolerating situations and behaviors I told myself I would not again. Double-edged sword indeed.

The big conclusion was to stick to my guns and keep following my intuition. When the ex/exes came calling, I had to put my foot down and imagine fireworks dancing on the horizon.

CHAPTER 19
UPGRADE

I kept ignoring the international texts from Andrew. You'd think he would get the message with my silence. I felt terrible when Christmas Day arrived, and against my better judgment, I wished him a Merry Christmas too. Of course, that opened the door for a series of texts that flooded my cell phone, and I decided to be brutal and tell him that I was not at a point where I needed a complicated person. I wanted easy, after all. How about normal? That would be nice too. But as time passed, I felt like there was no such thing. You might as well be seeking the Holy Grail. Was that treasure ever found? Only in legend, correct?

In my mind, when someone claimed I was the best thing that ever happened to him and that our connection was unprecedented, they would treat me right, not hurt my feelings, and do everything in their power to make amends and genuinely apologize.

But from Andrew, I only heard words. I like words. Words are my best friends. I think they are excellent. I love using them. Language was one of the universe's most remarkable creations. Language allows us to interact, communicate, create connections, and forge relationships. Words were one of the most powerful tools ever invented. But words became superfluous when they stayed in the air and were not followed by action or behavior. I was also a big fan of being proactive and acting according to your words. Andrew did not abide by his words.

The next step for the ex was to start calling me. Internationally. Every. Day. Until I returned to Boston. Again, all promises and words with no action. I didn't believe in unicorns. Thank God the telephone connection was through WIFI; otherwise, I would have turned off my phone. As I listened to his words, I wanted to believe him. I wanted to believe in our initial magic, forget the hurt, broken promises, and a grown man's immature and selfish behavior. I tried to set aside my not-neutral positioning as I couldn't admit that I was still feeling burned even to give this man a second or third chance. He told me he would prove his words with action once I returned to the United States. My gut was throwing me a red flag party. It was popping like balloons, and I wanted to pretend I didn't see or hear the commotion. As I tried to brush my hopes aside, I decided to upgrade my memberships to the two free sites I was on and sign up with Happiness Now. A friend of mine swore by it. This was how she met her husband, and she had several friends who were in stable, normal—go figure—and happy relationships.

I did the upgrades and got a new membership. I was beginning to take this whole online approach as an investment in my wallet. The Jokester reminded me how much I was saving from drifting from bar to bar to bar, which was something I wouldn't like anyway. He would, of course.

Going back to words and language. Words enabled me to start a connection in a virtual world, a mind-blowing fact. Maybe I could use words to find Mr. Right. I was still skeptical about the whole process. I was not one of those girls who was a serial dater or would agree to meet with every guy who messaged her.

I was visiting a friend who was going through chemotherapy. One of her male friends was also there. We were all single and divorced. Shocker! Our conversation quickly turned to the dating process. I was grateful to get a man's point of view. Granted, it was only one man and one opinion, but it was valuable. He told me he dated a lot and that many gorgeous women were available. And I even knew some of them.

Inside, I felt a little deflated. And I knew I was not everyone's cup of tea. He also mentioned that there was a demand for men. Some sites had contacted him and practically begged him to join. He wasn't all that. And he was not my type. Not that I had a type, but if I did, he wouldn't be it. The conversation reverted to the subject of sex, which was usually very prevalent in men's minds. I offered: "That's what all men seek. They're not looking for a relationship." His body posture changed, and he seemed offended. I told him about some of the messages I received. He was amazed that I had gotten so many photos of men's private parts without asking. I told him that was why I had my opinions. He told me, "Yes, sex is on men's minds, but ultimately I am looking for a partner."

I was left wondering if I believed a word he was saying. This guy had been divorced for fifteen years and was a serial dater. What kind of partner could he be looking for? He said that there were a lot of crazy women out there. I felt like I was in a focus group. This could be an idea. I should start one. Maybe it would give me more insight into the opposite gender, whom I concluded I could not comprehend most of the time.

I sighed mentally. Back to the drawing board. I was doing that a lot. And by the way, the ex-boyfriend vanished once I returned to the States. Ms. Diva was sharpening knives. My faith in words remained but not in his.

CHAPTER 20
STEVE

I got back to Cherub's Arrow. Plenty of Sharks made me nauseous with all the creepy messages. I was not interested in being anyone's submissive. I had enough Fifty Shades of Stress in my life to add that to my man-finding list. These guys looked good on paper, but when interaction commenced, I found out what they were after. Even though I was not going out that much, I liked to think of myself as no longer a novice in this process.

Steve emailed me. He was cute. His profile said he was forty-two and lived in Providence, RI. That seemed like a sensible age. He flattered me by telling me I must be getting hundreds of messages and constantly going out on dates. Yeah, I must be in high demand on everyone's list. NOT. As we talked back and forth, he seemed like an interesting guy. He was in Finance. Stocks, annuities, and stuff that was as foreign to me as math, Chinese, or Aramaic. Totally over my head.

I found out he had finished college, which was refreshing. My friend Rita told me I was being too judgmental and shouldn't just look at college degrees and PhDs. I was more inclined to agree with her. Look at where it had gotten me: two highly educated, short-lived boyfriends, a bipolar one, and one with an adolescent complex living in academic theory.

Very quickly, I concluded that Steve was only looking for a fling. He told me that he had had some crazy dates. My curiosity was piqued; I asked him to share. I should have kept my mouth shut.

He told me that a woman he was chatting with told him she was married and wanted him to go over and have sex with her while the husband watched. I almost fell off my chair when he told me he had gone. The Jokester was alternating between popcorn and beer. Ms. Diva was taking a nap.

I should have stopped communicating with him at this point, but I had to admit that this story sounded so outlandish that I felt I needed to sit back, get some popcorn, and watch this train wreck of a soap opera.

He told me more stories. My imaginary popcorn filled my curious appetite.

I kept telling myself I should click off and stop all communication. There was no future here. Steve was too wild and too crazy for my taste. But I was hypnotized by his stories.

I decided to lean back, relax, and observe.

During our increasingly shocking conversation, I found out some things about Steve.

One: he had a girlfriend.

Two: he cheated on his girlfriend. Occasionally, or so he claimed.

Three: she had no idea.

Four: she had no idea he was on a dating site.

Five: for obvious reasons, his profile photo wasn't him.

Six: he wasn't forty-two, but forty-five.

Seven: he didn't live in Providence but in Smithfield, RI.

Eight: his name wasn't Steve.

Curiosity got the best of me. And a potentially vengeful plot in my head took shape—all the ingredients for a very explosive denouement.

He was impressed that I could sift through his—pardon my French—bullshit. He said I could provide him with therapy any time, except I knew what kind of therapy he was seeking, and that kind I did not offer. So, in my nonchalant, non-caring, and borderline offensive way, I started to do what any woman would: give advice.

In my advice-giving moments, I further managed to extricate that the girlfriend was the wife, and they had a daughter, thus feeling obligated to stay in the relationship. There was too much at stake, even though his wife only slept with him once a month. I had heard similar stories before.

As I talked to him over a few weeks and continued to wonder why—I understood his predicament even if I didn't condone it. I didn't approve of his occasional trysts, and most of all, I didn't approve of him being on a dating site for singles like me who were looking for a mate.

My plan wasn't elaborate or intentionally cruel, even though others might think so. The premise for my plan was that I understood Steve occasionally had one-night stands to satisfy his needs. He had one night of passion and then returned to his life without ever getting involved mentally or emotionally with the woman. I felt like I was the perfect person to teach him a lesson.

My Machiavellian plan was, what if I could make him so wild over me that he would develop an emotional and mental attachment without ever being able to have his one-night stand? It would be revenge at its best. Revenge in the name of all women who had been cheated on. Could I pull it off?

The plan rapidly started going south when I realized a couple of things.

First, I would have to set in motion a meeting and unleash some concrete moments. I quickly realized that this was a risk for me. Not just in the moral sphere—I didn't feel as guilty about that as Steve occasionally lived outside the faithful parameters of marriage, but the risk was my heart. What if I couldn't keep my emotions in control? What if I fell in love with him? That would be a disaster of epic proportions, and there would be no going back.

I was not on the online dating roller-coaster to end with someone un-available and unable to give me what I wanted. Not to mention that going out in public would be impossible.

I saw this risk increase when I learned he was a nice guy (besides the in-corrigible unfaithfulness trait). Steve was charming, witty, and intelligent. He shared many other values with me and got my sense of humor. I began telling him everything, and I was filter-less with a man for the first time. I said exactly what I thought without worrying about how inappropriate it was. His sexual appetite exceeded mine, and I concluded I could never cross that line with him. I cared about him.

My second concern was Steve himself. He realized he had strong feelings for me and could not give me what I wanted. As much as he craved a physical experience with me, the more time passed, the more he knew that he would have to change his life to accommodate me in his, and he knew I didn't want that. He had been married for twenty years, and people get burned when they play with fire long enough. I asked him if he would continue "fishing," and he replied that he had learned his lesson. He had fished for too long and caught the Mother Fish, me.

Steve confessed that as much as he wanted me, he knew one night with me wouldn't be enough and would want more. He would want every night with me. That sounded like an ocean of trouble. I was not ready or prepared to deal with someone who could potentially be in transition out of his marriage.

But he made me promise that we couldn't break our friendship contract. I told him I wouldn't, and I. I occasionally talked to him through Face-book, knowing he'd be there to help me if I needed advice. He thought I was awesome.

So, my plan didn't precisely backfire, but it had all the ingredients for a major nuclear event.

I was still waiting for the Holy Grail and wondered in the back of my mind if the needle in a haystack might be impossible to find. But I came to a finite conclusion: I was the Holy Grail, the Ultimate Catch. If the One walked on this planet, whoever he was, he'd have to be worthy and waltz into my life at some point.

CHAPTER 21
XAVIER

While on Cherub's Arrow, I saw the profile of a handsome man. I scanned the contents and liked what I read except for a tiny detail: he had a kid and didn't want anymore. So, I moved on. That platform allowed the other person to see that you visited their profile, so he must have seen I visited his, and so he visited mine.

We started emailing back and forth, and I found myself intrigued by this man. He told me he was born in the United Kingdom, worked in engineering management consulting, specifically on oil and gas projects, and seemed bright. He also informed me that he had a five-year-old daughter who lived with her mom between London and Paris. He led me to believe that when he saw his daughter, he did so for a more extended period since he didn't get to see her very often.

He lived in Providence at the Regency Plaza Apartments, luxury condos near the Providence Place Mall. He sent me his phone number, but I didn't recognize the area code. Google had been my friend. I found out it was a California area code. I asked him about the California connection, and he mentioned he never changed his number, inferring that he once lived there at some point.

We texted a little bit. Then, the next day, he called me. To my surprise, he did not have a British accent. I could not quite place his accent, which frustrated me. It made me think that maybe he was not British at all. Aside from the accent, what struck me was the strength of his personality. I must admit that in my past relationships, I had been the one with a strong personality. Call it strong, stubborn, opinionated, bossy, annoying, and a plethora of other adjectives.

I wondered if that was a good sign or not. This man was so handsome that I asked him to send me some photos to my cell. He told me his phone had some sort of bug and that he could only do that via email. We exchanged generic email addresses, and he emailed me two pictures. He was making a face; the other, he was on a bed with his adorable five-year-old daughter. I sent him two of my own just to ensure he knew it was me on the profile.

I would soon leave for Las Vegas with two of my best friends to celebrate one of their birthdays. I told him this so he knew we could not meet right away. He told me he had to travel to New York and Houston.

He worked a lot from home as he had clients worldwide in different time zones, so there were a lot of phone calls, videoconferencing, and emailing. When I was in Vegas, he called me several times, telling me he was in New York with one of his clients from Dubai. I wondered why he lived in Providence and questioned him about it. He told me his offices were in New York, where he also had a place in the city and Providence and London. I was beginning to wonder if any of it was true.

He asked me a lot of questions and had not sent me any penis pictures or inappropriate messages. That was a good sign. He told me he had been single for four years because he was married to his job. He was building an empire and was very ambitious. Nothing was wrong with that, except I wondered if this guy would ever have time for me and if I would ever be a priority. I was sick of never being the priority.

I found his last name in his email address and googled it. There was a LinkedIn profile with his name, but I could not use my profile because there was a chance he might know I was snooping on his. My skills as a detective were not to be widely advertised. The next best thing was to use my houseguest's LinkedIn profile to snoop on his—lots of interesting information, including a past job with two Swiss companies. The light bulb went off, and I realized this guy might be French or Swiss. Why he had not mentioned that was interesting but understandable, as Americans didn't seem fond of the French.

Valentine's Day was coming up, and I wondered if I would ever meet him. That morning, he wished me happy Valentine's Day via text. I wished him the same. Later that day, he informed me that it was also his birthday. I stared at one of my kitchen cabinets where I had put a small Cupid Lara had given me for Christmas. Another irony and perhaps foreboding sign: I met him on a site called Cherub's Arrow. Lots of signs. If you believed in that sort of thing.

As our connection deepened through text and phone calls, I found out he was now in Houston, Texas, to meet with Shell. The more time passed, the more I realized this man was a workaholic, and I wondered if he would ever have time for a relationship like he claimed to want. The more we talked, the more we found ourselves connecting. It seemed strange to feel like you were in a relationship with someone you had never met.

Some friends warned me that it was too good to be true. This disgustingly handsome man had brains, a high-end lifestyle with chauffeurs and chefs, and multiple properties around the globe, and I found myself having seeds of doubt. Why would someone so successful be on an online dating site or have trouble meeting women?

While in Houston, he got sick with some sort of flu. I asked him when he was coming home to Providence. He told me he didn't know. He still would have to go to Chicago first, then New York, then to Providence. A week and a half went by when he didn't work and was sick as a dog, but in the meantime, he flew to Chicago, where he had an apartment in the Aqua building. I googled the Aqua building on Google: another giant mirrored skyscraper adorning the Chicago skyline.

While he was sick, I did not hear from him very much as he was sleeping a lot and losing weight, and part of me wanted to jump on a plane and fly to Chicago to take care of someone I didn't even know. Call me crazy. That was the understatement of the year. I knew he missed me, and feeling alone and not feeling well heightened the need for human connection. He had a doctor visit him in his apartment who admitted him to the hospital for a few hours to get more tests done and rule out anything else. As he got better, he realized he had to catch up on work, and even though he told me that as soon as he felt better, he'd be flying back to Providence, he did not.

My detective skills continued, and I found him on Facebook. At first, I could see his profile, but Facebook privacy settings changed all the time, and now, all I could see were his cover photos and any comments made on them. One of the photos was of a concert. One of his friends commented in French, and he replied in perfect French. I concluded I was right about the French connection, but I was unsure why he omitted the fact. In his comment to his friend, he said Belfort was his territory. Belfort was a small town about 180 miles east of Paris and 93 miles from Zürich, Switzerland.

When he felt better, he called me more often. One time, it was at eight o'clock in the morning on a Saturday, the only day I was hoping to sleep in, and he told me that he had an awful nightmare that I had not waited for him and that I had dumped him. He said he was experiencing this enormous fear of me leaving him. He even choked up, which I found endearing and alarming at the same time. I told him that I was waiting for him.

The gradually increasing pull toward one another was exciting but scary. I just wanted to make this a reality, meet him in real life, and see if our relationship was not just a projection. He still did not know when he was coming back to Providence. He lost the twenty-five-million-dollar deal to a German competitor, and he was now working on three different projects to try and make up for that loss. This was beyond my scope. I felt inundated with doubts and insecurities. I was not a doubtful nor insecure human being. Ms. Diva and the Jokester ate popcorn, but they, too, had doubts.

CHAPTER 22

XAVIER
Part Two

I was so intrigued by Xavier that I disabled my online profiles again. I received the usual emails on Cherub's Arrow and Plenty of Sharks. I got one that could potentially be interesting, but I told the guy I was talking to someone. He said that I could talk to him too, but coming from a European culture of twenty years earlier, where there was still no exact word for dating, let alone all the rules of it or lack thereof, I didn't feel right juggling more than one person at a time. I could multi-task lots of things, but I could not multi-task men. I knew some women could, and even though I felt Americanized more than I was willing to admit, I didn't feel comfortable with this process.

After two months of talking on the phone, texting, and the occasional email picture from Xavier, my anxiety increased a great deal.

I was still talking to Steve, the married platonic buddy on Facebook chat, and he told me that Xavier was full of it and that I needed to be smart about it. I tried not to pay attention to his advice until the unexpected happened.

I had been asking Xavier for more pictures. If I still couldn't meet him, I needed more visuals. He finally sent me four more, two of which he had already sent. The email address was the same, but something was added—Xavier Miller, not his French last name.

Now, the red flag party was on full blast. The red balloons were so glossy that I was bombarded with a blinding glare of doubt. All along, I thought he had the French last name. Once again, I enlisted Google's help. I plugged in Xavier Julian Miller, the last name attached to the email. Nothing. A whole lot of nothing. No images. No nothing.

I heard Steve's telepathic presence telling me *I told you so*. I called my cousin on Martha's Vineyard who had accompanied my online adventures. I told her the latest news. She asked me for his number and started doing some online research of her own. She alarmingly yelled out, "his number is a California number."

"Yes, I know this. He never had his number changed from when he lived there."

"It's a landline in Arcadia, California."

My stomach fell to the floor. Moments of agony ensued. I was in desperation mode. I started going through all my texts and now was questioning the validity of everything.

That weekend, my stomach was in knots. I felt nauseous and like an idiot. How could I have not seen this coming? The red balloons were dancing in my living room. Red glitter was everywhere. It was like the devil was the event planner of this drama unfolding. I stopped sleeping. I didn't want to contact him because I wondered what his motives were for talking to me.

My cousin said, "Sometimes, people are just disturbed. He might not want anything from you, just company or a voice at the other end of the line." I was looking for my darned soulmate. F-bombs suddenly started dropping at the devil's party.

My houseguest told me the next day she had good news. As I looked at her with permanent bags under my eyes, she offered: "I put my cell phone number online, and it says it's a landline from another town." I was stunned. The truth was that just because Google could be your personal assistant didn't mean all the information there was kosher.

Maybe there was an explanation for his last name change. I finally texted him. This was the actual exchange.

"What's your last name?"

"Miller. You wanna google me, I know. I didn't know yours. How about you?"

"You're not on Google. Lol"

"Yeah, 'cause I don't wanna be. Don't even try," he laughed.

"I thought your last name was something else because of your email address."

"No. Hell, no."

That was even an odder response. "Hell no" was what I should be saying to all this nonsense.

After a few days of that crazy agony, I called him.

Surprisingly, he picked up. He sounded sleepy, and I heard TV in the background. He told me how busy he was, that he had to travel to the UK to see his daughter, and that I needed to be patient. I told him that even though he hadn't met me yet, for those who knew me and knew that patience was not my forte, I had passed the test. He could not accuse me of being impatient.

Then, I brought up the email address. I told him that up until the week before, I thought his last name was something else, and now, I was confused about his last name being Miller. He brushed it off, saying that it's a family name but not his last name, and that's why he used it. Then, he started questioning me about my pictures and whether those were really mine, and I started getting defensive. He started getting defensive.

The lightbulb went off in my head. "I have a great idea. Let's Skype. You will see that it's me. And if you can't wait to meet me, you'll have the first taste on Skype." He started telling me he didn't have time for that. He didn't have Skype on his computer. His daughter used to FaceTime him when he had an iPhone, but she dropped the iPhone in water, and he just didn't have the time.

If the Jokester were a devil, he'd be laughing his ass off now and throwing his pitchfork in the air as if he were an Olympic athlete. If Xavier had time to talk on the phone for five minutes, he had time to sit in front of his computer on Skype with me. After a lengthy telephone conversation, I felt it was time to bury the hatchet. I was done with this guy. There was something very wrong, and now I was 99% sure he was a catfish.

The problem was I knew whom he stole his identity from, and I bet the real guy in Switzerland would not be happy to know that his photos, including the one with his daughter, had been stolen and were being used on a dating site. Now, what does one do with this information?

CHAPTER 23
THE DEATH OF XAVIER

"How could I be so stupid?" I bet that was a question many women and perhaps some men asked themselves as they went through the online dating process. The more I talked to people about online dating, the more I realized that not everyone was out there to find a love partner.

I was talking to a friend from college on the phone. She was no longer using online dating, but she told me that when she used it, she behaved like a frat girl and was just there for the meals and the sex. I laughed out loud, but deep down, I cried. That was precisely the antithesis of me.

I reactivated two of the profiles I had disconnected for a couple of months when I was so focused on Xavier. The best way to forget this whole sham was to get back out there. My troublemaker married friend Steve said, "I told you so." If my words could scream back at him, they would have. I told him to keep his thoughts to himself and that I did not need a lecture from him. He said he was trying to help me. I didn't need that at all.

When I got back out there, I had two scheduled dates back-to-back. Even though I suspected a friend connection only, I still agreed to go out with one of them. And my suspicions were right on. Despite his interesting personality, he was nice, but we had no chemistry. He wanted a second date, but I needed to figure out how to give him the news without hurting his feelings.

The following day, it was going to be coffee with Jake, a 6'4, slightly younger guy who had been a Boston firefighter for ten years, had attended Berklee College of Music, and owned a Karate School in West Palm Beach, Florida. I liked him, but his propensity for always trying to be his family's savior made me doubt date number two, which had been rescheduled a few times. Maybe the story of Jake would have another chapter, but my brother repeated to me that I should not put all my eggs in one basket, especially if the basket seemed a little flimsy.

In the meantime, shortly after, I came to the halting conclusion that Xavier had been a very well-connected fake identity. I thought long and hard about contacting the real guy.

I looked into communicating with him through LinkedIn, but I dismissed that idea the second I realized I would have to upgrade my account. It wasn't going to happen. I decided instead to reach out to him through Facebook. My message was simple. "Are you the Xavier I have been talking to for the past two months? I received photos of you via email with your name. Things that have been said over the phone to me don't match your profile on LinkedIn. I am concerned."

I didn't hear back, but my conscience was tranquil. Had I been the one whose identity had been stolen, I would have wanted to know about it. If the real Xavier wished to pursue it and try to identify the impostor, I would give him any pertinent information he wanted, but it was out of my hands.

I felt like I needed to rid myself of the impostor's energy. I was taking it out on myself. I felt stupid and dumb and didn't think either of those adjectives applied to me. If I were into punching bags, that was what I would become. Why did I fall like that? Why was I in a trance? Why did I have to be so naïve? How could I protect myself from disturbed people or people with intentions opposite mine? These were a lot of questions I had no answers to, and it wasn't like I could google them.

Imagine my surprise when the real Xavier responded through Facebook with very poor English two weeks later, as I suspected he was French or French-Swiss, letting me know that he had no idea who I was and had never spoken to me on the phone. He asked me what the profile was from the impostor, but I had to explain to him that it wasn't through Facebook. I also told him I was sure he knew this person, perhaps through his work or travels. I gave him more information but never heard back. I felt my good deed was done; at least he knew someone was impersonating him.

As far as I was concerned, Xavier was dead and buried. I texted a friend of mine for a Reiki session. I needed a spiritual detox. It was always great to be the recipient of some positive healing energy. I also tried a 21-day meditation cleanse, which seemed to be helpful.

In the meantime, I hoped to have some more news soon. But I was plowing ahead. I needed to acquire tougher skin and keep going.

CHAPTER 24
PUTTING OUT FIRES

I scored an A+ in patience when it came down to putting up with situations. Some of my friends accused me of not being patient enough and relatively inflexible, so I was doubly aware of what was at stake. I didn't want to become such an inflexible person at thirty-eight, so I worked hard to be more supple, get those muscles healthy, and the patience joints lubricated. I thought I had done well, but a fine line existed between being flexible and complacent. I had yet to find a happy medium. If I followed my nature of always being right and wanting things my way all the time, I was setting myself up for a very lonely future, and I realized that fact wholeheartedly. If, on the other hand, I put a smile on my face, breathed deeply as I had done many times before, and focused on being flexible, I became what some call a doormat. And I was not fond of anyone stepping on me, especially men not worth my time.

One of the things I discovered through this process was my sense of hope and resilience. It didn't matter how many disappointments I had, and I have had a few, which left me emotionally drained and without much motivation to keep these accounts open. I refused to go to bars and was too old for clubs. So, I kept at it. Someone decent was bound to come along. That was my hope.

Jake, who was seven years younger than me, sounded promising. He seemed to have his act together, or at least that was my first impression of him. We met at a Starbucks. He was 6'4. I loved tall men, and so did Ms. Diva. He was from Boston's Metro West area but had been in West Palm Beach, FL, running a karate school he started for the past few years. He was into some adrenalin-inducing activities such as car racing and motorcycles. He came back up for health reasons. He mentioned a blood disorder but gave me too few details. He was getting back into teaching at the Fire Academy in Boston as a Lieutenant Fireman. I felt the flames advance toward me.

But somewhere, Jake took a wrong turn. The second date got rescheduled. I didn't know how many times, too many for me to remember—showing my exaggerated flexibility, and finally, the last time, his excuse for canceling was that he hadn't slept much the night before and was still in bed. Ms. Diva choked on her dirty martini and swore she would start a blog.

If I had superpowers of telepathy and space transportation, I would have teleported myself and beaten the crap out of him, even though that was just wishful thinking, as he was much more advanced in martial arts than I was. Still, at least he would probably be too sleepy to react. Maybe. Perhaps. Maybe he was too young and didn't know that a real man would abide by his word. At least, that was what was on my mind, what a real man was supposed to do. I wanted to use a megaphone on my rooftop and yell, "Are there any real men out there? Preferably stable in every way?" I thought I put in my order with the Universe. I was very precise. It wasn't a long one, but it was very specific.

During a work event the day before, which was quite casual, I met this attractive female attorney from Boston who had been married for twenty-seven years. We started talking about dating and men without really meaning to. She couldn't believe I was single, and she called me beautiful and a catch. How was it possible that no one had swept me off my feet?

I was flattered. It's always lovely to receive a compliment, even though I had been more comfortable receiving those only recently. But here was an intelligent, attractive, normal, career-driven woman recognizing brilliance before her, and I agreed with her existential question: Why was I still single?

CHAPTER 25
JUNK AND MORE JUNK

I needed to travel again, so at that point, I was not too active in the online chaos. I texted a couple of guys of Italian descent, which was always troublesome for me. Chef Tom owned a café in Braintree or Quincy and was adamant that he wasn't looking for a fling. He was tall with blue eyes, a big nose, and medium brown hair, and we never met. I was not entirely sure why, but he didn't seem to have much time to devote to anyone other than his business.

He texted me while I was abroad and assured me he was interested but never pursued me like the deserving damsel I was. Hopeless: no. Determined: guilty as charged. And I was not chasing my knight. I was all for women's power, and I considered myself an egalitarian, but I still believed in romance and, regardless of my gender, I should not have to run after anyone. Plus, I wouldn't say I liked running. Ms. Diva concurred. Her heels wouldn't be conducive to such activities.

I was also talking to Marc, a contractor from Connecticut. He was cute, with kind green eyes and salt-and-pepper hair. Our exchanges started smoothly, but then I had communication problems with him. He needed clarification on what I meant. He got frustrated, and I was even more so. I have a master's in communications. I didn't have problems communicating. If at all, I communicated above and beyond. I could beat things to death occasionally. Just ask my friends. But the more time passed, the more I sensed this issue. I called him, and he didn't pick up. Instead, I got a voicemail with a sexy voice. I asked him when we were meeting and why he didn't want to talk on the phone so we could smooth things over. He texted me that I was rushing things.

A man in his mid-forties, scared of using his voice on the telephone, who was postponing a real-life meeting was never a good sign. That was one of my lessons from this online saga. Plus, the more time passed, the more I detected a mean streak in what he told me. Why bother? Why was I still talking to people who could not be kind human beings and were not normal enough to want to get to know someone in real life outside of electronics, where they never had to show their face, vulnerability, or soul?

It was true: looks weren't everything. I believed a certain degree of chemistry was necessary, but that had to be tested in real life and not through texting. I no longer wanted to waste time waiting for that required chemistry to develop. And chemistry needed to be at all levels: physically, mentally, emotionally, and spiritually. You were either in tune with someone or not. There wasn't a middle ground on this. I used to think differently, but time was fleeting, and this was a numbers game.

I was upset at myself for wasting time and wanting to put faith and emotions on people who couldn't keep up with me, even if they wanted to. I was at a point in my life where I knew very distinctively how I wanted to be treated. Why? I could treat others with respect, kindness, and the occasional snide comedic remark, but at the end of the day, I wanted and was willing to share my entire being with a partner who could inspire me and whom I could inspire in return. I wanted to build something together, knowing things would not always be perfect. Though I strived for that, things would not always be my way. I knew my limitations but knew I could learn and grow with the right man because I still had so much to learn and explore.

I needed to stop wasting time on junk. I believed it was a numbers game, even though I could have been more proficient at mathematics. I thought the more crap I went through, the more probability I would have to get to the finish line and get to the gold. In other words, to find a worthy partner. The hunting resumes. The Jokester put the recliner on max and changed the channel.

CHAPTER 26
BATTLEFIELD

I felt deflated. Should I have taken another break? There was so much going on otherwise, between family wars, business deadlines, friends with cancer, and my travel schedule, that I was losing faith. I knew the tiny flame of hope still flickered in the darkness of this quest.

Spring arrived. I needed to perk up and let the change in weather be a positive foreboding of times to come. I went home to visit family. My father's birthday was two days from mine, and even though he was recovering from bronchitis, I tried to relax in the familiar surroundings, representing my past, my present, and all that was secure.

I checked my Cherub's Arrow profile and had a message from Antiquesman from Long Island, NY. It was not around the corner, but I glanced at his profile, and everything sounded normal until I saw what type of relationship he was looking for. The site gave you several options, and he chose short-term dating, long-term dating, and casual sex. Pissed off, I decided to get rid of him by replying. "Hi, I don't think we are looking for the same thing. Good luck with your search." I imagined it would end any communication, but he emailed me back with a question on how I could make such a determination. "Um, have you read your profile on your chosen options of casual sex and mostly monogamous?" On chat, he informed me it was a mistake, that he was indeed looking for a relationship, that this was the first time he was online dating, and that he was still learning to navigate his profile.

All right, I could bite. So, we kept talking, and I determined he had made a mistake. I mentioned I was overseas during our conversation, and we spoke briefly about that. Then he mentioned he was also overseas. I asked him where. "Kabul."

My jaw dropped. I heard a crash and thought it must be Ms. Diva's martini glass breaking into a million pieces. WTF? I asked: "Afghanistan?" He said yes. I asked him why he thought it would be a good idea to be on a dating site and why he contacted me. I thought that Long Island, NY, was already a haul, and this man was on the other side of the planet. Yeah, I sure could find them. So, it turned out he was in the military and had been there for a year. He would be home soon.

He asked me if I was freaked out. I didn't give him a yes or no answer but told him I did not believe in long-distance relationships. In general, relationships are hard enough, let alone at a distance. I neglected to accept that this man was in a dangerous place. It didn't cross my mind then, and I didn't consider the repercussions.

But three weeks later, things were different. How did I get myself into this situation? Again! I knew I was an overachiever. I knew that I was not willing to settle. But it never crossed my mind to take on what could be the biggest challenge of my life by starting a relationship with an army man who was at war, protecting us all on the other side of the world nine and half hours ahead. With the securities in place, we could only communicate via email or Yahoo messenger, without cameras or voice. The more we got to know each other, the closer we became. I had no idea how I would pull this off or if I was strong enough to tackle a potentially dangerous future of losing someone I didn't even know.

When I traveled again, I was busy, but with him in the back. He didn't want me to worry. He told me about a week after the fact that one Monday, while I was having fun with friends, the Taliban attacked a US base and Kabul Airport, and twelve died.

He mentioned marriage. I did warn him about my anti-marriage state of mind, as I just got divorced, and how signing papers didn't make a good relationship. The Jokester almost choked on a Cheeto.

Now, I was going through something I had never imagined. Feelings of fear of losing someone and not knowing about it. Feelings of desperation. Of uncertainty. He could not tell me much about his work. I knew he loved it. I knew nothing of the Armed Forces or what life could be like in the future. I didn't even know when he was coming back. Neither did he. He said, "soon." I guess I could be the light at the end of his tunnel. I was hoping that he wouldn't struggle too much psychologically when he returned. He told me he was fine, but I wondered what it would be like for a soldier to adapt to being back home and to a new relationship. I must do research. There was a lot to learn.

For now, all I knew was when the sonar sound dinged on my phone, I was on alert and felt the adrenalin rush of relief. He was still alive for now.

CHAPTER 27
RESILIENCE

I arrived at Lara's door on a Wednesday night with my head down. It was 9 PM, and her three kids were in bed. She gave me a big hug and took one look at my face.

"What's wrong?"

I knew the bags under my eyes were dark and spoke volumes. I unloaded my purse, jacket, and cell gear on her loveseat.

"I just found out Barry in Afghanistan is a fake profile...."

Lara plopped down on her couch, and I followed her. I was defeated, and she was defeated by association. Or maybe it was shock. Maybe her mind wondered about her friend's propensity to find troubling situations.

"Not again," she sighed. "What happened?"

I told her about my conversation with Long Island Barry, US Sergeant in Kabul.

We had been chatting back and forth on Yahoo Messenger, and he mentioned something about my video. I had sent him a video link of a few filmed minutes I had previously uploaded on YouTube and then later deleted. It was me rambling again and wondering when he was coming home. While on chat, he mentioned coming home. Then he asked me if I had heard of a Transit. I told him I had no idea what he was talking about.

He explained that as his "girlfriend"— a bizarre title for me as we had never even met or seen each other, I was entitled to send a request letter for him to come home earlier. Another red flag party started popping up. The Jokester doubled over from so much laughing. It made no sense to me that if a soldier had been deployed for a year and knew he was coming home soon, I, someone he had never met, could petition the Army for a more impending leave from combat. How would the United States of America weigh in on that one? Staying in action or sending a valuable soldier home to meet a woman he had never met? Ms. Diva inspected her armory. A bazooka might be her weapon of choice.

My heart sank. Again. I knew that Lara felt poorly and understood.

"What did you do?"

I continued. He was allegedly going on patrol, which I knew was bogus, and urged me to consider the Transit request.

Once again, I enlisted Google. Right away, the search engine was good.

I found sites and forums about military romance scams dating back to 2005. The stories were similar, and some women (and men) went as far as sending the impersonators from Nigeria money. I knew what would come next for the request. I found a site that had kept a database since 2005 of all the Armed Forces photos, their handles, and even the false forms sent to the scammed victims to initiate this Transit process. Some had been swindled out of thousands of dollars.

Aside from being minimally enraged, I felt disappointed. How could I fall for another fake identity? At least this one was only one month and not two. I knew I had to confront him. I knew that, most likely, this person was in West Africa operating this very elaborate identity from some internet café. I even considered it might be two individuals using the same persona due to the time difference and to keep their character's story plausible. After all, Kabul was eight or nine hours ahead.

My messenger went off right before I went to Lara's house, and I knew he was back on. This was it. Barry's photos (or whoever the real Army sergeant was) kept flashing in my mind. The buzzing alert that this soldier was as much a victim as me. The only difference was that he had no idea his photos were being used for this scam.

As I suspected, the Fake Ass Scammer sent me the information I needed to email the Armed Forces (also an email address flagged by Google) with all his data. Why bother continuing this? My exact words left nothing to the imagination.

"It is ridiculous that you are impersonating an Army sergeant and think that someone with a brain was not going to research this. I am baffled. I feel like I wasted my time and energy on a lying scam. And what you are doing is absolute theft and crime. The internet is full of complaints and information about these scams."

"Ok," was his reply.

"It's not ok."

"Lol, what do you want me to say?"

"It's not okay," I repeated. "If you were a real Army man, you would send me an email from your military account. You can't do that, can you?"

He said he couldn't.

"Because you don't have one. Just admit it." I countered.

"Yeah," he finally said.

I had indeed lost too much time. I submitted all the photos, email addresses, messenger handles on Yahoo and Skype, and a brief paragraph to the volunteer victims who ran the database site so they could add him to the list of thousands of impersonators. I tried to track the IP address on the headers of his messages through Gmail, but they were all ghost locations. I was mad.

He contacted me the next day to try to send me an encrypted file through Skype. His audacity shocked me. "Do you think I'm stupid enough to open this? You probably sent me a virus!" I should have added 'fucking asshole,' but not sure why I contained myself. Maybe it wasn't an asshole. Perhaps it was a bitch. I would never know.

My heart was turning into an icicle. How many more hits was I going to take? Or, more importantly, should I even continue with this nonsense? *Elementary, my dear Watson.* I heard Sherlock in my head. The Jokester and Ms. Diva looked at purchasing a bazooka. Back to the drawing board.

CHAPTER 28
BARRY'S ARMY BUST

The sun hit my face. Summer was coming. The weather got warmer, and it was almost time to get those air conditioning units in my windows. The nagging feeling that surfaced every year that I should invest in central air conditioning was still present. I shrugged it off as if Ms. Diva, temporarily assigned as the AC fairy, was on my shoulder, one hand on one hip and tapping the opposite high heel, looking at me with crazy eyes. She was rolling her eyes at my perseverance with this soap opera of online dating. The NO TRESPASSING sign on my love life and the cobwebs around my heart were dead-on clues that I should throw the towel in. In my case, the nuns had probably gotten word of the warning on my forehead, which read something like *Fake identities, losers, and scammers welcome*, and I bet several convents were battling it out for me to join one of their sisterhoods.

I was not the only one extra skeptical these days. Some of my friends had the same opinion. Others thought that this was still an outlet that would allow me to connect with someone awesome whom I would otherwise never meet.

Sergeant Barry's fake identity left me off-balanced once again. After much research, I was convinced even more that this scam was probably headquartered and operated in Nigeria by teams whose job was to obtain foreign money with this military romance angle. I wouldn't say I liked the feeling of powerlessness because there wasn't anything one could do. I must consider myself lucky that I caught the fraudulent scheme. I would never mindlessly send any money, regardless of how noble the cause was.

I felt so jaded with my emotions that my mind hadn't started thinking clearly. Aside from the Google research rampage, I hadn't taken a minute to think about the information I already had in those photos. A friend pointed out that some stuff in the images could be relevant. I realized that in some, he was wearing a couple of different Iowa State University sweatshirts, which was a huge clue. I slapped myself for not questioning the alleged NY residence when a lot pointed to Iowa.

I talked to another friend of mine who was an Armed Forces veteran and showed him the photos. He thought the patch on Barry's military uniform was an Airborne Patch, but he would do some research himself.

Another light bulb went off in my head. One of my good friends was a Lieutenant Colonel in the Army National Guard. She could help. I may be able to warn the real guy again.

I made the call to my superheroine friend, who years ago was stationed in Afghanistan herself. I cringed at the thought of having to tell her the whole story and avoided the call for a couple of days, but then I got brave.

I told her everything. She asked me to send her the photos and said she would do some digging.

Before the day was over, she had a name and a Facebook profile for the real guy.

I didn't have the guts to check out his profile that evening and waited until the next day.

Of course, he was in a relationship. There was no way a guy that handsome could be single. I didn't have any hopes of that. I sent him a Facebook message, but in the back of my mind and knowing how the social media site operated, there was a high probability that he wouldn't get my news as we weren't connected, and the message would end up in some other folder. I asked my friend if she could get me his military email address. She did. The actual detective was her. Of course, she had more resources than me, but still.

I copied and pasted the Facebook message I had sent him and emailed it the following day.

A few days go by, and nothing. Then, an email came through.

"Thank you for the information. I am aware of someone using my pictures. A few months ago, a lady contacted me from Arizona and said she spoke on the phone "with me." This stuff ticks me off. I apologize that you had to go through this; I assure you it is NOT me. The best thing is to gather as much information on the person as possible who is posing as me. Maybe you should try and scam them for money or something lol...or if you can get a phone number, please let me know. I would enjoy a conversation with this person. Thanks again, RJ."

I sent him all the information I had. I doubted he could do anything else with it, but at least I told him to set his Facebook photos to private so no more could be stolen. I didn't hear back, but my conscience was at peace. I did all I could. It was no longer in my hands.

In the meantime, summer was around the corner. It was time to get back in shape. I had run out of excuses. I recently read: "Life is no dress rehearsal." Borderline depressed, saddened, and disappointed, I needed to return to the gym. Thursday would be the day. I needed my hair to stay put until then for work meetings.

CHAPTER 29

FULL SPEED AHEAD

I had been so very close to giving up. It would be so easy just to shut down all the accounts. However, I decided it was time to approach this online thing more methodically. Get the more objective scientific mind out. Plus, I doubted I had much of a science brain in me. Even though my mathematical self was practically non-existent, I wondered if it was true that there were just not a lot of quality men available, if I had terrible luck, or if I wasn't going out enough. I couldn't make this my full-time job even if I thought that to be effective, I needed to devote more time to the search for the elusive life partner. It sounded like the search for the Holy Grail, much pursued, never found.

Two of my accounts were about to expire their upgraded version, and the third was set to expire. I did not renew Happiness Now, the most expensive one. I didn't even communicate with a single soul from that site, and my membership lasted six months. Considering all the fake identities Cherub's Arrow had made available to me, I wouldn't continue with the upgrade. And I was still debating Plenty of Sharks. As much crap as I got on that site from sifting through millions of irrelevant messages, I could consider upgrading again, but I was moving at a snail's pace on that. So, I decided to restart my membership to Catch. Let's face it. It had been almost two years since I had used it, and the ads on TV claimed it was the most effective dating site. I hoped they had improved in the meantime, but I had my doubts. I found a coupon online and got significant savings, so I didn't feel guilty.

I emailed people away. I went through lots of emails, primarily uninteresting. I started talking to someone from Middleboro, MA, who owned a restaurant. We communicated easily, and the whole thing looked promising. We went out Saturday night to Federal Hill, the Italian neighborhood of Providence. It was a nightmare to park on the weekend, especially on a beautiful day when the temperature was just right.

A friend of mine advised me to wear a black dress. I was not feeling super sexy these days, but I took her suggestion. All dressed up, I wore these tall platform wedges I could barely walk on, questioning why women wore super high heels. I was the proud owner of a medium-sized collection that I mostly stared at because these were not shoes made for walking but more made for gazing. Yes, high heels made a woman taller, slimmer, and sexier. I couldn't deny that fact. I was so envious of women who pretended to walk comfortably and elegantly in these. I was not one of them. Ms. Diva was the expert in that department.

Brent and I met at Pasquale Square, quite a romantic spot with a water fountain, surrounded by live music and happy people out on the town. I decided to valet my car, even though I had no idea which restaurant we were going to. We texted each other and met at the corner of Venda Ravioli. I was pleased with how he looked; we walked to a nearby restaurant and decided to have dinner outside at a high table. I let him take the lead and order us dinner from various delicious appetizers. The conversation flowed, and no one was running away. I would need an ambulance ride to do that in these shoes. At the end of the evening and after five hours on Federal Hill, we hugged goodbye and told each other we would communicate once we got home safely. We did so. He told me he was home and said he had a nice evening.

Imagine my surprise when I never heard from him again. I was left wondering what went wrong and still had no answers. I imagined he wasn't physically attracted to me. That was the only thing I came up with. I told myself I couldn't take it personally. Yeah, right, because I was an emotionless robot from another planet! My pride was slightly wounded, but I moved on to the next adventure.

Chapter 30
GOING PORTUGUESE AMERICAN

I started talking to Jim, a Portuguese American. I have never dated a Portuguese man, let alone a Portuguese American. But Jim was good-looking and sexy, and I felt the chemistry would be off the charts. Ms. Diva was excited. The Jokester, not so much.

We met up for dinner. He pulled up in a new black BMW 3-series and looked even better in person. We had one point of contention: I wanted to have kids, but he didn't. Deep down, I knew this was a deal breaker, and at the same time, I wondered if my desire to have a child was due to my biological clock ticking. Let's face it: I was not prepared for a child. I could hear my ovaries screaming, "What is wrong with you?" But at the same time, I wanted nature to take its course and not a man to dictate that type of meaningful life event.

The chemistry was off the charts. We were making out in the restaurant less than half an hour before the food arrived. I had been living the life of a nun, and I knew the convent was calling, but Jim was tempting. I considered seeing him again and doing other things too. He commented about my two dark purple hair strands, and I laughed it off. An older couple was sitting in front of us. When they got up to leave, the man approached our table and asked how long we had been together. I smirked but let Jim tackle the answer. "A couple of weeks." The man smiled. "You look really happy together."

By the end of dinner, he wanted to go somewhere else, so we went to another restaurant for drinks. He drove. As we were walking in the parking lot, we passed a whole family, and the grandfather turned to him and yelled, "You have a beautiful girlfriend."

Two good omens? We had another drink, then left. After another make-out session in his car, my willpower almost faltered. I needed to be strong and not give it up too soon.

I went home to find that Ms. Diva manifested a black lace negligée and was impatiently sprawled on my bed. The Jokester was so tired of all the red flags he saw that he downed another beer, followed by a loud set of burps.

I needed to learn to listen to these two angels on my shoulders and to my intuition. I got into many situations because I overlooked red flags in the desperate need to find love. I wondered what Jim was thinking when he didn't text me immediately. How could that be? The chemistry was even evident to strangers.

A couple of days later, I received a text from Jim telling me we could only be friends. I was in shock. I asked why. He told me he didn't like my purple streaks, that it bothered him, and that I wanted to have kids, and he didn't. I replied, "The purple, really?" He said he really could not stand my purple hair, even though he admitted he wanted to have sex with me. I was in shock. How shallow could one be? I thought, "You didn't seem to have a problem with my hair when you were kissing me!" I didn't even text him back.

Next!

CHAPTER 31
THE BIG APPLE

For the Fourth of July, I drove to New York City to spend a few days with my brother, who lived in midtown Manhattan.

On Monday morning, three days after my arrival, we checked the street parking hours where I had parked. My brother couldn't remember if it was Mondays or Tuesdays when one had to move the car, and I didn't want to experience a disappearing car act. Thank God my car was still there, and it was a good thing we checked because I would have to move it before 10 a.m. We were forty-five minutes early. If I lived in the Big Apple, I would have to get rid of my car.

I wondered how long it took to find a parking spot on the Upper West Side on a Monday morning. Well, we couldn't find one with a Tuesday sign. Otherwise, I would have to repeat the same shenanigan the next day. So, we needed to be strategic and ideally find one with a Monday sign on a street that had already been swept. We circled and circled.

My brother on the passenger side was starting to get on my nerves with "this way, that way, straight ahead, left." I'm not too fond of taking orders, and I got aggravated. My blood simmered. I could see veins bulging in my hands as I gripped the wheel. Finally, after an hour and a half, we found one on 71st Street. It was pretty perfect, with a Monday sign, and we only had to wait in the car for ten more minutes, safe from the trash trucks and hefty fines. I would be okay for another few days before the Thursday deadline.

In the meantime, I had a twenty-one-year-old from Cherub's Arrow who wanted to become my boy toy. I was unsure when the cougar trend started, but some of these boys had either mommy issues or wanted to experience an older woman. I was not in the mood to train anyone, and I knew there were double standards as an older woman with a younger man was frowned upon instead of the reverse, which was seen as a trophy.

After all, I was in New York City to see old friends and spend time with my brother, whom I hadn't seen in over six months, plus the weather was fantastic.

On the last night, I decided I wanted to have dinner somewhere local without having to take the subway or have my makeup melt any more than it already had, and I was not that hungry. It was a Tuesday night, and we went to a fusion tapas restaurant, not specifically Spanish food but a variety of European cuisine. My brother checked to see if his landlady, who usually went to that restaurant, was inside, as he didn't particularly want to hang out with her on the last night his sister was in town. It was safe to go in, and so we did.

We got seated, and our very handsome waiter came to our table to get our drink order. He looked like one of those Spanish matadors, except he was all dressed in black, and I could see his biceps bulge from his button-down shirt. He had a short ponytail, and I found myself mesmerized. He was beautiful to look at. And he had a striking smile. After we were alone, I turned to my brother and whispered, "I need a boyfriend." My brother laughed. "You need to aim higher."

Ms. Diva knew he might not be boyfriend material but thought he had a striking smile. She couldn't stop gazing at him and slightly drooled out of the corner of her bright red lips. She imagined what she would do to him. The Jokester chimed in with utter disapproval, "She's never going to see him again."

Our evening continued. I was surprised to see my brother tipsy, a man with an alcohol tolerance of a bull. It was probably because he was mixing four different types of liquor. I stuck to two glasses of Sauvignon Blanc, and since food was involved, I felt fine.

I was unsure when our waiter started chitchatting with us, but I realized he was flirting with me. He mentioned he was from Turkey, and since I had been in Istanbul a year earlier, I managed to utter "thank you" in Turkish—the only thing I learned after four days on that side of the world.

I observed that he was hesitating to say much, and after a while, I understood that he thought my brother and I were a couple. I somehow mentioned that he was my brother. He laughed and said he thought my brother was my boyfriend or husband. Ms. Diva saw this as carte blanche to flirt with him.

He mumbled something in Turkish, and I asked him about it. "You are beautiful," he translated. I laughed softly at the comic quality of the situation when a Turkish waiter at a restaurant was flirting with me in the presence of my drunk sibling. It was preposterous.

He introduced himself as Ishmael and flashed that smile again. "My shift is ending, and I would love to take you out for a drink." My brother and I exchanged a glance. I smiled at the Turkish Adonis. "Sure, I'd like that." Zigzagging out of his chair, my brother conveniently bowed out and informed me he would walk home.

I couldn't believe I would do this crazy thing. Go out with a stranger who had just served me food. But I realized I was not made of steel, that I was a woman who needed to feel wanted and appreciated. We went out for a drink, and Ishmael had an exciting story.

He was a personal trainer by day and a bartender by night. Being a Turkish martial artist who traveled the world and won competitions, he ended up in Miami, where he lived for a couple of years, and had recently moved to New York City. He also proved to be a good kisser. He tried to convince me that I should drive my car to his apartment in Queens and that I could leave in the morning to go back to Massachusetts. I refused. The Jokester whispered, "Do you want to get murdered?"

It felt like a scene from a rom-com when he pinned me to the side of the building and almost had his way with me. I thanked the Jokester for not letting that happen!

He then walked me to my brother's place and asked for my number. I wasn't sure what he would do with it since I was not planning on returning to New York anytime soon. As good-looking as he was, he turned out to be a nice guy, but I had to return to my reality. I was leaving the following day for western Massachusetts to attend a wake for a friend who had just died of cancer. Fucking disease.

CHAPTER 32
WEEDING

I read an article about online dating that greatly saddened me. It discussed the daunting negative statistics of success and blew the whistle on the business side of things. It shed light on how the dating sites skewed statistics and sent you wrong matches so that you extended your membership.

It didn't make any difference now that I had been at this for a while, but reading it before I started this journey would have been helpful. I had no idea there was so much shady business with these sites and apps. I concluded that most men (and maybe even women) lied significantly on these profiles. I never lied. That statistic might be lost in the haystack. The Jokester nodded as he chugged down another beer.

I decided to keep going. I just needed to do some weeding and pay more attention to my gut. Every time I ignored my instincts, I got in trouble.

I met Chris at the Boston Public Garden after finding him on Catch. This was going to be the first guy this time around through that site. Our texting chemistry was off the hook. He was a service consultant for a car dealership north of Boston and loved to travel.

We met and had sushi on Newbury Street. Now that I thought about it, I noticed some things that were red flags right away. For instance, he sure drank a lot for someone who had had a heart attack when he turned thirty and had poor cholesterol, so bad that he had a thin white rim around his iris. I had two glasses of wine for his six cocktails. Then we walked over to Cheers on Beacon Street, and he had two or three more beers while I drank water. Granted, he didn't have to drive, and I did, but still, that was high consumption. We ended up having a second date, and I concluded his lack of manners wouldn't match my deck of full manners, so when he reached out again after a week and a half, I politely passed.

Then I started talking to Sam, an Army Reservist on active Air Force duty. I was not attracted to him; he came with the heavy load of four daughters. He had a medical emergency and ended up canceling our date, but I noticed from his texts and phone calls that he was attaching himself to me a little too fast in a matter of days. I was not ready for that. I didn't hear back from him, and that was for the best, thank goodness. The Jokester gulped some more beer and ignored me. Ms. Diva sat at her vanity, increasingly frustrated, as she applied cat-like eyeliner.

Then came the twins. Well, they were not twins, but they shared the same first name. The first Mike was divorced with two daughters, better than four these days, and he worked in Boston as an army recruiter. I was unsure what about me screamed armed forces, but I had a thing for uniforms and enticing authority. I knew many women did. It could be because my mother was always authoritative, which made me want to defy any authority in moderation. So, Mike set our first date in Quincy, where he lived. On the way there, I texted him I would be a few minutes late. I didn't hear back, but I had confirmed the date that morning. As I entered Quincy on Route 93 traffic, my phone dinged with a text. "Not going to make it tonight." This was way past our meeting time. I replied with question marks and got no response until a couple of hours later, stating that it had been his daughter's sixteenth birthday.

I didn't know what to do with the lack of common courtesy. I told him I wished he had saved me an hour of gas driving around and could have canceled or rescheduled the date earlier to save me the trouble. He replied that he had thought he could have made it.

What a jerk! No, I was not going to reschedule with him. He texted me the following day as if nothing had happened. He asked if I was going to stop talking to him. I didn't respond.

I took the high road. Instead of ignoring him as I wanted, I told him it was best we left things the way they were, and that was the end of that Mike.

This Mike and the next shared another unexpected characteristic, which still perplexed me. Why were men in their forties willing and able to send a dick pic to a stranger? I never asked for such a thing; I couldn't imagine why anyone would do that. I also concluded that it was a sign of poor character and that they couldn't be serious about meeting a normal woman for a possible relationship.

This Mike went a step above and beyond an inappropriate penis picture. He admitted to me that he enjoyed porn. Borderline porn addiction. He sent me several emails with links to porn sites, and then he wanted to have phone sex while watching these porn clips. Ms. Diva rolled her eyes. In addition, he made a request that I was highly unlikely to accept. Mike was a successful mortgage broker, and one day, he had to fly out for a business meeting to New York City, but due to weather conditions, his flight got rerouted from T.F. Green Airport in Warwick, RI, to Boston's Logan Airport. He would have some time to kill when driving through my area. He divulged his fantasy of meeting at a public parking lot—he mentioned Home Depot!—and wanted me to meet him there to bestow oral sex. I politely declined.

Ms. Diva lowered her fake black eyelashes and lit up a long cigarette. I didn't think I had seen her smoke in almost ten years. This was out of our league.

Delete, delete was my new motto. I was removing weeds. The gardening continued.

CHAPTER 33
POTENTIAL DAN

I didn't feel like an expert on online dating, nor did I want to win the title for most online dates under my belt. This process was exhausting enough. I hoped my weeding ability improved as time went on.

I wondered if the other half had as much difficulty as I did. Most of the single and divorced women I knew were remarkable: They had careers, were often single moms doing an incredible job with their kids or grandkids, and had so much to offer. I had one friend who did the online thing for a while, and when I recounted some of my experiences, she almost fell out of her chair. She said she had never had anyone text her inappropriate pictures and that none of the guys she met lied to her. The kicker? She was on the same websites as me. She said her short hair must have given her a more serious appearance. Well, I was not chopping my hair off, not because of online dating. That was just my preference.

I rotated between sites but didn't spend much time on them. I got a message from Daniel on Cherub's Arrow. I looked at his profile, and it seemed interesting. I was not greatly attracted to his photos, but I replied anyway. We switched to phone texting, and he asked me out for that night. It was Saturday, and I wasn't busy, so I decided to go. He chose a restaurant in Providence he loved and told me they had valet parking—and who doesn't like valet parking?—and I went.

It was a beautiful summer night. A slight breeze in the air, not too hot or too humid. Maybe it was a good omen. I got to the restaurant by the Providence River, and he was waiting for me outside. We had talked about what roles each gender takes on a date, and even though the whole thing still seemed foreign to me, I let him take the lead and be "the man." He recommended a specific dish since he had been there many times before. I noticed it was quite pricey, and the Jokester snickered at me, snorting. "Watch this idiot stiff you with the bill." I poofed him away. That hadn't happened yet on my dates, but it was always possible.

Daniel was high up in corporate marketing for a national bank. In addition, he had been in the Army for almost two decades and served three tours, two in Iraq and one in Afghanistan. He regularly saw a therapist for what he called "maintenance," which I found to be an excellent idea; he loved to travel and had been divorced for quite a while.

He was a hero, not only bright—he had an MBA—but a man who could fight. He was an insurgence specialist, recruiting and training locals on his tours. This was no chicken shit of a man. And I didn't mind uniforms.

There was something of concern, however. He had just had a year-long relationship that ended a month earlier, and I told him that perhaps he was not ready to date yet. He disagreed. He said it was a mutual decision, and they were not a match. The Jokester had a bag of popcorn on his lap and laughed his butt off, probably screaming obscenities and things that made no sense, like "Have another drink, wise ass."

The conversation was great. The dinner was very nice, and we adjourned to a second location for just wine, and the conversation continued to flow. We were intrigued by each other. He gave me a good night kiss, which was surprising, as I never expected one of those. I preferred not to exchange spit with a stranger, but I understood why it happened.

So, I left. He didn't wait with me as I was waiting for the valet, which was a bit disappointing, but he texted me when he got home and asked me on a second date four days later. I agreed.

The day before we were to meet again, he told me how excited he was to see me.

Then, on the day of the date, he messaged me, canceling the date indefinitely. He said that he was dealing with some issues in the next few weeks, that I was a wonderful person, and wished me all the best in life and love.

I was dumbfounded. The Jokester was lying on my shoulders, holding onto his belly, laughing his tush off. "He probably went back to the ex-girlfriend, you silly girl."

Miss Diva was MIA and probably thought Dan was AWOL.

I was left wondering if I was doing something wrong or if something was wrong with me that a seemingly normal guy pulled another fast one.

I was speechless indeed.

CHAPTER 34

WHAT IS NORMAL?

I met Ian, a design engineer for a very well-known company. He was forty-three, recently divorced, and co-parenting his seven-year-old boy. He seemed to have done a little online dating. By the time we started talking, he had a trip planned to San Francisco to visit a friend who was turning forty. They had played golf the entire weekend. And because of that, he scheduled our first date upon his return.

So far, I was impressed. He hadn't sent me inappropriate photos; his conversation seemed normal, and he could spell. All good things in my book and rare to find. He worked for the same company as James (from two years earlier), who had Cornell and Georgetown degrees. I wondered if they knew each other. I could already imagine if this relationship panned out, going to an office party, and meeting the guy who had sent me the second penis picture I ever got. What would I say? Nice to see your face?

The timing of meeting Ian couldn't have been more inconvenient. I had decided to do a food detox and was barely eating anything, shy of grilled fish or chicken and salad. But he chose a place not too far, which could accommodate my requests. I realized I had become *that* person with specific demands, who custom-ordered at restaurants: dressing on the side, no cheese, hold the condiments. Like me, the Jokester found those people highly annoying.

Ian drove a Prius. Environmentally conscious. I liked that. Now that I thought of it, I didn't know anyone who drove a Prius. He was tall, 6'2, lean, with glasses and kind eyes. He hugged me, and I realized he was more nervous than me. He seemed fidgety.

He was a gentleman, I could tell. Maybe it had something to do with the fact he was from Michigan.

The conversation flowed well. I realized he had traveled more than me; he went around the globe with his previous job. He was a foodie, and I was eager to learn more. He lived in the same town, ten minutes away, thus closer than most. He said I was the first normal woman he dated. I'm not sure what he meant by that, but on my end, I could say the same about him as a man. Or I should say Ian was abnormal, judging from the other male samplings I had been in contact with.

We adjourned to another restaurant for one more drink. I stuck to seltzer with lime, and he chose a glass of Cabernet Sauvignon. Afterward, he reached over and kissed me. And... What a good kisser he was. That was a checkmark on my list. Ms. Diva's left eyebrow raised to the moon. He set the second date for Saturday as he had his son that week.

The communication deepened throughout the week, and he asked if he could pick me up on Saturday. I agreed. Then I realized I had never allowed a man to pick me up at home. I told him that if I allowed him to do that, it wasn't a green light to see the inside of my house. He understood and told me he hadn't assumed that.

I let him pick me up, and we had dinner at PF Chang's in Providence, RI. Again, it was a lovely time. Date number three was somewhere local, and he picked me up again, which was great. Every time we saw each other, it was better and better. I found him more interesting, and our chemistry was escalating.

For Labor Day weekend, he flew to Colorado for a three-day Phish concert but texted me the whole time, telling me how much he missed me. We had date number four scheduled on Labor Day, and he came straight from the airport to have dinner with me. I hosted. I was a little nervous as this was my territory, and it was always dauntingly nerve-wracking to let someone into your own space. I was clean but cluttered and collected lots of crap I didn't need. It could be a turn-off for a man, but Ian seemed okay with it.

Date number four was so good that date number five happened the next day. We were scheduled to have date number six a few days later after I returned from Europe to see my family.

I felt good about Ian and liked him more and more. Ms. Diva was optimistic as she lounged on the couch with a sexy black negligée.

A couple of days later, my intuition started flaring up. I sensed a distancing but couldn't quite put my finger on it. On date number six, he wanted to take me out to dinner and emphasized the words "dinner only." My eyebrow lifted. Ms. Diva's as well. "Why did I put this negligée on? What a waste!" But I still shrugged it off. Almost immediately, he said he'd been having a tough time at work that day with his boss.

He still picked me up, and we drove to a nice Japanese place about forty minutes south of us. I still sensed something wasn't quite right, but I was not sure what it was, and maybe it had to do with his bad day at work.

I talked a lot. He didn't speak as much. Then he took me home and realized he left his cell phone at the restaurant, so he had to drive back. We kissed good night a few times, he lingered and told me he already missed me. I questioned him. "Really?" He said yes.

The next afternoon, I left for the airport. He texted me a little, but I felt his communications were not as fast-coming as they once were. I was positive something had changed and just didn't know what.

The next day, I arrived in Europe and told him I had landed safely. Ian wished me good luck with my dad. I was bringing him to a neurologist as we suspected something was off with his memory.

I asked Ian if everything was okay with him. "Yes, I think so." Then, he went on a few paragraphs about how he was wondering about the whole dating thing and how it started great, and then his commitment issues started peeking into his brain. He said he was trying to get past that feeling with me but wanted to be honest.

"Do you want to date other women?"

"I don't know." That was not quite the answer I had hoped for. How could he say that when he was dating *moi*? He said he was not actively pursuing others, but it was too early to say one way or the other. *Seriously?* I was devastated and sad. He said that this had nothing to do with me. I had previously heard the "it's not you, it's me" statement.

What did I do wrong this time? Why come to my house and be wined and dined if he was experiencing these feelings? He didn't break up with me, but I felt these were just excuses not to pursue me.

I felt tears of rage and disappointment stream down my face and decided to enable my online dating accounts. I should have just kept them on, or I would be doing this forever at this rate. A few days later, I saw he was online, so I guessed he thought changing the woman was still the right strategy to overcome his commitment issues. *Yeah, right. Good luck, buddy.* He should have come with a disclaimer.

Ms. Diva was pissed and ready for combat. She immediately manifested camo makeup, a sexy military outfit, and held a bazooka, prepared for war. The Jokester sighed and simply plugged his ears to listen to a podcast.

CHAPTER 35

FULL SPEED AHEAD

I returned to the US a little wounded, fearing that my heart was hardening from all these disappointments. I had a date scheduled two days after my arrival. I convinced myself of the mindset that to overcome heartache, the best thing was to move on quickly.

I started talking to Tim, who lived an hour away on the border between Massachusetts and Connecticut. I was not overly attracted to him from his pictures, but he seemed nice. There were two red flags that I thought doomed the whole thing even before the date occurred. One was that he didn't have a job, as he decided to switch careers a few years earlier and return to school. He had finished his associate degree in accounting and was now working on his bachelor's. The other thing was that he lived with his parents at thirty-seven years old to save money. He wanted to move out and most likely would have to get a roommate once he got a job.

I was already having nightmares of supporting a grown man who would, at the first chance he got, move into my house. He had too much time on his hands because he found me on Facebook and was probably digitally stalking me with nothing better to do. Or texting me. He was very eager and said all the right things. Ding, ding, ding, the warning bells in my brain rang loudly, and I felt all these things as huge turn-offs. My big-belly

Jokester was cracking up. The little devil wouldn't stop laughing and, in between snorts, called me names like "sucker," "sugar-momma," and "loser." Yeah, because I would be the loser if that happened, and he would hit the jackpot, just like my cats.

Nevertheless, I went and met him for a drink. How did he think he was ready to take women out on dates or for a long-term relationship and kids when he didn't have an income and lived with his parents? Perhaps I was too judgmental, but I still agreed to meet him. I cost him a miserly $6.49 for a glass of mediocre red at TGIFriday's.

I knew immediately that there was no chemistry, but he was excited about me. He swiftly mentioned a second date, and I dismissed it with the excuse of jet lag and the eye infection I had gotten when I came home. Eye infections greatly affect the brain. The Jokester also had red, bulging, bloodshot eyes, but I suspected his were from laughing so hard at my expense. And maybe too much beer.

I had to break it to Tim the following day when he texted me that I only felt the friend vibe. I knew he was greatly disappointed. On the other hand, after a few minutes of guilt, I shrugged it off as, "This is my life, and I cannot waste time on something that I already know won't bear fruit."

I started talking to Mike on a different site. He kept me on my toes. He was in medical sales, traveled a lot, and had houses on the Cape, Maine, and upstate NY, where he was from. He had two golden retrievers, never asked for my number, and just emailed me from the site.

I wondered about this because, typically, this meant the man was either married or had a girlfriend.

With his erratic travel schedule, he convinced me to drive two hours to Portsmouth, NH, for sushi. I agreed that even though this was a little too far for a first date, I wouldn't do that again.

He was much better looking in person than in his one photo.

We had a nice lunch, and the conversation flowed easily, albeit not too deep. On the way out, he asked me if I wanted to meet his dog in the car, as she was recovering from a minor surgery to the eye. I loved dogs, so I said yes. Then, out of the blue, a woman getting out of her jeep came over and started talking to him or us—the jury was still out on that one. She also had a golden retriever in the car and did private rescue of the breed. They started talking "Golden," and I felt alienated. I wondered if they knew each other and if the whole thing had been planned. I guess I was concocting conspiracy theories as I noticed how beautiful she was. Should I leave? They probably had more in common.

She eventually left, and we said goodbye. He had mentioned at lunch that he only had a work phone when I questioned him about not asking for my number. He said he didn't want his boss looking at his phone, so he didn't use it for personal communication. Hm. Okay, but I was pretty sure he was using it to go on the dating site. He asked me to send him my number through the site inbox.

We hugged goodbye without any plans, and I left. I heard from him several times the next day, and then that was it. It was a law of numbers. Indeed, the probability of finding a needle in a haystack was minuscule. And I hated to admit and accept this fact, but I couldn't change it.

I reached out to Steve, my married friend from Cherub's Arrow. We occasionally communicated through Facebook to catch up. I checked on him to see if he was behaving or still cheating on his wife. He had his eyes on two women at the two gyms he belonged to. I scolded him and then told him a little bit about my adventures. He always wanted to know the dirty details, but ultimately, he thought I was trying too hard and wanted to see me happy.

Maybe I needed his help. He said he'd be glad to. I just needed to tell him about each guy, and he would give me his opinion. Every time I shared with him, he was right on the money. We talked about getting together as friends for a drink at some point, but he knew that would be it. The look-but-not-touch approach was the best. My Jokester smirked and shook his head. He did not approve at all. Ironically. Ms. Diva was in a sleep-slumber party of one.

CHAPTER 36

BLASTS FROM A RECENT PAST

They all came back. For one reason or another, they all reached out to me, either because they missed the intimate moments, missed letting me go, or wanted something from me, which boiled down to the same.

Imagine my surprise when Juan, the Latino hunk from last spring, emailed me. I dated him for two months. The honeymoon phase decreased. It went from what I thought was the typical three months to less than two. Magic was just not extendable anymore. I was not sure if it was because people were more cynical, older, more scarred, intolerant, or just plain crazy. I was going to vote for a combination of all the above.

At first, the emails were one-liners, and I still wondered why.

"What do you want from me?"

"I miss talking to you." *That must be true because it had been over a year of silence.* I didn't buy it. The Jokester opened a bag of Cheetos and went at it. Ms. Diva decided to give herself a manicure out of boredom. Neither believed him, so I pressed on. He said he was sorry he hurt me.

"What do you really want from me?"

"What are you willing to give me?" Was this guy for real? Was he bored? What was his deal? I told him I was done with games and wished him luck with his life.

"I want your forgiveness." WHAT? Ms. Diva, on my right shoulder, curved her back like a cat and was sickened at the fact that I was replying to these stupid emails.

I told Juan he had my forgiveness, that I had closed the chapter, and moved on. Ms. Diva was pissed that I was still talking to him, and rightly so.

He proceeded to tell me what he wanted from me.

"Thank you for forgiving me. I am just going to come out and say it. You asked what I want from you." He paused. "I need a place to stay. I have to be there for work from September 29 to October 3, and I don't have a place to stay. The kids' grandparents moved and retired, and the kids' mother moved to Puerto Rico. My friend Sammy got engaged to a girl from São Miguel, Portugal, and she doesn't want him bringing any friends around. I am being honest. I understand if you can't, but it's the truth."

Little conniving piece of fecal matter! I could not believe this. The guy was baking a fancy cake with bologna, lies, and con artistry. After I called him out on his deception, he said he was joking, that his job was putting him up in a hotel in Boston, and that he wanted to take me out to dinner. *Not even over my dead body.* Ms. Diva slammed the door on that poor excuse of a man.

I should have had my head examined. Why did I always give people the benefit of the doubt? Or second chances, and sometimes third? It was counterintuitive and unproductive and created a whole batter of aggravation.

But I had not learned my lesson.

Daniel, the Purple-Heart-two-Bronze-Stars veteran, sought me out. I liked him, and he claimed to have resolved his issues. I was hesitant to see him because I suspected he had gone back to an ex-girlfriend. Plus, I thought it was too soon for him to start dating, even though we had a great time together in Providence a few months back.

Imagine my surprise when he disclosed that the reason for his absence was that he had been laid off. The national bank he worked at for twelve years wasn't doing that great, and the fact that he was a high-paid executive and had deployed twice in that period made him a target for layoffs. I didn't think companies could do that, but he seemed satisfied with a one-year severance, and with his resume, he could find a position in no time.

I agreed to go out with him. We spent a beautiful day in Newport, RI. We visited the Vanderbilt mansion, and with his top clearance, we got inside the Navy Base, which I had never visited. We went out for a drink, then dinner, and another drink.

His history was mind-blowing. He embodied the quintessential hero and sacrificed a great deal to protect us. He joked that he was most likely the most lethal guy I had ever been with. I pondered this fact. Ms. Diva crossed her legs and lifted an eyebrow while smoking a long cigarette. "Yup, he is!" I was unsure if I should feel alarmed about this, but I felt safe, proud, and appreciative.

We saw each other a couple of times in the following few days. I made him lunch one day.

He was going to a PTSD program through the VA in Providence, and one day, he came over very stressed out because he was going to have his first group session with seven other veterans who had been in combat. I helped him relax, and he left with less stress, even though he just got the news that his brother-in-law, who was still active, was being deployed to Liberia thanks to the Ebola crisis. I informed him that my friend Gabby was coming over for dinner, and I hadn't seen her in a long time.

He told me that on that Thursday, two days away, he would make me Teriyaki salmon, couscous, and asparagus. I was enjoying this. I liked him more and more, and even though I still didn't know how his PTSD manifested other than anxiety and shakes—which I was confident I could deal with—I was cautiously optimistic. We said goodbye.

Imagine my surprise when, the following day, he texted me, canceling the dinner and wishing me the best. Yet again. I asked him to call me. He did.

The conversation wasn't good. He implied that I was with another man. Let's recap. I was entertaining my girlfriend, read her excerpts of these pages, and we laughed our butts off until midnight, and here was Dan accusing me of rolling in the sheets with some other guy. He became defensive, and I could hear in his voice that he had already decided to discard me. Ms. Diva changed into a red Flamenco dress and high heels and furiously shredded the cigarette she puffed on, stomping on it.

Well, another one bit the dust.

Mercury was going retrograde. Planets gave me a false sense of alignment, and something needed to be corrected. This was not quite right. So many in a row had been such a disillusionment, and I felt beat. I knew I should stop. At this point, maybe I should keep going because I felt like these stories would never end, and I would be writing the longest manuscript ever written... there sure was enough content.

Ms. Diva's wooden castanets rattled in her hands. She was rocking long red fingernails and looking at me like she would hit me. I doubted Dan was the most lethal one.

On top of it all, the week ended with someone breaking into my house and stealing my iPad, two of my grandmother's rings, a diamond in white gold, and a green tourmaline surrounded by small diamonds set in yellow gold. I was not happy. Freaked out was more like it. I could become a hermit or join a convent. Maybe it was safer there in all respects.

CHAPTER 37

TWOFER

Never have two dates on the same night. That was my conclusion after experiencing it.

I met Adrian from Plenty of Sharks at a dive in Milford at 5:30 p.m. and had another date scheduled for 8 p.m. in South Easton with Fred, a forty-minute drive from one another.

It was going to be tight. Ms. Diva sat on a chaise longue in a leopard-printed nightgown, chewing gum like a street worker waiting for her next show. I knew what she was thinking. She shook her head at my complete and utter idiocy.

Adrian was 6'2, muscular, and bald. I had no idea what he looked like apart from that. I knew he was smart, had a Ph.D. in sports medicine research, and was quite the world traveler. Never been married and had no kids. I often wondered about that one.

He only had far-away photos because he claimed to be private and never exchanged numbers with me. Again, the whole work-phone excuse and I imagined a wife or a girlfriend hidden in the mix, accounting for the mystery of no facial pictures.

The dingy place in Milford will remain nameless, but suffice it to say, it was not a popular spot for dates or much of anything. He must have googled it and come up with that lovely hole.

This guy was tall and muscular, wore glasses, and was nicely dressed. I could tell he was happy with how I looked. We went in and sat at the bar. Ms. Diva looked around and tapped me on the shoulder, reminding me of the non-toxic antibacterial sanitizer in my purse. Germs must have been partying it up in this joint.

We ordered drinks. They only had two kinds of red wine at $4 a glass. I didn't even know if that generic wine was of a particular label or some concoction made in someone's basement by dirty guys stomping on red grapes.

Soon enough, however, we were laughing and having a good time. Then, I was downing a second glass of nasty wine, hoping my empty stomach could withstand the wait until my eight o'clock date. In the back of my mind, I wondered if second-date-Fred had wanted to do drinks and appetizers or just drinks. If the latter, I just hoped I could digest the stuff before I had to drive anywhere.

Adrian made eye contact, making a point of touching me here and there, and his conversation was intelligent. I could detect an accent; his parents lived in London, but he was born in Marrakesh, Morocco, where his mother was from and where his Turkish-German father had been stationed as a physician. He grew up in international schools, and his family valued education.

The mood started to shift when he started interrogating me about everything. I felt like I had a light bulb on my face where each of my wrinkles was analyzed for movement, scrutiny, and judgment. Ms. Diva was in a panic as she sat in an FBI interrogation room with an unattractive bead of sweat slowly trickling down her temple.

Adrian asked me about my dates and how far they had gone physically. When I refused to answer, he started analyzing my body language.

I warned him. "You ask the same question a thousand different ways, and if I don't want to answer, I won't, and that's just the way it is."

"I am curious."

"Curiosity killed the cat, and I don't think you're a cat."

We laughed a bit, but even though I knew he felt chemistry with me, I didn't because I was not attracted to him or his line of questioning. If this was only the first date, I could only imagine the polygraph tests to follow.

Ms. Diva rolled her eyes, got up from her chair with her cat-like rhythm and curvaceous bottom, and whispered in my ear, "I am done! Stick a fork in me. This cheap meat is dead."

We left. I decided to omit the fact I had another date right after. Adrian would probably maul me if I shared that, so I told him I was meeting a girlfriend for dinner. Technically deceptive on the gender and the type of meal, but prudent.

He gave me a hug that lingered too long and felt too intimate, and I left. I texted Fred that I was going to be late. I arrived fifteen minutes late, and since he lived near the restaurant, I was surprised he was the one who showed up after me.

I sat at the bar. Fred came in. He was different from the type of guys I had met and my first redhead. He was very friendly and polite, and it was refreshing not to be bombarded by questions and treated like a criminal.

The scary thing about Fred was that he had three young children, and I was unsure if I was prepared for that type of baggage.

I had another glass of wine, of much better quality this time, but still no food. I knew the next day my head would hurt. And it did.

I heard from both gentlemen again. Adrian insisted on going out several times, and I had to tell him that I wasn't fond of his interrogation tactics and would like not to repeat that experience. With a hand on her hip, Ms. Diva tossed her hair over her shoulder.

Fred wanted to see me again, but it didn't happen. I must admit that three children and a lawyer for an ex-wife were not great selling points in my book.

Ms. Diva wore a sexy pink negligée and tapped her foot. It might be that time of the month. I shrugged and told her, "Back to the drawing board, darling."

CHAPTER 38

FINISHING THE BOOK
Mission Possible?

P art of me lost total faith in this debacle. I decided that even if I was to finish the book, I needed to continue to submit myself to these ridiculous, laughable, and disappointing situations. Hopefully, my mission was not impossible! And hopefully, Tom Cruise was not secretly reading my book and laughing his tush off. Maybe he might even sit with my fat-bellied Jokester and Ms. Diva on the couch, devouring popcorn that was way too salty and drinking super cheap wine. Ms. Diva would naturally be eyeing Mr. Cruise as dessert, but the Jokester would shake his head and remind her he was too short for her.

So, in the name of research, I needed to prevail and continue. There were two more days of Mercury Retrograde, so I should have stayed put. But I thought there was no harm in digitally talking to people. Yeah, right. I should have known better.

I needed to be more proactive. I wasn't very lucky when I emailed the guys I was interested in. They usually didn't respond. And only a tiny percentage of the ones who initiated communication did I reply to, and then, I'd get immersed in these maniacal situations with questionable characters where one could laugh at my expense because even if I wanted to be creative, I couldn't make this shit up.

One of the guys that I emailed responded. I was very excited. His name was Peter. Handsome, forty-five, divorced, 6'2, college degree, district manager for Staples, and one twelve-year-old son. Our conversation flowed for a couple of days through Plenty of Sharks, and then we decided to exchange numbers and text.

Texting, the form of communication I was highly addicted to. It might have something to do with the writing part. Talking on the phone with strangers was never my forte. I always hated cold calling. So, texting could become a drug, and I didn't want to overdose at this point with a stranger for several reasons. One, it built a false sense of intimacy and, in that case, left room for boldface lying with the protection of a handheld device. Two, one wanted to meet as soon as possible to avoid reason One. Third, it could get rude to constantly glance at your phone while in the company of others. Fourth, it was a distraction when you had more important things to do. Fifth, it opened the door for creeps to send you inappropriate pictures.

Peter emailed me a couple of photos. Of his face. I was already asking in advance for guys not to send me penis pictures. If I had kept them all, I would present you with a very illustrated book of penises from different angles and sizes. And I could safely say you'd be observing over a dozen appendages. One should be glad I deleted those and asked for a written waiver when I started texting someone. Sometimes, even an explicit request was ignored!

Back to Peter. I got a few face photos and thought he was very handsome. I had yet to determine if he was normal overall. He asked me if he could call me.

Oh my! An actual person who wanted to have a phone conversation with *moi*? Ms. Diva changed into her sexy bubble-gum pink lingerie and was practically humping a very alarmed Tom Cruise on the couch. Snorting, the Jokester was obviously under enormous alcoholic influence.

I had an enjoyable conversation with Peter, and he asked if he could call me later. I texted him back, "Sure."

In my mind, a voice from deep below whispered this was too good to be true. So, I decided to Google his profile photos. I went on Plenty of Sharks and saved his two photos onto my desktop. I opened Google, clicked on Images, and then dragged and dropped the first photo. Matches were found. My eyes trickled down the populated list, and I got a distinct metallic taste in my mouth—it could have been bullshit if bullshit ever had an actual taste.

I clicked on one of the links, and it was a dating site from Norway with the same two photos and the two others he had texted me. My mood changed instantly.

The Jokester woke up from his drunken stupor and manifested a Glock in his hand. Ms. Diva pushed Tom Cruise off the couch and morphed into a black ninja with matching cat-eye makeup, holding a black leather whip in one hand and a bazooka in the other.

I shook my head. Without even a moment of hesitation, I went back to his profile on Plenty of Sharks and reported Peter as an abusive user. There was a window of comments I could fill out, and I wrote, "These are stolen photos from a dating site in Norway." Within the hour, his account was deleted.

I texted Peter. "I don't do fake profiles."

"What are you talking about?"

"Your profile photos are fake."

The phone rang. It was him. I picked up. He started getting very defensive, blamed me for having issues, and accused me of being crazy. I explained to him that I Googled his photos and discovered they were stolen. He swore they were his, even if he was a little older now. Exclamation point squared to the infinite! I told him that there was a very easy way to solve this. He could take a photo of himself right then, text it to me, and if it were the same guy, I would be the first to apologize. He said he would and then countered that it would be his choice afterward whether he would continue talking to me. I responded, "Fair enough." But my gut was not budging.

Then he emailed me a photo. It was not the same guy—similar features and older. I told him that. He didn't try to convince me any further. He got caught. He said he was not confident. I told him he needed to deal with that on his own and that it was not my problem. I explained that lying like he did was a deal breaker for me. He asked me if we could remain friends and if he could text me from time to time. "My friends don't lie to me." So, that was a big-fat-Jokester-Ms.-Diva no, with capital letters.

When will these men learn that, eventually, the truth will come out? Don't they plan on meeting the woman face-to-face? Maybe not, if you recall the two extensive fake profiles I had to deal with in the past.

However, it may also be that I was developing a more ninja-like intuition and was extra alert. Or maybe I was just less hopeful. It might be a perfectly balanced cocktail of the two.

CHAPTER 39

INTROSPECTION AS A SIDEBAR

I might have needed some introspection. I wondered if I was just too cynical. I had done some individual therapy (and couples' therapy) while looking for solutions to save my marriage. I was assured I was a reasonably normal woman with my head on my shoulders most of the time.

I had a vast network of friends who confided in me, and vice-versa. I also had a bunch of female friends who were in the field of psychology; some were in private practice, teaching, profiling, or providing therapy to law enforcement officers. They all thought I could have been a psychologist because I gave good advice. It worked. And it was free.

So, if there was such a consensus and I was deemed a reasonably normal human being, then it would logically and plausibly follow that I could figure out my love life or find an equal or suitable partner. Of course, there was an assumption that I could find an equal to me. That could be debated at great lengths. I also considered that perhaps I needed a matchmaking committee of girlfriends who would meet once a week (over drinks naturally, preferably wine, vodka, or some other cocktail) and would analyze my progress or devise a different strategy than this online dating saga.

They could consult with my Jokester and my beloved Ms. Diva, as they had divergent opinions about the men I had been dealing with.

One of the guys who sometimes talked to me on Plenty of Sharks told me that the world of dating, not just online, had changed a great deal. He said that no one was bothering with commitment anymore. That the process was a "rinse and repeat" one. The thought of all of this was quite depressing.

We could all second-guess ourselves when our self-esteem screamed doubt at us, especially in uncomfortable or familiar situations. Online dating was a souped-up rejection center, full of deception and people looking to get lucky. The Jokester raised his eyebrow and nodded at the same time.

I was tolerant and patient with this process. I continued it even though grown professional men in their forties, some of them fathers themselves, sent me pictorial portraits of their private parts as if they were some sort of trophy or toy they were proud of.

And I agreed with some of my friends who asked me why in the world I was still doing this. I'd tell them that aside from information-gathering for this manuscript, which was never my intent when I started this online thing, I was not going to go to bars or clubs in the hopes of meeting my next life partner. I started this as a log on my mini iPad, where I could keep track of first impressions of my first dates so I could distinguish them. I have the memory of a seed (no offense to seeds), and I found that keeping the log would be a helpful tool to help me navigate the online dating waters. But once I started experiencing some of these looney toons, I had to do more than write down simple descriptions to help my memory.

There were no rules or protocols, but I learned that I couldn't take people's information, profile, or stories at face value. Some were doing it purely for entertainment. Others were in relationships and looking for extracurricular activities. Ms. Diva knew what I was talking about. She was not wearing her shimmery couture red gown and six-inch patent leather designer heels for nothing. And those sparkling diamonds around her neck and ears were real, darn it! She probably got those from past lovers, and now she was in your face with the glitz and the glam without a care for anyone's opinion. I envied her nonchalant poise. She didn't give a crap about what anyone thought of her.

As time trickled away, I reflected on all of this. Did I have some regrets? Sure. If we were honest with ourselves, we all did, even if we have accepted and let go of them on certain levels. The last thing I thought would happen to me was that as I approached the fourth decade of my life, I was divorced with no children. I honestly did not see this coming and didn't plan it. Life threw you curve balls. Some people knew how to roll with the punches better than others. Others just got thrown many challenges. I was fortunate that when I wrote this, I was healthy, did not lack anything, and was content with my life. Could I have improved lots of areas of this journey? That was a resounding yes. Had I learned a lot so far? Yes. Did I still have a lot to learn? Double-yes!

But I thought that time didn't forgive certain things. Your experiences branded you, even if you had little devils on your shoulders, no matter how loveable they were. Your story could give you scars and shake up your ideals. Some could shake up your morals. Others could cause you to behave in opposite ways than you ever thought in a million years. You may become less idealistic, hopeful, more cynical, and intolerant. Sometimes, you became more confident about what you wanted because, having gone through unpleasant, out-of-your-comfort-zone experiences, you got a sense of appreciation for opposite extremes and were no longer willing to settle for average. Plus, walking in someone else's shoes was impossible, especially if they were the red patent leather designer kind.

CHAPTER 40

SIFTING THROUGH MEDIOCRE SAND GRANULES

I used Plenty of Sharks. I used Catch. I scheduled two dates for the same week. If I aimed for that number, I could sift through the frogs quickly. Maybe not. One was from Catch. Let's call him Jerry. He lived north of Boston, forty-five, divorced, had three children, and was into mergers and acquisitions. I had no idea what he merged or acquired. Yeah, I know—even the Jokester got off the couch and started bolting for the door. I knew he was 5'10", which was borderline too short. I was a "heightist" for sure, which was someone who discriminated against short men. I admitted it. I couldn't help it. But I was tolerant of many other things and was the first to admit I was not perfect.

Jerry set a date for Thursday night, and he wanted to take me out to a costly restaurant near Gillette Stadium, home to the New England Patriots. I was always hesitant about dinner because that could mean two hours of boring conversation.

He told me he had to travel to Texas for a few days and would return on Wednesday, the day before our date. The conversation was smooth and intelligent, sometimes flirty. I looked forward to meeting him.

I didn't hear from him, so I decided to text him on Thursday morning to confirm our date. He told me he'd only come back that night at 9:45 PM and had deleted my texts and lost my number. That was the most ridiculous thing I had heard, as he could have warned me or canceled the date through the site.

Ms. Diva was reading a book and lifted her pencil-thin eyebrow as she lounged on a velvet emerald-green chaise from the early 1900s. She slowly turned the page and whispered, "asshole."

I had a message on Plenty of Sharks from Bruce, forty-seven, divorced, and in the animal field. It was Jokester's turn to raise an eyebrow as he was momentarily distracted from the Real Housewives of New Jersey Reunion. "Animal field? What the hell is that? Is he a farmer? Does he live in a barn? Does he enjoy being put on a leash?"

It turned out that Bruce had three children—I heard the alarm sounding in the distance again, and he was an animal nurse. He was 5'11". Okay, that was better. Not great, but better. He asked me out for dinner on Saturday, and the same happened. He never got back to me. I emailed him through the site that morning, as I never had his number, and only got a response at 11 at night. Something about how he "couldn't deal with others," gibberish I didn't comprehend. I snapped out a reply that he could have given me a heads up, also known as common courtesy, but the only word I got back was, "Sorry."

Ms. Diva slightly changed positions on her chaise longue and turned another page, muttering again, "asshole."

I got an email from someone else on Plenty of Sharks. His name was Jeff, and he was forty, divorced, with a five-year-old son. We exchanged numbers, and he called me a few times. We had some great conversations. He worked as a service advisor at a dealership, owned two Pitbulls, and was active in a non-profit to save the breed. He owned an antique car, worked on it, and participated in car shows.

He asked me out on a date for Friday night, the only available night I had that week. And then, the same happened. I didn't hear from him. The Jokester got up from the blue recliner and twirled his middle finger.

Yup, he sure did. So, when I texted him on Friday morning, which was starting to be a stupid routine I didn't want to have, I only heard from him later that day, telling me that he was trying to reconcile with his ex-wife. I wished him good luck. Then I noticed him online on Plenty of Sharks. The ex-wife's tale was smelling wickedly foul. Ms. Diva licked her ring finger and turned another page from her book, muttering once more, "asshole."

CHAPTER 41
THE COUGAR EFFECT

I had a hard time with the term "cougar." It was such a double standard. People applauded twice when an older man was with a younger woman. I sometimes used to refer to myself as a trophy wife as my ex-husband was sixteen and a half years older than me, and for the sake of reality, I was a trophy—a treasure. Remember when Hugh Hefner, in his eighties, dated twenty-year-olds? But if a woman dated a younger man, you heard snide remarks. It was a matter of pride that the younger guy got a "cougar," but honestly, everyone else didn't look well upon a woman with a younger man. What was wrong with her? She was deemed a hunter looking to entrap Bambi. It was ridiculous.

But there was a trend, judging by the younger guys who emailed me. I laughed it off at first. Ms. Diva was intrigued, however, and magically donned a spotted animal print outfit with matching lingerie. She also wore a big smirk, probably concocting something in that devious mind of hers. I was not sure I was ready for it.

According to Wikipedia, a cougar was "an older woman seeking a sexual relationship with a younger man." So, what did you call a younger man seeking a sexual relationship with an older woman? Was it a cub?

I didn't know the exact answer, and I found it laughable at first. Why would a younger man be interested in me? Girls their age had fewer scars, wrinkles, or stretch marks. And they hadn't been as corrupted. Had they? Times had changed, and from what I heard, people were having sex younger and younger, but still, it perplexed me that a younger man would want an older woman.

Imagine my surprise when Neal, a twenty-one-year-old from Connecticut who had begun contact during the summer, re-emerged. He was now a ripe twenty-two. And he still wanted a sexual relationship with me. I laughed it off a little. Ms. Diva licked her lips as if she was about to have some dripping-hot BBQ ribs fresh off the grill.

I was not the first one in his line of cougars. He had even dated someone who was forty-four. That was five years older than me. I pointed out to him that she was double his age. He laughed. He explained that he preferred older women because girls his age were emotionally immature, and the true crux of the matter was that they were sexually not as experienced. Our age difference was... ready for this? Seventeen years. If I had a clone, she would beat the crap out of me for considering this.

Neal had been in the army for four years. Here was another army boy, literally. From the photos he sent me, he was beautiful. 6'2. I was in trouble—blue eyes, muscular, delicious. I waited for lightning to strike me. He was now a full-time college student and worked full-time for Lowe's. In his spare time, he tutored history, his specialty being American history. And he was politically involved with rallies.

He was intelligent and seemed more emotionally mature than most mid-forty guys I encountered. How was that possible? But, of course, he was not what I was looking for. He was just too young.

However, he did make me a proposal that was tough to refuse. He wanted us to have a monogamous sexual relationship; "friends who bang" might be the term he first used. He wanted to become my boy toy. He would drive a little over an hour away and be naked in my house, where

I could use him for sex as much as I wanted. He still wanted me to get a boyfriend and go on dates, but in the meantime, we could play. He wanted to do sexual things in every room of my house. He wanted me to be loud and even mentioned something about outside. He took it back when I told him I had neighbors, but the gist was that he preferred older women because they were more experienced and knew what they were doing. He said he wouldn't question it anytime I wanted to stop this arrangement. And he told me that if he found a girl he wanted to date seriously, he would tell me, and we would stop everything.

He also pointed out that we were both in our sexual prime. He was right, of course. Wasn't it God's humor at work to make the man be in his sexual prime early on and the woman in her mid-thirties to mid-forties? Ms. Diva started taking off her clothes. She was ready for this. She almost bopped me in the head. "What is wrong with you, you idiot?"

The truth was that I never did crazy things like this when I was in my twenties. I was a very shy, late bloomer, and then I met my ex-husband. In the two years I was single, I didn't go crazy, and I only had a couple of short-lived relationships, if I could even call them that.

I agreed to meet Neal at a TGIFriday. He was very handsome and so very incorrigibly young. We had a great rapport as he drank water, and I sipped on a delicious Malbec. Our conversation was easy, and I was secretly excited to delve into the waters of cougarship, even if it was to have a little taste. Ms. Diva drooled in anticipation.

The more I thought about this, the more I realized it was not a good idea. He would require training, judging from his kissing skills. I guess the other ladies didn't bother with grooming him for me. And I didn't have the patience. Ms. Diva was dressed for the classroom. "What else would I have to teach him?"

Highly disappointed, Ms. Diva pouted in the corner. She knew I was not going to go forward with this arrangement. Deep down, she understood. It wasn't what I was looking for. And I had to keep an eye on my end goal if that was to ever materialize. From time to time, I heard from him. He graduated college and entered the workforce.

CHAPTER 42
SPEED DATING

S o, my friend Gabby, who lives in Rhode Island, told me about a speed dating event in Warwick. I mentally rolled my eyes. The Jokester and Ms. Diva snorted simultaneously, showing me how vested they were in this ordeal.

As much as these two shook their heads on speed dating, I told Gabby it would be a good chapter for the book, as I looked at this as field research. Gabby was coming out of a thirteen-year-old relationship and hadn't dated much, so we signed up online.

This should be interesting. I had been to speed networking events, ironically based on speed dating, but I hadn't considered it. It couldn't be any worse than what I had already experienced.

Gabby told me this was open to professionals, ages thirty-four to forty-six. What I concluded, however, was that there was no pre-screening. Regarding age, one could lie, and no one asked you for identification, so I already saw room for deception. Ms. Diva's nostrils started flaring in a crescendo.

We had a drink at the bar first as we were early. Not a great idea to drink on an empty stomach.

This happened in a separate room at the restaurant, and the event coordinator, a much older, disheveled woman, explained that we all had a badge with our first name and a number, the ladies remained at the same table, and that one had six minutes with each person. She would then return to the room at the six-minute mark and ring a bell. Since there were twelve women and twelve men, we talked at least 72 minutes, or an hour and twelve minutes. Probably a little more than that, as people relocated to the next table.

We were given two sheets. One was for our notes, and the other was to give back to the coordinator at the end of the event with our answers, specifically, 'Let's talk' and 'No, thanks.' She also placed a sheet of questions on each table in case we ran out of things to say. How could one run out of things to say in six minutes, I wondered?

Right before the event started, I looked around the room and tried to absorb first impressions. Some of the ladies were quite beautiful, some were curvier girls (I fit into that category a little bit,) and others looked washed out and perhaps over the age limit the group allotted for.

Surprisingly (or not), the men could be more attractive at first glance, and most were short. When I say short, I mean shorter than me. I was almost 5'8, but I was more like 5'10 with my boots, and the bulk of these guys were under 5'7. This was a massive problem for me.

Not so much for my friend, who was 4'11.5. She was also four years younger than me but looked twenty-five and had the face of an angel.

So, the rounds commenced. There were no breaks. At the end of the night, I identified a couple of potential men for her and none for me. There might be one who was a wine distributor (shocker!), but we were talking about a very slim maybe. I couldn't get over the poor soul who was getting his CDL license the following day, was missing a few teeth, and didn't have a job. I ran out of conversation with him. I glanced at the questions, but even so, there were long and awkward silences. In six minutes.

At the end, I looked at my sheet and wondered what the hell I was going to turn in. I felt bad about turning in a paper with all "no, thanks," so I wrote "Let's talk" with the wine distributor. If there were a match, the coordinator would email you information about each other. If you chose someone who didn't choose you, they might get your information, but you didn't get theirs.

At the end of it all, I realized I wasn't very popular. Only three of the twelve chose me, and one was Mr. Toothless. The Jokester bent at a ninety-degree angle and couldn't stop laughing. Ms. Diva tried to contain herself. But laughing could be contagious. The expression on my face was very serious when I found out that Gabby had received eleven emails back. I knew this was not a popularity contest, but I felt right back in middle school. If there had been a loser stamp, it would be on my forehead.

We had dinner afterward, and by the end of the night, we both went home with headaches. Hers lasted one more day, and mine turned into a six-day migraine. I hadn't had one like that in years.

I looked at my two other suitors and decided neither would do the trick for me. On the other hand, Gabby got two dates and dated one for a bit. She ended up brokenhearted but met someone on Happiness Now, whom she dated for a long time but didn't last as she had hoped.

Ms. Diva shrugged and wrapped herself in fleece. Winter was here, even if not officially yet. This was the time for layers and sexy boots with tight leggings.

I took a nice deep breath and thought of the habitual *back to the drawing board*.

The three of us agreed that Speed Dating was not to happen again.

CHAPTER 43
THE DISAPPEARING ACT

I took advantage of a highly discounted rate on Happiness Now for three months, over 60% off (isn't that how they get you—waiving before you what you think is a great deal when in reality is probably the same old crap?). A friend who lived in New Jersey met her husband that way, and she insisted I give it a shot.

The Happiness Now process was trickier than the rest because you could not email someone directly.[1] You had to send them five pre-selected questions, and only if they answered would the lines of communication open, and you could start using HNmail.

The first time around, I felt no connection with the guys who sent me their questions, and the rare ones I had sent my questions to, which was a rare thing, had yet to respond. It was this permanent miscommunication. I seriously doubted their marketing campaign and efficacy claims, but I promised to be more proactive this time.

---

1. This is at the time that I wrote this chapter.

I got five questions from Ethan, who lived in Southern Rhode Island. I knew it was a stereotype, but most people I knew from Rhode Island didn't seem to travel very far. It almost seemed like if they had to drive to the town next door, they had to pack their entire household, or they commented things such as, "Providence? I am not going into Providence, it's way too dangerous." So, traveling overseas, which was one of my things, might sound like traveling to outer space to a Rhode Islander, but I had to keep my mind open and be judgy. This was plain hyperbole.

Ethan and I emailed back and forth for a few weeks, at least one email a day, and he decided to ask me out for drinks. He told me he would drive to Providence. Shocker! After exchanging phone numbers, I discovered he had traveled much outside Rhode Island. He had even gone to Asia! I was impressed. He had gone to different places as he liked to surf and climb mountains. I warned him I was not at that level of being adventurous and probably never would be, but I had a bucket list in my head, not *1,000 places to see before you die*, like Patricia Schultz's best seller, but a few.

From the photos on his profile, he had at least one son. 6'2. Check. Well-traveled. Check. Apparently stable. Check. It seemed safe to meet. We set up coffee at Caffe Dolce Vita on Federal Hill.

My top might have been too revealing, even though it was a wrap navy top, and I had to keep glancing down to double-check that there were no accidental mishaps. He occasionally looked in that direction, and I started feeling self-conscious. But it all subsided as the conversation flowed and coffee turned into dinner. I felt hope's gentle breeze on my cheek. We seemed to have much in common.

We talked a lot about traveling. He told me he had two sons from two different women. His youngest was eight and lived with his ex-wife. His oldest was a twenty-year-old college student and part Native American, which explained why Ethan was on the Board of a Native American non-profit. He had raised him by himself, and he mentioned that the son's mother had not been up to the task. I was unsure if it was because they were both very young or something else.

He made it sound like it was a big happy family, where he now got along with both exes and saw their families too. This was a lot to take in. I wondered if I could ever fit in. I was having flashbacks of my ex-boyfriend in Maine with his clan-like family, and I started getting warning goosebumps. He talked about his parenting skills. He also said he was in the Navy for a while and had gotten the travel bug from that experience. He had been and still was a contractor, and you could tell he was successful. Not sure why he felt the need to tell me he had picked up an $800 tab at a Foxwoods steakhouse for his friends at some point. I was not looking for a sugar Daddy and found it borderline idiotic to boast about money that way. But I let it slide.

We ended up spending four hours together, and when he hugged me goodbye and told me we should do it again, I had a nagging feeling that I would never hear from him again. For some reason, my four-hour dates always turned to post-dating silence, and I was never sure why. All I knew was that Ms. Diva and the Jokester blinked a few times and didn't have to say a word. I was right. I never heard back from Ethan.

CHAPTER 44
VIDEOGAME ADDICT

December crawled up, and Rick started communicating with me. He was in IT for some big company. He could spell, which was a bonus. Ms. Diva rolled her eyes. She was so sick and tired of my grammar snobbism.

Rick was originally from Massachusetts but lived in California for a while.

He decided to call me. And we talked for hours a few nights in a row, so much so that I was not getting enough sleep.

The red flags kept coming, and I looked the other way.

I called my brother in NYC. He always had a way of pulling me back to the ground, even if it was rough sometimes and not in the most soothing way, but that was tough sibling love.

I told him Rick's story. Rick was a very eloquent speaker. He sounded like a Californian, smooth-talking me in the wee hours of the night as I became more sleep-deprived each day. I told my brother that Rick only started getting his life straight eleven months earlier, coming out of a lifetime of video game addiction. His addiction got so bad that he got fired two or three times, neglected to pay his rent, and eventually got his car repossessed because he didn't bother paying his bills. He was too immersed in the alternate reality of gaming to be present in our earthly reality.

I assumed that video games were the culprit for his failed relationships from the past, including a four-year one where his fiancée cheated on him and left him for another.

After he lost his wheels, he decided that he needed to grow up and quit video games. And he did it cold turkey. He got rid of his computer at the ripe age of thirty-six. That was eleven months after we started talking.

Ironically, he got a job in IT, but he was determined to succeed and beat his habit. Everything he had described to me was classic signs of addiction. I asked him if he sought therapy for this, and he said, "No."

He replaced his addiction with martial arts and was thoroughly immersed in studying those, going to the gym, and getting in shape, which I found admirable.

The other red flag my brother scolded me about was that he was now a super fan of UFC or Ultimate Fighting Championship, a mixed martial arts company that held fighting events throughout the country. Just like wrestling, football, or baseball, they had televised events. It was the football of mixed martial arts fighting, not a martial art in my eyes, but pure sport and competition.

Nevertheless, although Rick seemed emotionally immature for a thirty-six-year-old man, he asked me out on a date, and I agreed. What was I thinking? I didn't have a clue about reforming someone like that, nor why I would even want that challenge.

The dinner date was set for a Saturday night. Two days before, he called me and said he had forgotten about a UFC match that was supposed to start Saturday night. I told him we could reschedule since he didn't want to miss that event. He insisted on keeping the date and told me it was more important to meet me than to watch the pay-per-view event.

The day before the date, he changed his tune. His friends wanted to get together to watch UFC and celebrate a birthday simultaneously. I gave him an out, and he told me he was thinking about it and would tell me his decision the next day on Saturday.

My mind was churning. Ms. Diva swatted her faux fur scarf in my face to wake me up from my stupor. Rick texted me on Saturday afternoon to tell me he would hang out with his friends and asked if we could get together the next day. I concluded he was another one to place in the "predictable box."

The next day, Sunday, I was going to go to a giant bonfire, and I planned to meet up with a friend who would be with her family there. I asked him if he wanted to come along, and he was more than welcome as it would be a big crowd. His answer was, "We'll see."

My brother told me, "I told you so." I did hear from him again. I mistook his call for someone I had recently been talking to, who shared the same first name. I only realized later in the conversation that it was him. He asked me out again. I said maybe. He kept insisting in the following days, and I finally told him no because I felt that he was not emotionally mature enough and was still hung up on his ex-girlfriend. We eventually became Facebook friends, and he is now married.

CHAPTER 45

CHRISTMAS BREAK
The Curse of Always Being Right

Around mid-December, the day before I went home to Europe for Christmas, I squeezed in a date with Joe, a divorced forty-seven-year-old. Very successful corporate guy with a somewhat shady past. He told me he had been a drug dealer in his twenties. I should have just walked out, but I realized this was all for a greater cause: manuscript content, and I couldn't make any of this up. I felt at times that I was in my reality show, and no one was watching, apart from the Jokester and Ms. Diva.

Joe was a nice guy. He had a goatee, which was not the usual type of guy I went for, but I was trying to think outside my box. And my open-mindedness seemed to have no limits. The date overall was great, over a couple of lemon twist martinis, which he suggested, and I approved. And because it was great, I predicted I would never hear back from him, and I was right, yet again. I hated this curse of mine.

I had been ready to throw in the towel many times. I questioned myself. I questioned why I was determined to make this online dating thing work. Theoretically, it could work, but the equation of quality people wasn't panning out. I knew quite a few online dating success stories and figured I could be another one. But the third anniversary of being online was coming up, and I had nothing to celebrate other than shit, more shit, and shittier shit.

I didn't even have a theory of why that was, and if I were honest with myself, what I should have done was forget about finding a partner online, shut down all my accounts, and maybe focus on getting more work, a job change, or learn something new. All good possibilities and time potentially better spent than on this stuff. But I wanted to finish this book even if it was to conclude, "Hey, I tried this, but it didn't work for me. I gave it a good three fucking years."

I could imagine being interviewed by Ellen DeGeneres or Oprah after the book made it to the New York Times Bestsellers' list. "Why did you put yourself through this torture? You beat a dead horse." And I would blankly stare at the audience and say nothing as if I were a deer blinded by headlights on a wooded road in the middle of nowhere.

During the holidays, I found myself automatically checking Plenty of Sharks. I had been talking to Cam for about a month, a FedEx driver for the past seventeen years who lived in the same neighborhood as one of my best friends in Warwick, Rhode Island. He sounded good, but all he did was chit-chat, and like the countless guys I emailed online, he was all talk and no action, and I knew I was wasting my time. I decided to cut communication shortly after that. The New Year was coming, and it was time to start from scratch.

I laughed when two twenty-year-olds from Cherub's Arrow and a twenty-three-year-old from POS emailed me the same week. I ditched two of them immediately. One, however, let's call him Dan, was intelligently debating why I should give him a shot. He was a college graduate with a full-time job who lived a couple of towns over... at his parents, of course. I thought to myself, 'I probably know his mom!' We talked about traveling.

I also told him that I was not interested in twenty-two-year-olds, regardless of how much stamina they had and how much fun they thought they could give me. So, even though Dan occasionally texted me, he also concluded that he wanted to date girls his age, which I encouraged him to do. He texted me when he needed advice, and of course, I concluded yet again I was in the wrong profession. I should have charged for my time.

On Christmas Day, I got a surprise email from my ex-boyfriend from Maine wishing me Merry Christmas. Instead of not responding, and because manners were branded in me from the get-go, I emailed him back and wished him the same, which was basically like shooting myself in the foot because I knew he would think that I was opening the doors of communication.

And yet again, I was right. Ms. Diva had a red tinsel-fitted gown, which could blind Santa. Her hair was blown out in high volume, and she looked like a red Christmas tree, with matching lipstick and color-changing nail polish that went from sparkly red to sparkly burgundy. The Jokester dressed up for the first time in honor of Jesus's birthday and was sporting an ill-fitted dark suit, making it clear that Ms. Diva wasn't his wardrobe stylist.

Both were watching my reality show. Andrew emailed me back, saying, "Hope you're doing well." I was happy with that sentence. It had a period in it. There was no need to reply. My conscience was clear, but two weeks later, he emailed me a question.

"How have you been?" If I didn't reply, I felt like I was being rude, so instead, I said: "Amazing. Couldn't be better. Why do you ask?"

"I'm happy to hear that! I still think about you and how you are doing.. ..to be blunt, I miss you." *Well, I don't miss taking out your trash from your car because you are too damn lazy to do it.* I didn't reply that, but I thought about it. Nope. That chapter was closed. I decided not to add fuel to the fire and ignored his last message.

Many of them wanted to come back. But there may be a reason why they call the past the past! It's supposed to remain there, and only a dumbass brain attack would have made me go back there. I didn't see anyone throwing me a three-year online dating anniversary party.

The New Year came with resolutions, and I was adamant about finding a partner. I had to become as aggressive as ever. And more open-minded. I may even have to open the exception of meeting people under six feet tall. Maybe there was a good needle in that haystack.

CHAPTER 46
THE ARTIST'S WAY

So, my first date of the New Year was with Nick, a Renaissance man who dabbled with a guitar, singing, bartending, and juggling two teenage daughters as a single dad.

Our very intellectual communication on Plenty of Sharks piqued my interest. As a word artist, I tended to choose different kinds of people in seeking the elusive life partner. However, I looked in the mirror and telepathically said, "You need to choose differently and completely outside of your box of predictability."

There was always quite a risk in choosing outside this box because I felt I had lost my filtering abilities and feared that the more time passed, the more I thought I became pliable on specific deal breakers of what I was looking for in a relationship. I demonstrated countless times that I could be too flexible and too tolerant, as if I were watching a storm coming right at me, and my legs were paralyzed and unable to react. I could only become the victim of my plight.

I was unsure if Nick was employed, and I didn't ask him, which was me overlooking one of those deal breakers. I dismissed both my shoulder companions. I knew Ms. Diva was high maintenance, and the Jokester was a glutton, emphasizing how their addictive habits were proof of my culpable negligence.

There was something quite fragile and beautiful about Nick. We had been going through one of the worst winters ever, and he offered to shovel and get wood from my shed. Of course, yours truly was not going to allow a stranger, regardless of how beautiful and angelic he appeared, into my home, my sacred space. The guns would come out blazing from Ms. Diva and the Jokester.

However, I had been looking for fireplace kindling all over the region, as I ran out and could not find any for sale. I mentioned something to Nick, who told me he had kindling all over his property in the woods and would pick some for me and bring me a bag on our first date. It struck me as a sappy, romantic gesture. And my thoughts couldn't help but drift to the possibility of this relationship working out and me uttering the words, "you had me at kindling."

The bitter cold quickly snapped me back to reality and my daily chore of shoveling at least twice a day, blizzard after blizzard, and accepting the harsh truth that living by myself sucked when you had no help. It certainly would have been nice to have a knight in shining armor, or whatever attire, to help me with New England winters.

We met at Panera. Nick was attractive in his rock-and-roll black leather jacket, blue jeans, and messy hair. He was tall and skinny, charming, and witty. I had a coffee, and he had nothing, making me wonder if he had any income. He appeared nervous. This was his first online date since his last brief relationship with an old high school flame after a long marriage gone sour.

He told me that he had been married for over eighteen years and that he used to work for an event management company. He then discovered his boss was having an affair with his wife, and thus why he'd gotten divorced. That couldn't be easy for a man's self-esteem and ego.

We had a great time, and he told me he wanted to see me again for dinner and a movie. I said yes, but we didn't make definite plans. We went outside, and he moved a giant bag of kindling into my trunk. I thanked him, hugged him goodbye, and we became Facebook friends. I didn't post anything too private on there anyway, and I didn't have a relationship status like many there.

We texted back and forth a little more. We scheduled a date and ended up canceling due to another blizzard. Winters were not romance generators in my book, and for someone trying to date, this time of year was challenging.

We never rescheduled. I was a big believer in being pursued and not the pursuer when it came to romance. Thus, I was not chasing anyone for a date or a relationship. Maybe I'd hear back from him. Perhaps I wouldn't. Both were fine with me. And Nick's kindling was great. I learned through Facebook that Nick found his match and was super happy. Last I knew, he welcomed a third daughter.

Perhaps I should have kept thinking outside of the box.

Chapter 47
Navy Seal

I should have avoided a Navy Seal with over twenty years of career and constant deployment. It was not like the glamorized GI Joe movies, where you had these incredible men of steel who were lethal, effective, and stable. Not in real life.

In addition, Larry was a widower, having lost his wife of twenty years to cancer in 2008. That was traumatic enough, especially if they were your soulmate, and you knew you would never be able to recreate that person.

Not sure which part of his résumé made me think getting involved with him was a good idea. I was extremely grateful for his service, but at the same time, I realized that his life experience had been a sacrifice, and there was no way I could relate any of mine in comparison.

Royally fucked up might be applicable as a description. I could not picture this man as a mechanical engineer. Being court-martialed three times to protect his men (all charges had been dismissed), this Master Chief was a broken and massive gladiator at 6'3. Having been shot multiple times, his liver cocooned with bullet remnants, his pancreas had been damaged to transform him into an insulin-taking diabetic, his teeth blown out, his thyroid unable to function correctly, his ears and eyes were affected in numerous ways, even though they didn't look it, and I still found this man beautiful.

Part of me admired him, and part of me felt sorry for him. I had no idea how in the world this could work. He now lived in Boston, was a Union steel worker operating heavy equipment like cranes on the sides of buildings, and plowed for the State of Massachusetts every time there was a need, and this winter had been a never-ending state of emergency.

He was lucky. Even though he hadn't fallen into alcoholism or heroin addiction like many, he took a lot of medications, including mood stabilizers, and occasionally attended group therapy for his PTSD, which manifested through nightmares about war.

I was over my head on this one and unsure if this had any type of future potential. He immediately fell in love with me, which could be misconstrued as a giant red flag. I ignored it. It had been a while since a man had professed love for me.

I was cautiously optimistic but terrified at the same time. Larry carried a gun and a knife concealed in his vest, and he never separated from it, even while sleeping or going to the bathroom. He counted his money obsessively at times. He barked orders at me, and I verbally fought him back, telling him I was not one of his soldiers. I quickly said to him that if someone gave me orders, I would purposely go out of my way to disobey. I believed in equal partnerships and couldn't be told what to do without having childhood flashbacks of my own and feeling voiceless. The other thing that worried me was that Larry was angry. He said things without thinking, and he did the same in writing. I knew that whenever that happened, I had to disengage. I wondered if my willingness to be open-minded and flexible allowed for too much tolerance.

I knew I was learning a lot, but what was I willing to sacrifice in the name of tolerance and peace? And for how long?

CHAPTER 48
FINAL CATCH

I joked a few times with Larry that I went fishing and caught myself a seal. We laughed at it. I had been burned out by the online dating scene and had suspended all the online dating profiles. I wanted to delete all the accounts, but it was as if I heard my brother's voice yelling at me not to delete them or put all my eggs in one basket. Well, that's what I did—put all my eggs in one basket. I didn't think I knew how to live any other way. Maybe it was not brilliant, perhaps it was the behavior of a potential gambler, thus why I didn't gamble. However, I started this book to keep a log so I could remember the details of my dates and not try to date multiple people simultaneously. I couldn't have juggled that. If I had turned dating into multi-tasking men, I would now be in the looney bin, along with the Jokester and Ms. Diva, the three of us shackled in white coats.

A couple of weeks into dating Larry, I was positive I would break things off with him. He was way too complicated, way too strong, and way too stubborn. Sometimes, he would text me horrible stuff because he was having a bad day, and I would start feeling red smoke coming out of my ears, but something told me to stay steady and give him a chance. I was intimidated by his strength. There was no way I could manipulate him. Even though I was not a liar by nature, I knew I couldn't even get away with a white lie with him. He was used to actual combat, war, death, and suffering, and I had no right to challenge anything. For that reason, I also knew we might not stand a chance. Let's face it. How could I possibly relate to anything, not even a remote speck of his life experience?

My complaints about stupid stuff seemed preposterous compared to the suffering, maiming, and hardship of war, losing a wife to cancer, especially the aftermath of being shot, and PTSD. How in the world would this have legs to stand on?

I tended to overanalyze things. I always needed some explanation; I needed to understand things to death—no pun intended. Maybe even measure pros and cons, which sounded wild as I was no math girl. Both Ms. Diva and the Jokester nodded simultaneously.

Being with someone with such life experience might have been a challenge. I could learn a lot. And because Larry was still such a beginner in his adaptation to civilian life, I knew I could help him. Maybe it was because he shoveled four feet of snow from my roof after the worst winter ever. Or perhaps it was how he was always ready to give of himself and help everyone.

I also knew this was not an easy relationship, but I had always taken the road less traveled. It was the stubbornness in me. The fact he was just as stubborn and just as strong as me was what took me out of my comfort zone. I pushed, and he pushed back. He pushed, and I pushed back.

Some things about him made me cringe, but I also had a period of adaptation. I had become used to being single and having things my way all the time, as I no longer had to compromise in my personal life.

With someone used to giving out orders without *please* and *thank you*, I had to set boundaries and teach him a new way. I still remember the first time he had dinner at my house, and I politely asked him if he could do the dishes. His blue-green eyes opened round like marbles as if I had asked him to jump off a plane (something he had done), and he reluctantly got up, mumbled something under his breath, and complained about my request but did do the dishes. When he was done, he proclaimed: I have never done the dishes for anyone in my entire life.

I looked at him, with invisible fumes coming out of my ears again, and muttered, "Well, in this house, if I cook, you do the dishes. If you don't like that, you don't have to eat here, and there's the door." He was taken aback by my response. But he now did the dishes without asking and sometimes even cleared the table without me getting up. I called that progress.

I knew he was doing therapy, and there might be hiccups down the road, but I had to have faith in my feelings and his. We passed the honeymoon phase of the two-month mark in a relationship.

We grounded each other. He didn't take my bullshit, and I didn't take his. I felt safe with him, and he felt safe with me.

I learned to take things day by day, not make plans, and I tried to live in the moment.

Maybe the Jokester was experiencing bliss, and Ms. Diva had found her man, even if he was completely different from what she could have imagined. And I never imagined ending up with a soldier. It didn't hurt that he called me *Princess*.

So maybe there was a light at the end of this online dating tunnel after all.

CHAPTER 49
THE TRAIN DEPARTS

I might have felt like the end of this online dating journey had arrived. It had been three months, almost four, which, in my book, was a damned good record for any relationship I had in the past three-plus years. It was the second longest relationship outside of my marriage. I had fallen in love with someone, unlike anyone I had ever met, with a life experience so different than mine. The road ahead would have some obstacles, like all relationships.

There were still moments of significant doubt. We weren't kids anymore, even if our life experiences couldn't have been more disparate.

I wondered about combining lives. There was something serendipitous about opening the doors to your space, especially if you had been alone for a few years.

Was I an independently stubborn person, or was it a stubbornly independent one? Either way was probably right. Despite this, my home wasn't completely my own for most of this time. First, my ex-husband and stepson moved out because of separation and, ultimately, a divorce. As an unforeseen circumstance, my brother got stuck in Europe and could not get back into the United States, and as a good sister, I felt it was my duty to help him out. Therefore, I spent an entire week packing his apartment in

Manhattan, rented a U-Haul, and moved his entire home into mine. I had a surplus of storage and stuff between my living room and my basement.

Then, a good friend of mine was going through an emotionally abusive marriage, and she needed to get divorced, and for her protection, I housed her for a year. So, all her belongings ended up between my basement and living quarters.

I accepted and felt that I was more set in my own ways now, which would only worsen as time passed. I liked the toilet paper a certain way, and the sharp knives, after they'd been rinsed, had to be placed downward so I didn't slice my hand or lose a finger. I couldn't leave any piece of clothing on the floor because one of my cats might have his way with it. I didn't want to find hairs or anything inside my bathtub. All caps had to be tightly fastened or closed. My stove could not have any grease droppings on it, and the list went on.

These lists annoyed Larry, especially on the days when his fuse was shorter than usual because he was either having a bad day, a night haunted by war and death, or a change in his medications. I could see how my lists and pet peeves could become explosive, and he, like me, had no problem telling the other one in a very rambunctious way that something wasn't right or felt uncomfortable. Our communication styles could escalate because two alpha personalities were bound to clash, and I was under the nutty impression I could go head-to-head with a Seal.

Anyhow, when I had my friend living at home, there were times when I did feel I had lost my privacy. She was like a big sister/mother to me, and it didn't feel right to entertain any male guests and take advantage of my singledom while going through crazy online dates.

A few weeks earlier, after four years of storing his belongings, my brother finally came to pick up his things, including his couch and the entertainment center I used in my living room. I found myself with a basement emptier than ever and a living room with nowhere to sit.

I remedied that by buying a new living room set, which was an ordeal due to the many delivery issues I had to endure, but I finally had somewhere to sit.

I cringed when I saw Larry's clothes on the floor. I had a fit when he was eating some crackers, which pooled on my kitchen floor to be later cleaned by me, muttering obscene words and then yelling out loud about crumbs. He had better excuses for why that easily happened to him. On the other hand, I didn't have a good reason other than my charming Southern European personality.

I could see the Jokester on my new power reclining loveseat with a center console for drinks, eating Cheetos, making a mess while grinning, sipping a jug of beer, and watching reality TV on Bravo, and Ms. Diva, leisurely sprawled in the best lacey negligée on the new matching soft brown couch, with her shiny high heels carefully hanging off the edge so not to damage the furniture with semi-closed eyes, the best Hollywood smoky eye shadow application ever seen on Earth, and a perfectly delineated shimmery pink pout, smirking, and pleasantly content. Voices were raised, and tempers flared. She purred. "Don't sweat the small stuff, darling."

CHAPTER 50
SPRING

Spring was finally here. And so was spring cleaning mode. Due to an annoying chore called work, the to-do list kept getting put off. Not to mention, I was in a new relationship, solidifying and blossoming, even though it felt like we were still trying to get to know each other. We knew we were bull-headed, and that could be because both of us had similar blood coursing through our veins, or perhaps—we found out we were type A positive. Yes, I was talking about blood and not the personality type.

Ms. Diva's eyes were semi-closed, rolling towards the back of her head, lips folding into a semi-sarcastic smirk, and the Jokester sat too busy channel surfing, looking for a more entertaining program to watch, sifting through hundreds of channels on cable TV.

I was retraining, not training Larry into my life but retraining me into being in a relationship. I had to be lenient about certain things, even if I held myself to some high standard of propriety that was ingrained in me from my mother's womb. As thick-headed as I was, aside from the assertiveness of my classic, exotic Southern European charm, I had to learn the steps of crossing the bridge to the land of compromise. It was not as easy a task, but one that I would gladly take because it might be worth it—a thousand-fold.

CHAPTER 51
WAS IT WORTH IT?

On the Saturday before Memorial Day, we visited Southeastern Massachusetts to take his mother to dinner. We met up at the restaurant. I was not expecting to see anyone I knew, so imagine my surprise when an acquaintance showed up. I had just traveled on business and been overseas with a huge delegation of which this acquaintance had been part. I knew this man had been in law enforcement and was now involved in government. I also learned from Larry that they knew each other from the past. He talked to the three of us, and right before we left, he sat down with a friend to have dinner.

I was happy to see him, as he was always very pleasant.

After dinner, we went our separate ways.

The next day, we skipped church and went to the beach, not expecting the cold wind to blow in our faces. We used my car as a shield from the strong breeze for two hours. We realized we should have stayed in the backyard when we got home, where the sun felt like a heating pad on our skin. I was content. At some point that night, I thanked the angels for my happiness and asked them if there was something in the dark for them to please bring to the light.

Memorial Day fell on a Monday, and we got invited for lunch at my cousin's (she's a cousin of a cousin), about an hour away. I was simultaneously apprehensive and excited that my cousin would meet Larry for the first time.

Lunch was delicious as she was quite the chef, and Larry and her husband went outside on the porch to bond. I could hear Larry's stories through the window, stories I had heard many times before.

We spent a pleasant afternoon together, and we were all surprised that my cousin and Larry knew some of the same people. She thought it strange that he knew these people, as he gave the correct information about them. My cousin's 90-year-old aunt came to visit, and through that conversation, he realized he also knew one of her grandsons, a personal trainer.

The more time passed, the more I realized that the world was small and everyone was somehow connected.

We adjourned and then came home, as I was hosting a significantly reduced number of my writing group due to the library being closed on national holidays. We typically rotated houses to hold a session when that happened. Only four of the nine members were present, and Larry decided to sit in and give constructive feedback as we read our short pieces.

He told them about his house-sitting experience for me when I was traveling and what had happened to one of my cats on the night I left. For some odd reason, or a rodent one, my older cat Lucky ran into the fireplace and down the chimney. He ended up getting stuck between the first floor and the basement. Larry called the police, fire department, and animal control, and chaos ensued. My other cat, Rocky, was missing in action with all the commotion, and for hours, the fire department and animal control tried to get Lucky out of the chimney. Because the owner was away, the fire department didn't want to destroy property and get sued to save a cat, so Animal Control tried to use their equipment to grab him, but in vain. The cat was stuck. Meowing in fear, Lucky was breathing in ashes and probably covered in soot, as my chimney had often been used after one of the worst winters. One of the firemen asked Larry what the cat's name was, and when he replied, "Lucky," he said, "he's not so lucky tonight."

Everyone left, and Lucky was still stuck in the chimney. Larry didn't sleep and couldn't contact me, as I was stuck on a plane mid-Atlantic.

When I landed and turned my cell phone on, there were dozens of texts from Larry, every single one more panicked than the previous one. I called him from the airport and heard about the chaos in my house, feeling jet-lagged, tired, powerless, and estimating that my fourteen-year-old cat was probably going to die that day and that I hadn't said a proper goodbye.

I got to the hotel, defeated, and hadn't even started my workday. I tried to get some sleep, but it was useless. Larry called me, giving me updates. He decided to call his boss, as he worked in construction, to convince him to lend him some equipment to break into the chimney in the basement; otherwise, the cat would perish. One or two guys came to help him, and he jackhammered the chimney and made a hole so Lucky could get out. He tried to grab him, but since Lucky was scared and traumatized – and not fond of Larry to begin with, he ended up getting all scratched up. He had to go to work, and Lucky would hopefully be able to get out of the hole on his own and into the basement.

I told Larry I had to bite the bullet and needed to call my ex-husband, who was very familiar with Lucky, to try and see if he could retrieve the cat from the basement and find Rocky. Larry said he couldn't find the other cat and kept yelling at the fire department and police to keep the doors shut because there was a second cat in the household, but they ignored him. Larry asked me to have my ex give him a call. I didn't think that was such a good idea. It was bad enough that I would have to call my ex-husband and tell him I was dating and that I needed his help saving Lucky from this incident.

I made the dreaded call, and I was lucky that he answered. He said he would try to leave work early, as he worked third shift, which was the equivalent of 4 or 5 a.m. Eastern time. Luckily—pun intended; they did not cross paths. My ex entered the basement, looked in the hole, and didn't see Lucky. He found him somewhere else in the basement, covered in soot and scared. He tried to grab him, but the cat was out of reach, so he used a hose to get him out of his hiding place, leaving the poor animal soaked. This cat had been traumatized for over twelve hours in a chimney, and now he was getting hosed down. I received a photo, and my black and white four-legged tuxedo looked terrible. Poor thing. His white fur was now brown, and he looked wet and cornered when he was taken to my laundry room so my ex could wipe him down with paper towels.

In the meantime, he found the other cat inside a laundry basket in my closet. After Lucky's semi-paper towel clean-up, he spent time with and fed them.

After the cat-in-the-chimney debacle, I managed to work without much sleep. Larry called me after he got home and told me that all seemed well and that I shouldn't worry because the chimney would have been rebuilt when I got back, and I wouldn't see a sign of disturbance. I thanked the sky above that he knew how to do that stuff. I told him to save the receipts.

I felt terrible for him that the three-week housesitting had to start so wrong for him. I wouldn't know what to do, and I knew I wasn't good in crisis mode, so I was glad someone was taking care of it.

CHAPTER 52
TRUE COLORS

The day after Memorial Day, I got a few texts from my cousin express-ing concern for me, and in those texts, she voiced her doubts about some of Larry's stories. I got defensive, even though I knew she meant well. This man was complicated. I had no doubt my plate was full, and he was unlike anyone I had ever met, totally out of my dating norm, but the last thing I needed were seeds of fear to be planted when I felt content with him.

We had plans for the summer to go to Martha's Vineyard, go to the range where I would learn how to shoot, go for walks, go to the beach, and have BBQs. I didn't need someone to plant doubts in my mind or undermine my life with Larry.

Later that day, I went on my laptop. Maybe the Jokester whispered that I still had access to his Facebook account and could go in, as we had changed his privacy settings together. I knew that if I did that, I'd be invading his privacy.

I sat down and opened my laptop. The Messenger appeared. My stomach received a few punches by an invisible hand as I read through thirty-three different messages, most of them addressed to porn-looking women, and sifted through "God, your beautiful," "hot," "you drive me crazy." No, he didn't know the difference between "your" and "you're." These messages span a little over a month, including when I was away and after that. You could tell these women were total strangers to him. Some didn't reply, and I was confident some of these profiles were fake anyway. A lot of these women weren't even in the country. A few replied, and I read through messages where the conversation was two-way and where he gave them his cell number. From the messages, it was implied that pictures had been exchanged via text.

My heart split open. Trust was broken, and I knew, in my heart, this was the end. I thought back to my cousin's texts and the doubts she had expressed. They were legitimate now. If he lied about this, I wondered what else was being kept in the dark from me. I knew the angels had heard me, but I didn't expect such devastation.

I wanted to know why. We had a good life. I thought we were happy. We talked about a future, even if it wasn't clear what it would be like due to all his health issues.

I needed to confront him. I took pictures with my phone of most of the messages. I felt betrayed and disgusted. I wondered if he brought women into my home, into my bed.

Even on the day I landed in Boston, he communicated with women. He had been almost two hours late, and I had been so upset. My head spun, and I knew we had to talk as soon as he came through the door.

He arrived that night after work. I sat him down at the dining room table. With my heart practically coming out of my chest, I could hear palpitations in my ears. Perhaps the oxygen in my lungs was supplied by Ms. Diva's panting and the Jokester's infuriated cheeks.

I started reading the messages from the photos I had taken. By the third interaction, he stopped me. He was upset. And he started raising his voice, mad at me that I had violated his privacy.

I thought to myself: What if I hadn't? I would have remained in the dark, like someone who did not know the sun's light was shining outside.

"You have no right to be mad," I barked. "I am the one who has the right to be mad! Not you! Me! You're mad because you got caught."

"I never cheated on you," he replied. Then he gave me some crazy excuse that some of those girls he knew from the gym, when clearly from the conversations I had read, he was the one who had requested friendship of strangers on Facebook based on their looks, and most of them weren't even stateside. There were girls in West Africa and the U.K.; some spoke only Spanish or French. He was clicking on their profiles based on looks alone.

I told him that trust was broken. In a four-month-old young relationship, trust was the only thing that could be the foundation for sustainability, and he, alone, destroyed that. The kicker was that he complained about how he wouldn't hear the end of this, so he was giving up.

"You're breaking up with me?" I asked.

"Yes, we are done."

If the Jokester had woken up from his stupor, he would have gotten up from his recliner, closed his mouth, and punched me right in the face to smack me back into reality. I could imagine Ms. Diva was back in her stealth mode catsuit, guns blazing, waiting to pounce on Larry and shred him to pieces. He deserved total annihilation.

Larry plopped on the couch to spend the night there. My mind was racing so fast that I remembered I blurted out, "Are you even a Navy SEAL?" to which he looked highly insulted.

I went to bed and could barely sleep, drifting on and off until about 4:30 a.m., when we usually got up. I got out of bed like a robot, and in the dark, I went to the kitchen, passing by the couch, and he asked me what time it was. I replied, and a cathartic energy overcame my body. Like a sniper, I went to my kitchen closet, picked up a few trash bags, and started filling them with all his belongings: clothes, shoes, trinkets, bullshit. I lined up my driveway with giant black bags within half an hour. He was getting ready for work and realized all his belongings had exited the premises.

He dared to comment. "That's a lot of stuff. Maybe we can put some of it in the trunk of your car and drive it to my place later."

"Um, that's a big fat no. Nothing is staying here. I don't want anything in my driveway. When your friend comes to pick you up, you can take everything. My driveway will be empty."

He didn't dare utter a word. I was mad. I was sad. I was confused. He still claimed that he hadn't cheated on me. The thought that perhaps other women had been in my bed while I was overseas sickened me to the pit of my stomach. I found myself crying. He said that he wanted to say goodbye to the cats. Now I understood why my cats were always missing in action when he was around. They had always hated him. I told him to forget about the cats. They weren't going to come out, even if I called them. I told him, "Cats are sensitive to energy. They know what you have done."

He hugged me and started tearing up too, and said he wanted to work on our relationship so we could move past this. He said that he was going to talk to his therapist. Deep down, I knew it was pointless. Whenever he picked up his cell phone, I suspected him of talking to some girl. I couldn't feel sorry for him. He had destroyed us.

CHAPTER 53
UNVEILING

After Larry left that Wednesday morning, something in me told me I would never see him again. I didn't feel it then, but I could imagine it as I stood in my doorway when his friend picked him up that morning, looking defeated in my pajamas, and I waved goodbye to him, were both the Jokester and Ms. Diva. They were devastated for me. They were perplexed and angry. I didn't feel the latter. They did. I was sure Ms. Diva was still dressed in black but had bags under her eyes. And the Jokester wasn't even hungry or thirsty.

Later that morning, my cousin texted me, asking me to go to lunch. She told me she needed to see me. As the blinders started stripping away, I knew she probably had more bad news for me and wanted to share it in person. She felt terrible about how she told me about her suspicions over her text messages, and even though her way might have been a tad overbearing, I knew she cared and was looking out for my well-being. I also knew she had a detective streak, and she had likely dug up some dirt on Larry.

I agreed to meet her at one of the chain restaurants two towns over. In the meantime, Larry texted me several times, apologizing, and he finally called me seconds before my lunch. I told him I needed to heal, that he needed to give me time and space. I also asked him why. He said it was a mistake. And I said, "Thirty-three women is not a mistake. That's thirty-three deliberate ones." I told him I didn't understand. I was under the impression we were happy and that things felt good. He told me some girls were from his gym, and I yelled, "Stop! Stop lying to me because I know that's not true." And I told him I had to go. He still professed his love for me, and that felt like another slap in the face. I wanted to believe him, but the blindfold was coming off. Deep down, I knew he must have been lying about other stuff too.

My cousin arrived at the restaurant. I had been sitting at a booth waiting for her, and I got up to greet her. She started crying. And I asked her why. She said she had been afraid I would never talk to her again. I told her to stop being silly.

We sat down. I took a deep breath.

"I know you have more bad news. What did you find out about him?"

"I know from two sources that Larry is not who he claims to be."

My heart dropped again, even though I didn't know how bad things would get. She continued.

"He's never been in the armed forces. He's not a veteran. He's a drug addict and has been in jail. Listen, on a scale of 1 to 10, he's a 10. He's dangerous, and you need to cease all communication with him. I was even advised that you consider returning to Europe for a few months."

My emotions were going around in circles in chaotic turmoil, a tornado of sorts, as I was trying to wrap my brain around this newfound information. I told her about the Facebook girls. She seemed relieved that I, on my own, had discovered some of his deception. I started crying. Uncontrollably. In public. I was always in such control, and now all hell broke loose. It seemed that the gates of hell had opened; some evil demons had escaped and brutally attacked Ms. Diva and the Jokester, and there was nothing I could do to defend them.

I could not stop the tears from flooding my cheeks, so much so that from an adjacent booth, a woman got up and came to our table. She had been sitting with her adult daughter, and both had tears in their eyes.

"I am so sorry to disturb you, but my daughter and I saw you crying. I have no idea why, but I know that I needed to come over and give you a hug. Can I give you a hug?"

This kind stranger embraced me with her love for humanity. I felt that my pain was creating a ripple effect inside the restaurant, which had been palpable to these two sensitive earth angels. I thanked her and was speechless by her outpouring. There were kind, honest, and beautiful people in this world, and even though I thought I was in that category, I felt utterly broken in those moments. I didn't feel myself. That was what usually happened when your heart broke into little pieces, and you could not simply glue them back together. There would always be scars, zigzagging seams of sutured emotions, remnants of past hurt.

My cousin also mentioned that she had Googled him and found a court case of a sexual offense in the 1990s. Ms. Diva and the Jokester were both sharing beds in a psych ward, comatose, and under heavy sedation. I didn't hear a peep from them. I shook my head, unsure if I was being overcome by denial, rage, or a cocktail of both, but I still hoped I would wake up from the nightmare.

"We should go to your house, and you should stay with me for the next few nights. I don't think you're safe right now."

I nodded, robot-style. We went to my house, and I packed a bag with one change of clothes. I would have to come back the following day as I had an appointment in my area, and she lived an hour away. On top of that, I could not abandon my cats.

My cats! Like a lightning bolt in my mush brain, it was clear why these cats had always hated Larry. They had known. Had they spoken English, they would have said something four months earlier. I was sure of it. They were such sensitive creatures, and I knew I had been the only one in that household immune to energy fields.

We drove back to her house at the tune of my on-and-off sobs. Her husband made me breakfast the next day, and both tried to cheer me up. I was going to go through the grieving process of losing a relationship. I also knew it wasn't just the loss of a relationship but the betrayal and the lies. I thought I was all savvy with online dating but had been immersed and living with a false identity.

My cousin took me to lunch at a nearby restaurant in the town where his parents and brother lived. This was way too close to home for me, and I felt uneasy. I told her that I had bumped into that man I knew from work who had known Larry and his mother when we happened to be at the same restaurant. I told her I thought it was strange that for someone who had been a police officer, if he had known his identity, he wouldn't have reached out and told me. Had he thought I had known? We weren't far from his office. My cousin had known this man since she was a teenager and whispered, "I think I see his car."

"Stop the car!" I yelled. I looked in her passenger sun mirror at my disheveled face. I had no makeup on. My hair was a mess, and I wore workout clothes.

We walked into his office and asked his assistant if he was in. She recognized me as she had been on that trip with me. She hugged me, nodded, and walked us to his office in the back. He saw my cousin, then he saw me trailing behind her, and his face froze. I said hello.

"I know you know the truth. Tell me everything."

"When I saw you at the restaurant, I thought you had been sitting there having dinner and that he and his mother had just sat at your table. It never dawned on me that you were there together. He is dangerous. On a scale of 1 to 10, he's a 10."

I recognized him as being one of my cousin's sources.

I told him that I was under the impression he had been a Navy Seal, that he had told me he had been shot, and that he was a widower.

This man kept shaking his head and denied all that information. It was all lies. He confirmed he had been in and out of jail and advised me to spend the summer overseas. He said, "Get rid of your cats and get out of here." He thought that I was in danger. I couldn't leave my home or my cats.

I started dealing with a growing and highly daunting emotion—fear. Never in my life had I been afraid of anyone. I never found myself checking my surroundings like a scared animal about to be slaughtered. I became terrified. I had no idea if, while overseas, Larry had made a copy of my keys, but now I needed to be diligent and focus on my safety.

We returned to her house so I could go home, feed the fur babies, go to my appointments, and get another change of clothes.

I called a locksmith. He could only come on the following Monday. I was going to have to stay at my cousin's. I was worried about Sunday because that was the only day Larry had off, and if something happened, that would be the day to avoid being home.

CHAPTER 54
GOING DEEPER

Larry kept texting me. Sometimes, he called and left a message. Sometimes, his texts just went on and on. Monday came, and at mid-day, so did the locksmith.

While I was at my cousin's, I called one of my best friends, who's a retired chief of police who is now living in New Hampshire. I told him what had happened. He heard the fear in my voice and sensed my tears as I told him everything I knew. He told me he still had contacts in my town's police department and would have a detective call me. This guy would be able to tell me what my options were.

The truth was that, at this point, Larry's dangerous persona was all conjecture. I had no real evidence of what he was capable of because I didn't know what was in his past, but I also had no idea if he could suddenly turn on me, show up at my house, and do something irreversible. And the other truth was that he never threatened me in the four months we were together, despite his imposing stature and rough-around-the-edges personality. On the contrary, Larry was always gentle and loving towards me, and I had difficulty matching these two identities.

That Monday night, the detective called me. He had been slightly briefed by my friend, who asked me to email him some photos of Larry.

I told him I didn't want to do anything officially because I hadn't been threatened, but I needed to feel safe.

I didn't recognize myself in a state of fear. Borderline paranoid at times, I drove around my house to see if anyone was lurking in the shadows of my backyard. Where had the strong me gone? Where were my sidekicks, Ms. Diva and the Jokester? Surely, they were still in the psych ward, heavily medicated, because, at this point, I felt crumbling, like an old muffin disintegrating into little specks of nothingness. I knew that the fear and the pain I was experiencing needed to be deconstructed and analyzed once the emotions calmed down, once the storm passed, but I felt like I was still inside the tornado.

The next evening, the detective called me past 9:30 p.m.

"I have some information for you. It's not good. Can you come into the station?"

"Sure, I'll be right there."

I walked in at 10 p.m. and met him in an interrogation room, which was ironic because I was not being interrogated. I was not even supposed to be there.

He made it very clear that this was off the books. I neglected to mention to him that it was not off *this* book.

He brought some papers with him, and the top page was a letter-size photo of Larry I had taken of him at the beach. He was a good-looking guy; there never was any denying that. But weren't all con artists charming in some way? He started reading off his record without ever giving it to me. The big thing was that he had served five years in prison in the 1990s. There were a couple of shoplifting incidents, an assault charge dismissed, and several violations for failing to register as a sex offender. My hands shook.

He told me that he thought I had two choices. First, I could text Larry and tell him he needed to cease all communication with me, or I would be forced to seek law enforcement assistance. Option two: He could call him. I didn't want to do that either. He also suggested that I block his number for peace of mind. In the back of my mind, if I did that and something happened to me, there would be no trail of threats or his state of mind.

I didn't tell the detective that I was still invading Larry's privacy by going on his Facebook account and monitoring his conversations with his mother, which were by far, and apart from the information I obtained at the police station, the source of his volatility and eye-opening into his dysfunction. At one point, I considered that he might be delusional and believed his fake identity, but by the conversations with his mother, he knew exactly what he was doing. It was calculating. His stories were detailed and consistent. He must have perfected these stories throughout the years, and with his incredible memory, he had studied and could recount minutia, making the storyline believable.

Larry had even fooled some of my friends, including my minister's father-in-law, a Vietnam and Desert Storm veteran who was about to retire from a job at Veteran Affairs in Rhode Island. But he had raised red flags at my cousin's. Both she and her husband told me they suspected something had been off.

I knew he wasn't delusional when he asked his mother to lie for him the next time she talked to me via Facebook Messenger. She said he needed to stop lying and that she was done talking to me. She also called me some nasty names that I will not repeat here. Names I didn't deserve. I didn't deserve any of this. I had been her son's loving, supportive, and caring girlfriend, and now I felt the four months were a charade. To what purpose? I still didn't know.

While I was at the police station, I asked the detective if there was any way I could find out if the police and the fire department had come to my house during the whole chimney incident. I suspected that story was manipulated and twisted too, and there was only one way to find out. The detective said the police system was linked to the fire department, and the computer would quickly show any incidents. He told me it would show a whole history by just inputting my address. We walked over to the computer, and he typed in my address. As expected, there was no incident at all. I just shook my head in disbelief—another story Larry made up. I could imagine my cat Lucky had run away from him and that he somehow ended up in the chimney. I would have to ask my ex-husband if he had seen any evidence of chimney destruction or rebuilding in my basement when he had helped with that situation. The made-up stories never ceased.

As I left the police station and crossed the parking lot in the dark of night, all was quiet. I was not sure if I was becoming numb to my reality—the reality that had punched my face and the reality that had stabbed my heart. I felt duped. There was no doubt about that. Part of me felt stupid, but I knew I was not stupid. Kind, gullible, too trusting? Definitely. But not stupid. How was I to recover from this one?

CHAPTER 55
WAKING UP

It was not healthy for me to read Larry's correspondence with his mother. I read some things about me that were highly offensive. Not only did words hurt my feelings, but they gave me a brutal beating to my self-esteem, which was usually above average. Some of my closest friends who knew what was happening told me I needed to stop snooping and cut ties.

Larry sometimes texted me, and the thread on my cell phone remained a monologue because I stood silent in mourning. All the words were personified lies, and as much as I was a word lover, his words of professing love and nostalgia for me were poisoned daggers to my heart. I was mourning the death of the relationship, which was what happens with break-ups, but this time, I experienced betrayal at different levels. I had lost trust. I lost a relationship that I had thought would keep going, even if I knew, deep down, that he was never my forever person.

I wondered if this would destroy my outlook on men and my trust in people and if it left any room in my heart to love again. This could be the end of online dating for me. I couldn't risk being in such a predicament ever again.

Ms. Diva and the Jokester slowly woke up from their doped-up sleep. Ms. Diva wore a nun's habit. I couldn't believe she was considering joining the convent. Granted, black and white looked good on her, but still. Did she think she could last more than five minutes in there?

The Jokester was now drooling in front of the television in a deep state of depression, compulsively channel-surfing and not finding anything suitable, fun, or joyful to watch. He was on a binging streak. There was junk food everywhere, and he was consuming massive amounts of alcohol. He might have been finishing the Heineken Larry left in my fridge. I didn't even drink beer.

I decided that I was in no danger. The blindfold was off. Judging from his record, I didn't find him going in and out of jail for violent behavior, and there were no restraining orders on him. That had been my biggest concern. Had he had a trail of violence, I would have felt the urgency to take an extended vacation in Europe. But I didn't want him to win. I didn't want him to have that power over me. I needed my power back. I needed to replenish and heal. I had no idea how or when this would happen, but I knew time was on my side. As annoying as the saying went, time did heal. Time helped soothe suffering. It might not mend the wound of hurt, but it certainly placed distance on the reality of pain.

Sitting on my recliner, I looked at the side table and found a folded paper. I knew what it was before I even unfolded it to reread it, as I had endless times before. It was my "list." It was not in list form, more like a piece of paper in paragraph form. I didn't know how old it was. I knew it had moved around from my bedroom to my living room. I added some line items to the back not long ago. Those were in bullet points.

This piece of paper was like a treasure. I wrote it to describe what I wanted in a man and what I envisioned was the right relationship. As I read through it, I was baffled that Larry didn't fit most of what that piece of paper described. I didn't think he ever did, even when he was a Navy SEAL, or rather, playing one. Where did I go so off track? Why did I forget about this piece of paper?

I knew immediately that it was as if it had become stale and lifeless because I hadn't read it in a long time. Ms. Diva looked at me, lifting one of her perfectly delineated eyebrows. I knew what she was thinking. She wanted me to write a fresh version, and she didn't believe that words like "I want" should be in it. "I want" implied a lack. She wanted me to use the present tense. She would never admit it in public, but she loved all the law of attraction stuff, and she knew that things should be worded in the present tense as if they were already yours or as if that reality was already happening.

She was right, of course. I scrambled throughout the house to find lined paper. I ended up using a fine-point Sharpie. Writing it with a permanent marker would solidify it. Maybe it would manifest what I wanted faster.

It was apparent to me that Larry wasn't the right guy for me. My mind and intuition knew it. My heart needed to catch up.

Another friend of mine offered to do a shamanic ceremony to ask the universe to bring me a healthy relationship with a healthy and wonderful man. I was unsure what the ceremony involved, but she asked me for a list.

I didn't have a list per se, so I scanned my two new pages of what Ms. Diva had urged me to rewrite, and I emailed it to her. She said that her daughter's dating life had changed since she did a shamanic ceremony for her. I had nothing to lose and everything to gain. I loved this type of stuff, and I believed that the more people put positive energy out there on my behalf, the better the odds, and I would only help with the process. Thankfully, I had many great friends, but I was not sure how many of them were praying or visualizing on my behalf. After all, they were not entirely privy to what I wanted. They only heard about my adventures in amazement, and I knew some of them just shook their heads, wondering why I was still determined to continue this journey. I sometimes asked myself the same question, but the answer was never clear enough for me to stop. That would signify giving up. I didn't do that.

Well, that was not true. I stubbornly stuck in my marriage long after I should have because I was determined that I, alone, could fix it.

The Jokester was still on the couch, stuffing his face and rolling his eyes, mumbling, "When will you ever learn?"

Maybe the shamanic ceremony would work. I should have taken a break to heal. I felt stronger every day. It's as if I was waking up from a deep sleep I had been under for the past few months. Wasted time.

CHAPTER 56

RESURGENCE

I ended up spending the Fourth of July by myself at home. It sounded depressing, but I was not depressed. I saw the light at the end of the tunnel, and Larry hadn't communicated in over a week. I felt a little relieved. I started working out diligently, and I got busy with work. It was kind of nice not to have to share my recliner with him and be able to watch whatever I wanted on TV. Larry had loved war shows and documentaries, and I was looking forward to renting some movies and spending the holiday in pure relaxation.

But the stars didn't align. He texted me. I was not sure what propelled me to answer, and obviously, I didn't think it through, but I felt empowered and no longer in the dark. I told him to stop communicating with me. That, of course, opened the door to a flood of messages, and he called me.

Without divulging what I knew, I told him there was no point in communicating with me. He needed to move on, and there was no longer a need to lie to me anymore. I knew everything. He asked me what I meant by "everything." Ms. Diva twirled her finger in the air, and I said, "Oh hell no, I am not playing this game."

After words were exchanged, he told me that he was relieved I knew everything. Now, we could start with a clean slate. That he missed and loved me and that the time away from me had been excruciating. I told him there was no going back and that he needed to take this experience as a lesson. Lying was never the solution to anything. He begged me to get back together, and he even started crying. He cried in different instances and on various phone calls.

As much as my emotions faltered, I was convinced that compulsive liars were hardcore manipulators, not to mention actors, and the whole thing saddened me. He urged me to reconsider and begged me to tell him what to do to be convinced. I replied, "Nothing."

He also said that I could ask him anything.

"So that you can feed me some more lies? I don't think so. I don't have anything to ask. I already know everything I need to know."

"Are you still in love with me?"

I responded, heavy-hearted.

"I was in love with a figment of your imagination, with a character you created. That person is not real. I don't know who you are." I also told him I didn't believe he loved me for one iota. He was trying to get back something very convenient in his life, so he could simultaneously keep doing what he was doing, with the other girls, the bullshit stories, the drugs, and whatever else he had going on in his life, and keep a girlfriend who was probably the best thing that ever happened to him.

I genuinely believed that this man was not capable of love. His words had selfish motivations, whether due to his sociopathic nature, his addictive behavior full of impulse, compulsion, and extremes, or the lifestyle of a manipulative narcissist who could, in one instance, badmouth his mother or the girlfriend he allegedly loved. I didn't think he even loved himself. He might even hate himself. The addiction reigned above all else, and I was not sure or even interested in knowing what pills he was addicted to. I knew little about addiction, but I knew enough to know that all the people the person with an addiction surrounded himself with were either addicts or victims of this awful epidemic.

I was a fixer. There was no way I could fix the mess that was Larry. It was so beyond my abilities. There was a morbid curiosity to see his dysfunction on social media, constantly friend-requesting these porn-looking or body-building women, plastic and fake. I bet a lot of those were fake profiles on their own. How ironic! He was a social media novice, and I had the upper hand in following his digital footprint. The activity was telling. The erratic messages showed his volatility and egocentric nature of portraying himself as the victim or pretending to understand any emotion. This was a human being who perhaps lacked compassion. His selfish desires propelled his good actions. How could I have been so blind?

I wish I could have minimized the memories and removed the mountainous pain I was feeling, but there was nothing I could do. I needed time to heal, and replying to his texts and phone calls after over a month of silence was a royal mistake. I felt vindicated because he knew I was no longer a fool. I was privy to the truth, and the truth had been what tipped the scale. Naturally, the truth would continue to be his demise because, in my heart, I believed he would continue to lie to me and everyone. He could not help himself.

A part of me was still holding on to the fact that maybe a sliver of him cared. I was mad at myself that I still cared, but I could tell that Ms. Diva was in workout gear, and the Jokester just smirked, taking a swig of his more refined *La Fin du Monde* beer and muttering "You can't fool this fool anymore. We will be having the last laugh, asshole."

In the remote chance that a baseball bat hit me in the head, suffered permanent brain damage, and took Larry back, my sacred circle of friends and family would never accept him, tolerate his presence, or forgive the hurt he caused me. Taking him back is not an option. I found out soon enough that he moved on even though he occasionally texted me and called me, begging me to give him a second chance.

It took me a while to peel the remnants of this man from me. I beat myself up to try and deconstruct the reasons and analyze my utter fuckedupness. In my logical mind, I could not fathom why I was giving any more time or energy to this man, who mismatched the way I lived, thought, and conducted myself in society and wasn't remotely close to sharing any of my values or integrity. It made no sense. Ms. Diva and the Jokester were baffled and close to beating me with baseball bats. Or maybe I just needed a therapy intervention.

What was wrong with me? I didn't lack self-esteem or confidence. I was the complete package, as several people had described me. I needed to let time do its thing. I needed to control my curious behavior and cease all communication. I couldn't afford any more emotional hits. I asked myself if this wish for a healthy relationship was becoming an obsession, even though I knew many people had the same desire. After all, it was only reasonable to want a healthy partner in one's life and a balanced romantic relationship where each could grow individually and as a team. Or was this another great expectation I had, and was I not fully able to accept it as an impossibility?

CHAPTER 57

PICKING UP THE PIECES

Letting go can be challenging, even if you are letting go of something so wrong for you.

I was so determined to find my match through online dating that I drowned in a bad situation. It was time to pick up the pieces, my pieces, and just focus on me. I knew this was a good idea, rationally speaking, but when you had a desire so deep in the abyss of your being, it was hard to release any attachments about it.

And then, I did something foolish. I agreed to meet Larry because he told me he wanted to come clean about everything. He did. He looked good, and I could slap myself.

I was still in love with him. A professional therapist could have had a field day with me, and given a chance, this time, it would be Ms. Diva and the Jokester checking me into the psych ward. He asked me for a second chance, and I concluded this was the worst idea ever. Maybe because of it being so, I reluctantly agreed.

I know this dumbass decision had no legs to stand on. Even though I still loved him, he could never fulfill most of my needs. Even if in my forgiveness, I was no longer in a state of denial. I was sure that could also be debated at great lengths.

The few people I told about being back with Larry weren't happy about it. I understood. If I were looking for people's blessings and approval, I would have never agreed to give Larry a second chance after everything that happened. Part of me questioned my sanity. My state of mind was dubious, at best. I didn't take drugs, except the occasional glass of wine, and now, I had a feeling people thought I might be a good candidate for some experimental narcotics.

No, thank you. I had seen what drugs could do, even if I wasn't aware of it at the time. If I didn't need them, I wouldn't take them.

But was I not treating Larry like a drug? He was the worst possible male candidate for me. The trust was shattered, and now, with ears and eyes wide open, I was still not sure this was a good idea. I knew it was not, and I wondered why I was putting myself through it.

While we weren't together, I went out on one date with Max. It was probably one of the best dates I have ever had. Ever. Max had retired from the Coast Guard—I swear I wasn't deliberately picking uniforms—it was pure fluke. He had finished his career as an officer in Hawaii and was spending the summer with his parents in Rhode Island before commencing his second master's degree in Budapest, Hungary.

When I met Max at a tapas bar, we talked non-stop for three hours. We laughed, and we got each other's sense of humor. Like me, Max loved traveling. Talking to him was easy and seemed like a walk in the park compared to my interactions with Larry. Max wanted to see me the next day, and as both of us had day commitments, he asked me to contact him when mine was done. I did. He was practically non-responsive and non-committal, and after a couple of text messages, I realized I would never hear from him again, which was very mind-boggling. I could only attribute it to the fact that, perhaps, he had not felt a physical connection with me.

However, it wasn't my job to speculate the reasons. I had concluded long ago that the more time passed, the less I understood the male gender.

Or perhaps my sense of logic did not apply to online dating. Logic and sensibility went out the window a long time ago and were now floating around in a different constellation light years away.

Only an idiot with a strong sense of masochism would take Larry back. Granted, the likelihood of him lying to me was extremely high, and I told him I could only take things day by day. There was no way I could fathom future plans. All I could do was measure my happiness one day at a time.

I realized that I was the best thing that ever happened to him. But did I not deserve the best thing to happen to me? My skepticism grew leaps and bounds, and I was no longer sure I was making good decisions. I had gone from someone with no trust issues to someone duped by several men, and in this case, deceived by the man I had decided to take back, who was probably the last man on the planet I should consider for a life partner.

CHAPTER 58

MAKING SENSE

A wise friend told me the other day, "All that matters to me is that you are happy." I thought about these words for a long time. As much as Ms. Diva and the Jokester wanted to see me in a mental institution, I needed to focus on my state of happiness, which could be measured by the passing of each day. It's sort of like the tide coming and going.

I did not think that things with Larry would last. And it was not because I didn't care about him. I probably cared a lot more than he deserved. However, I loved myself more. And I thought I was sane enough to recognize a few things. One: This would be a distant memory in a year or two as time was fleeting. Two: He did not have his life together as I did because, in a way, he was going through challenging things I never had to deal with and hoped I never had to. Three: Just as combustible as this relationship was, the fuse of patience shortened by the minute, and we were at an age when tolerance for certain things significantly diminished, even though my tolerance itself was questionable.

I told Larry that I'd measure the future of this relationship based on my daily level of happiness. Ms. Diva raised her perfectly delineated eyebrow. I should say my overall level of happiness started after I unveiled the truth and accepted him back into my life. This journey had been a lesson. The

Jokester was huffing and puffing a profound statement, "Ain't that the truth?"

I went to a Natural Living Expo with a girlfriend, which was full of cool presentations. She and I were on the same wavelength on many of these topics, and at the end of the first day, Larry mentioned he wanted to join us. My face must have been momentarily paralyzed because I could not see him fit into any of these topics I was interested in, which ranged from mediumship, oracle readings, energy healing, meditation, accessing the Akashic records to obtain information on your previous lifetimes, meditation, or dowsing with L-rods and pendulums, to name a few.

I also allowed Ms. Diva and the Jokester to panic for a few seconds, and my statement to Larry must have had a tremendous impact on him.

"If you come, one of two things will happen. We'll either break up, or you will wake up."

I didn't even have the guts to tell him what he might wake up to. I judged that the term "spiritual awakening" might be too much of a bombastic and intimidating statement for him. I didn't have to explain it further since he decided to watch football the next day and have a lazy Sunday instead.

I was relieved that my friend and I could resume our personal development classes and return to the second day of the expo.

However, my meditated and relaxed self returned home to find the refrigerator wide open, and I lost all my cool. It was true that one person could have many facets, just like a diamond. Ms. Diva agreed. And the Jokester suspected he had been a shaman in a previous life.

CHAPTER 59

FAIRYTALE ENDINGS

Some of my close friends accompanied my progress through the ups and downs of an imperfect relationship. And some asked me when I would finish this book, or better yet, they asked me how the ending would be. Wouldn't it be a total spoiler if I divulged that information?

At the Natural Living Expo, I sat down with a medium. The convention center was packed with psychics, and as a lightworker myself, I had to follow my instinct and knew I was not meant to sit down with just anyone.

In addition, I didn't believe that the future was written down with a permanent marker, carved in stone for eternity, unwavering and unchallengeable. But I also knew that as pragmatic and scientific as my mind could be, I was wise enough to know there was something more, and just because our brains or our senses couldn't solidify it in a way that could be palpable and scientific, our intuition was the emotional guidance system that navigated as the proof tool of something beyond ourselves, and energy was one of those things.

My friend and I arrived so early to beat the crowds that there wasn't a mob sifting through the aisles yet. As I walked aisle after aisle, I kept glancing at several psychics, wondering which one would be the right one for me. I finally stopped at one table and felt this was the right place. The medium had an assistant as she was busy doing a reading in the back of the booth. After a few words with her, I glanced at my watch, as I could tell she was wrapping up with the person. I handed her my credit card and pre-paid for my fifteen-minute reading.

Shorter than me, her dark hair curly as mine when not straightened, she talked a mile a minute. One of the coolest things she did was record our session, which she later handed me on a CD. I was grateful she did that because at her speedy Gonzalez rhythm, not even Ms. Diva could have kept up with her. I was sure the Jokester's head swiveled around a thousand miles a second.

Of the plethora of things she covered during our session, one was romantic relationships. She pointed out my choices of remaining status quo, going all in, or jumping ship. She asked me which one I was feeling the most. I told her, very honestly, I did not know. She told me that if I jumped ship, other opportunities would arise, one being with someone I already knew. That information freaked me out as my brain scrambled to figure out this person's identity. The reading concluded that nothing was inevitable, and I had the power of choice.

I always had the power of choice; even if I made very questionable choices at times, I was still the boss of my world. Life was not a bed of roses, and it was hard to see the Jokester swimming in a pond of flowers.

I was relieved. The pressure was behind me. I had been putting so much pressure on myself to find the right person through online dating that I lost track of this simple truth. I always had a choice. I made choices every second, every minute, every hour, and every day, and there was no reason this should be any different.

I was a positive person. I had not always been like that, especially when I was married. Sometimes, I couldn't or didn't want to contemplate the future, that ethereal time label, which could be a source of hope, joy, fate, and doom. Part of me always maintained the hope for a better tomorrow, even though this path's experience had been winding and full of potholes.

Maybe that positive outlook came from reading too many romance novels throughout the years.

I should get back to reading romance novels. That's what my friend Gabby did. After our speed dating saga, she got on one of the sites for less than two months, and as we sat down for lunch, she shared with me that she had found the winning ticket. She had found her Mr. Right.

"He is even better than the romance novels. I can't believe I knew such a man could be out there."

I was slightly jealous. I knew jealousy was not a positive trait, but here I was, single for the past four years, double the time she had been single. She found the perfect man for her, and I was with Larry, a highly flawed Mr. Wrong, who, even though might care about me, I couldn't help but think we were just not meant to be together at all.

I felt happy for Gabby and wished the same for me. How was I ever going to feel that same feeling, that feeling Ms. Diva dreamed of when she immersed herself in her luxurious bathtub with coconut milk and the aroma of pure lavender and ylang-ylang essential oils?

I discreetly heard the Jokester snort in outrage as he rolled his eyes. He was the one who was not so positive in this journey after all.

CHAPTER 60
IN SOLITUDE

Click, click, click. No, it was not the sound of a computer keyboard. I heard Ms. Diva's sharp neon pink nails on my desk. The Jokester channel-surfed in the living room. I could listen to the TV changing sounds every two seconds. It wasn't enjoyable. There should be silence in solitude, but solitude was futile with these two hanging around me.

I could hear them telepathically telling me, "I told you so," "It took you a while," and "Why did you put up with Larry for this long or at all?" "You're such an idiot," and "A leopard can't change its spots."

It didn't feel like getting back to Square One, though. I hoped to learn from my mistakes and be able not to repeat them. At this stage in the game, things with Larry went kaput for good. There could never be any going back. That would be a sign of mental instability on my part or a pretext to have me institutionalized. Again.

So, in a nutshell, my tolerance barometer collapsed. I stopped believing Larry. I had warned him to stop lying to me. He couldn't help it. I had to accept that he had an addiction. Whether it was food, alcohol, prescription pills, women, sex, or lies, Larry was his own worst enemy, and I needed to jump off the Larry hamster wheel. The relationship scale had toppled over.

We were together for a total of eight months, and it was eight months too long.

It came to the point that I didn't have the time or patience to have him in my life. In adding another business to my plate, I rarely had nights off, and the few I had when I saw him weren't good. He would be giving me some story or excuse, making my house messier, scavenging the fridge and the cupboards, devouring everything he could find in sight at all hours of the night without asking me, including wine bottles, which would suddenly show up empty or with water inside. I knew that cutting the cord had to be done.

His mother reached out several times, and even though she might have had overall good intentions, she, as an enabler, always made excuses for the men in her life, starting with her husband's mistreatment of her and the constant disappointments of her two sons: one was an out-of-control addict, and the other, in a very profitable business of drug lording and using people, including her, who would clean his house and watch her grandson, if one of the drug runners/babysitters was busy. So, this time, her reaching out to me was bittersweet. She didn't try to convince me otherwise. She thanked me and said, "he will never find a better woman."

I knew she was right. He might find someone prettier and more affluent, but he already had the best, and you couldn't upgrade from there. Most likely, he would go on a downward spiral, as he had done many times before, until someone temporarily tried to rescue him. Well, this damsel was distressed enough and done with trying to save others.

Ms. Diva stared me down and muttered, "You're not planning on wearing those pajamas for long, are you? You have wasted time, darling. And don't think about letting go of your fashion savoir faire just because this was another asshole, which you have known all along. But don't you dare go out looking like this and without makeup!"

I shook my head and gave her the silent treatment. I had no clever words of retort, profound remarks, or funny comebacks. Getting back out there, online, offline, or any line, was daunting. I dreaded it. Joining the convent was not an option, so the mourning period commenced three weeks earlier, and for some reason, I foresaw it to be of short duration. Was I becoming desensitized to disappointment and failed relationships? Had my heart transformed into cement or steel? Maybe hope was vanishing. I never thought that day would come when hope would abandon me. Or had I left hope behind and become way too cynical?

The Jokester stopped channel-surfing and was now watching reality TV, specifically The Bachelor. I heard him snort and swear at the same time. The odds might even be worse in that show.

Chop, chop! I couldn't wait too long. I needed to finish this book, and that required more research. Now, it would be structured as in character finding to fill in this saga. I knew online dating worked. It had worked for so many of my friends. I had not been so lucky. But going out in the field one last time might be the distraction I needed. My problem now was finding the time to go out on coffee or drink dates. I was just too busy with work, which was not such a bad thing.

CHAPTER 61
SNAIL MODE

I forgot to mention that I didn't want to have to pay for trash disposal of the stuff Larry left at my house. So, what did I do instead? I drove for forty-five minutes and dumped the contents of my trunk on his unlocked porch at the sober house he was living in. That should now be a clue to Larry's life condition. I didn't judge him. If I had, I would have never stayed with him for so long, or perhaps my gullible nature and some twisted self-torture were to blame.

I have wondered about my standards. Was it because I hadn't been that lucky with online dating, or was it a deeper psychological hurdle? If it was the latter, maybe I needed to find a counselor or someone to analyze my brain or perform a painless lobotomy.

Both the Jokester and Ms. Diva nodded their heads. They needed it to be painless. I put them through the wringer already. It wasn't fair.

The more time passed, the more perspective I gained on this last relationship. I was browsing through one of my favorite stores, TJMaxx, and saw this block of paper in blue and white, beckoning to be bought. It was a list of Pros and Cons. It could have been so handy if I had found it several years ago. I would have used it for each of the guys I talked to. I might have needed more than one block—a page for each. The sifting might have been more efficient. Part of me was a massive proponent of efficiency, even though I could slide into both extremes of the efficiency scale.

Wasn't everyone made of certain extremes? Some might be in our nature, and others are acquired with time. For instance, I abhorred stagnation, incompetence, and apathy. And here I was, drowning in moments of despair and extreme apathy, even slower than snail mode, with fear that I might develop mold from all the emotional hibernation and healing I needed to do.

"It takes a village" is the saying. It only took me to be in defeatist mode, half depressed, half full of self-pity, and suspended in the deep waters of the black hole of the abyss. This might be a little flair of drama wafting through the cracks of Ms. Diva on my shoulder, in my conscience, or on the purple velvet chaise longue where she still rested in a full-length glittery gown as if she was on a break at the Oscars with all the A-Listers. However, Ms. Diva was also prepared. She glamorously lounged, even if she felt my pain, but she was ready for the unexpected moment. I hated when people told me, "Things will fall into place, and you will meet the One when you least expect it." Hell would freeze over before Ms. Diva was caught in an unprepared moment of opportunity, and that was why she always urged me to look good, have my makeup face on, and not lounge like a snail moping around the house.

The Jokester almost beat the crap out of my iPhone when Larry texted me from a new number. But I made him proud. I politely texted back: "Please do not contact me again. I am blocking this new number too. Good luck with everything." This time, I had blocked him on Facebook and my cell phone, so there was no chance of contact. There was no re-igniting anything at all. My standards were raised. I was evolving and recovering quite nicely.

Relief washed over me several times. I had a ton of work, which naturally kept my mind busy, but I also felt a certain lightness in the air. It was a leap year. Today was Leap Day. It was the perfect time to make a promise to myself. I promised to be wiser. I allowed myself to mourn and heal through this, but I was not staying in the hibernation of recovery. I would shed my shell and skin into a spring full of possibility.

Today was a day of spiritual enlightenment, a day when I could start to be kinder to myself, maybe a day of awakening, even if it was a raw and fresh awakening, but one full of efficiency and potential.

CHAPTER 62
THE USUAL SUSPECTS

I reactivated two of the online accounts. Neither the Jokester nor Ms. Diva found this amusing. Their tolerance had rolled down the driveway a long time ago. I already regretted it.

One of the more expensive sites had a three-month special, but there was only a little interaction between people, and I did recognize some faces. The other was the dollar store version; I was not paying for the upgrade this time. I didn't think the promotion gave me access to anything special, and I saw the usual suspects: Men I had either talked to, men I had gone out with, and men who had messaged me multiple times and still didn't understand that my non-responsiveness might be a lack of interest in them. How sad was that?

Coincidentally, a good friend of mine, Sarah, was on the same site. She recently became single and commented, "Now we are competing for the same guys." I loved her, and I would never want to compete for guys! Especially this crew. I could be competitive in other things, especially with myself—perhaps an OCD characteristic or my propensity to pursue perfectionism with certain things. Still, I would never want to be in this position. We had different tastes and goals, so it could get awkward if she ended up dating someone I already met, but since it was an ocean of possibilities, I was confident that perhaps that wouldn't happen.

However, she told me to look over her profile, and I was jealous; she had a photo of herself in a helicopter and all these active, fun photos. Her write-up was super funny and light-hearted. She said she had hidden her profile because she was getting too many messages. I asked her if she would look at mine. She was a sincere, no-sugar-coating friend, so I knew I would get great feedback. She told me my profile was too serious and intimidating and that I needed more fun photos, including of local places and things I liked to do.

I took this opportunity to upload some new photos, new to this site, one being a full body shot of me at Borderland State Park with a horse and its rider in the background, so I gave the impression that I wasn't on the couch all the time. Another photo of me in Vegas and another at a local restaurant sipping on a very high-calorie drink, which was not my usual, as I either had a glass of wine (or two) or a vodka martini, extra dirty with three olives.

But I was trying to look at this process with fresh eyes, and for that to happen, I was ready to start anew, with a slightly different profile write-up, and see what came to shore. One of the things my friend also shared with me was that she never approached a guy first. She was very passive about that; she looked at his profile, added him as a Favorite, as he would be notified, and waited for him to make the first move. I was not sure how I felt about that. It was the twenty-first century, after all.

Most of the guys sending me messages were short, appeared just to want to have fun, couldn't spell a sentence, were heavily tattooed, pierced, and had not read a word of my profile when they sent me an email with "Hey sexy." I noticed some photos of the guys that looked like mug shots and a plethora of shirtless selfies in the bathroom. I was not sure why grown men would do this, especially if they had it on their profile that they were looking for a relationship unless they were lying. Who would be taken seriously with a shirtless photo? Ms. Diva raised an eyebrow, contest-winning-worthy.

Sarah was going on more dates from Plenty of Sharks. I, on the other hand, had not. I didn't take any of these guys seriously. The last date she went on had gone well. She deemed him nice, but sparks were missing. And the next day, she texted me a photo of his profile, stating that he had met someone nice and wished everyone good luck. I told her I thought it was too soon after one date to publicize that he had found someone.

I told this story to a male friend, the only one I met through online dating I had remained friends with, and he said that Sarah needed to watch out as this guy sounded like a stage 5 clinger. I was unsure what a stage 5 clinger was, but I imagined it was the equivalent of a stalker. Hopefully, she wouldn't go out with him again, or she might have a pickle on her hands. It was the Jokester's turn to raise an eyebrow.

I wanted to remain hopeful, but it was wishful thinking. This could still work. I tried to convince myself that this might still take a while and when to throw in the towel. Would there be a moment when I would look in the mirror and say, "This has not worked for you. It's time to shut down all the online profiles." Wasn't online dating a medium selling a dream? The dream of finding your other half? Wasn't it comparable to any propaganda used by every other medium? It was worthwhile to ponder.

CHAPTER 63
ANOTHER YEAR, ANOTHER SPRING CLEANING

I felt so amazingly productive this past weekend. I wanted to tackle my office for months. I binged on half a season of House of Cards and simultaneously went through years of paperwork. I must have tossed four or five large bags in my recycling bin. There was still much work to be done. It never ceased, like the sun that would set and rise again, and so were the piles of clutter I needed to address.

The light bulb went off as I went through papers over six years old. This was the perfect metaphor for not finding the right guy! I needed to literally and figuratively clean house and dig through the cobwebs of my life. This was why I had been getting into situation after situation. No shoe fit just right. There were always pebbles in the red patent heels that Ms. Diva tried on. Something was always off.

In the middle of my cleanup, I went into my bedroom and glanced at my vanity. I bet I could have thrown away all the lipstick in there. It was probably a nest of bacteria that I didn't even touch. I hadn't worn them in years. I wondered if you could get a prize for holding on to things. I bet Ms. Diva would have the best award-winning speech. I held on to these items as a symbol of the past because they reminded me of mall trips to makeup counters my best friends and I made in college. The laughs we used to have when I'd pretend to be French (which I was), speaking English with a thick French accent and asking the makeup counter lady at Lancôme to show me something less "pinkkk," and a bunch of them behind me trying to contain their laugh.

So, this was it! I was holding on to this past that wouldn't come back. I knew holding on to these materialistic, outdated, bacteria-rich lipsticks made no sense. My rational mind intrinsically knew this. It was not a big reveal. There is no magic trick here. The Jokester got excited at the mention of the word "magic." I put things in a closet because they were out of sight, out of mind, and I told myself I would deal with them later, and then later came around, and it was an absolute no-pass-go. And I did this to every corner of my house. I focused on work and life; the cobwebs formed inside the cupboards of my home and the closets of my life without my realizing it.

I went to see Gabby in Rhode Island, and she asked me how things were going with online dating. I told her they were at a standstill. She asked me if I had heard from Larry. I told her I had blocked him on social media and my cell.

"I'm proud of you." She patted me on the back.

At the end of last year, Gabby joined Happiness Now and, within two months, met the love of her life, so I signed up again for their 3-month special—this was the third time around. What was annoying about this site, besides being the most expensive, was that it was still so challenging to communicate with someone. They made it so hard. You still had to send them five pre-selected questions, and if they answered, it would be their turn, and then the process continued. My patience had run out a few years back. However, I saw how this could potentially work, even though I still believed all these algorithms were stacked against you, so you'd renew the membership, but only a man truly serious about finding someone would pay money to be on there.

Gabby and I decided to go to my Happiness Now account and scroll down the prospects. She even agreed there was not much to go on. I had told her I had been emailing back and forth with one guy, but then he dropped off the face of the earth. He must have had his interest elsewhere and just ceased all communication.

"You don't want a guy that does that anyway."

She was correct. She also had me edit my profile and noticed I mentioned traveling six times and pointed out I needed to be "warmer and fuzzier." She meant I needed to appear softer, more approachable, more feminine in my wording, not so much like a furry animal.

I told her about my metaphor for spring cleaning and my epiphany on the correlation between cobwebs, clutter, and my dating life. She laughed out loud. Thank God and the Angels that we laughed more than we cried. We had bouts of tears before, but this was not one of those moments.

"Then, clean house and manifest this man. I suggest you read romance novels. I got exactly what I ordered, exactly the guy I wanted."

The Jokester snorted, and you could hear it for miles. Ms. Diva's hooded long lashes fluttered in pre-defibrillation mode. I turned to Gabby.

"You know what I don't understand? Why do I still have hope after all I have been through?"

"Hope is good," she nodded.

When would I ever find the time to read romance novels with all the de-cluttering I had to do, not to mention work?

CHAPTER 64

MR. TALL

I recognized Mr. Tall when he messaged me on Happiness Now. I had talked to him a couple of years earlier on Catch, and I couldn't remember why our conversation hadn't progressed. We exchanged phone numbers through Happiness Now's inbox and started texting. Jay was indeed tall and handsome. At age 44, he towered most at 6'6. He worked for a printing company and lived in Quincy.

Ironically, it was the same town Larry lived in. I secretly wished they lived on opposite ends. I barely thought of him these days, even though some of my girlfriends did muster the courage to ask me. And my answer was always the same. "I blocked his phone and blocked him from social media, so I have no contact." Their reply was always the same, "Good."

Jay had lived by himself for a long time. He had never been married and had no kids. He was disgustingly handsome, and I wondered if his photos were real or stolen from some international model's website.

He left it very clear to me that he wanted children. I wanted children, but I was honest with him that my clock was ticking 1,000 miles a minute, and I didn't know if that would be possible. He said his clock was ticking too, which I didn't understand, as there was no time limit on men's equipment, and I suspected he probably woke up one day and made that decision overnight. He said he wanted three kids.

The Jokester did the best eye-rolling stunt ever and contemplated a possible career in acrobatics despite the existence of his pot belly. Ms. Diva clenched her pelvis muscles just as the thought entered and exited her mind quickly. Three kids? She was totally against that. As for me, in today's world, that might not even be physically possible at my age.

Nevertheless, I was open to the possibility that I could start right away if I found the right person. Time was indeed of the essence.

This was going to be my first date in ten months. I was rusty and nervous. I wondered if Mr. Tall was also Mr. Right. As I headed to the restaurant in Norwood for drinks, I fantasized about what it would be like if Mr. Tall was the hero of the romance novels I still needed to buy, per Gabby's suggestion. I created in my head the perfect scenario, down to the moment when we first lay eyes on each other, and magic would happen. I imagined our hearts would intrinsically know even before we said a word to each other. The Jokester would start his first flip, Ms. Diva's lingerie would pop off in superfast motion, and the happily ever after credits would start rolling.

The credits didn't roll in this romantic comedy, and no fireworks started. As fate would have it, when I first lay eyes on Jay, he didn't run as fast as he could, nor did that spark ignite. As the night progressed, I concluded that Mr. Tall was indeed very tall and nice.

Jay rented his apartment for the past eleven years. He told me he hadn't slept in his bed in years and chose the couch with Fox News as background noise as his favorite to watch and fall asleep to every night.

"How come?" I took a sip of my glass of Malbec.

"The bed is too comfortable, and I don't want to sleep very much for fear of missing out on life," he explained, then gulped down his beer.

Jay was unprepared for the woman of his dreams or three kids. He was unprepared for a girlfriend, never mind the kids he wanted today or tomorrow. He asked many questions, and it felt like an interview, even though I never sensed he wasn't being truthful with me. He also struck me as a loner, and now I understood better why he had never married or been in a long-term relationship at age forty-four. He was smart, pleasant, and extremely attractive, but the chemistry was nonexistent. I suspected he felt the same.

I only drank one glass of wine and was appalled when the bill came, and he hesitated to pay for his two beers and my wine. He expected me to offer. I was not going to. Next time, when the bill came, at a girlfriend's suggestion, I would conveniently go to the bathroom. I was disappointed at his lack of gentlemanly courtesy. We left without words and barely hugged goodbye. He went back to Quincy and his couch by himself. My fantasy romance novel scenario vanished mid-air.

CHAPTER 65

JIM

A few days later, I started talking to Jim, whose profile stated that he was a builder. He lived twenty-five minutes from me and was only a few years older than me. He asked me out quickly, and I said yes, with the thought in mind of not having any expectations and that I would likely not connect with this one either. We decided to meet at TGI Fridays right after my writing group for apps and drinks. He texted me to let me know he was running a few minutes behind but for me to grab a seat at the bar, which I did. I was not expecting anything, especially out of Plenty of Sharks, where I had met Larry. Jim walked in and was bald—not typically the type of guy I went for. Not that I had a specific type, but usually, hair on the guy's head was the norm for me. He was much better looking than his profile picture. One of the things that I found weird about him was that before our meeting, he never asked for my name, which gave a new meaning to complete strangers meeting. I was a nameless somebody to him.

After saying hello, a couple of guys arrived, sitting adjacent to us. The two men looked at each other. One of them said to Jim that he knew him from somewhere. They couldn't figure out where they had met before. The couple introduced themselves to us, and I finally stated my name.

"I can't believe you never asked for my name," I looked at Jim. For some reason, that didn't seem normal to me and was a first for me. He didn't seem to make a big deal out of it. Perhaps he had no expectations when meeting someone from Plenty of Sharks.

At one point during our conversation, because we were at a bar with TVs all around, the news flashed some horror story, and I turned my head away. I then confessed that I never watched the news nor read the newspaper. He looked at me dumbfounded and said, "Same here." It was my turn to be amazed. Usually, people deemed my ignorance irresponsible when one chose not to know what was happening in the world. I saw it as maintaining my peace of mind and a more positive outlook on my life and community. That would change in the future.

I was able to have a meaningful conversation with him and was surprised as we discovered that we shared similar values and thoughts about life. I also noticed that he had manners while eating, which was extremely important to me because that meant that he could be brought out of the cave, which, believe it or not, was a rarity these days. He also asked if I would like another glass of wine, to which I politely said yes. There was no reason not to, as our conversation was going so well that I figured the night could carry on.

Imagine my surprise when it was midnight, Cinderella's dooming hour, and we were the last ones in the restaurant and had not even realized it.

Jim told me that he had not had a meaningful conversation like the one we had in over a year. I wondered what type of women were out there since I knew amazing single women who were online, but I took it as a compliment. I was shocked that time had passed, traveled in a sense, and we both had not noticed.

He walked to my car and gave me a light kiss on the lips. We promised to text when we got home safely.

Ms. Diva's eyebrow lifted at a sharp angle. The Jokester snorted. The jury was still out.

CHAPTER 66

JIM
The Sequel

I did not expect to go out with Jim immediately, but he asked me out for Friday night. We met at the parking lot of an Applebee's, and since his Saab had been having ignition problems and was about as old as my car, he had suggested we take mine to the comedy show he planned to take me to.

I realized there wouldn't be much chance of conversing at a comedy show, as the roster included several comedians, one right after the other. We laughed quite a bit, though I didn't understand why comedians needed to swear so much. Sometimes, I found the best humor was the cleanest, simplest humor. It made it even better when one could be naturally funny without resorting to harsh words. One of my good friends, a financial advisor, had a hobby as a comedian; she was one of the funniest people I knew and seldom used harsh words. The stories were naturally hilarious and didn't need the added neon colors of foul language to make them shine any brighter.

We decided to grab a drink at Applebee's, where he parked his car so that we could talk more. Talking to Jim was one of the easiest tasks I had experienced in a long dating history during the past few years. We shared similar interests. I told him about my newfound passion for essential oils, and he told me he used essential oils, as he had experimented with making his lotions with shea butter and coconut oil. I was dumbfounded again. He had been a builder for a long time but had to change careers the year before when he fell off a ladder and broke most of the left side of his body, including a hip, arm, and several bones in his left hand. After being in recovery for three months, his arm never fully recovered. He decided to return to school to become a chef, as he now ran his new baking business, and planned to pursue a culinary degree.

We were getting along so well that he asked me what I thought about dinner and a movie that weekend. I told him I thought it was a fantastic idea, so we first went to Tavolino's, a very pleasant Italian restaurant in Foxboro. He impressed me by ordering a bottle of wine. I must have had horrible dates, as they never ordered an entire bottle. Maybe one had, but that must have been a fluke. From the corner of my eye, the Jokester nodded profusely. We had a nice Italian blend, and again, we lost track of time and ran in the rain across Patriot Place to get to the movie theater. We arrived late, but we enjoyed the movie. As it drizzled in the parking lot, we kissed again. A less chaste kiss this time, then parted ways.

I had a busy week ahead of me, including my birthday on Thursday. On Friday, I was gathering my best girlfriends together for a dinner party an hour away. That Saturday, I was going to a wedding and thought about inviting him.

He ended up taking me out on my birthday. He asked me where I wanted to go, made reservations, and met at the restaurant. We had a fabulous time, and I asked him to be my date for the wedding. He joked that I sprang that on him at the last minute but said yes. In the back of my mind, I thought that he might stand me up. I realized now that my expectations for men were still very low.

On the wedding day, I decided I would drive. Again, his car was not in top shape yet, and he met me at my house. He wore a tan pick-stitch suit, a striped navy and green silk tie, and a perfectly pressed pocket square in his jacket. I told him he cleaned up well after he told me I looked beautiful in my black lace tan-lined dress. With a sly smile and fanning herself slowly, Ms. Diva approved of his style and wanted to see what was under the hood.

My comedian financial advisor friend was attending the same wedding with a friend, and I knew we would sit together at the reception. I was nervous because this would be my first friend to meet him.

A few minutes into their introduction, I knew I had nothing to worry about. She gave me a seal of approval with a look. I was pleasantly surprised that I was now interacting with him and other people and that he was extremely polite, engaging, and a total natural. Whenever the food platters came, he got up and served everyone. He was always asking people if they needed anything. Every time I got up to go to the restroom, he pulled my chair out, and when I got back, he helped me with it again. I also noticed that he opened the passenger door for me. I didn't remember experiencing this level of manners from men on any sites. I was taken aback.

At the same table was a family of four: a couple in their eighties who had been married for fifty-four years, their daughter, and their son-in-law. During dinner, eighty-year-old Sheila asked us how long we had been married. We paused midair and started laughing and chuckling. And I finally said we hadn't been together for long, without specifying it was less than two weeks. The four of them looked at one another, and the son-in-law commented that he thought we had been married for a long time because we were so comfortable with each other. Jim and I thanked them, looked at each other, and smiled.

He made a joke out loud that he had told me earlier at the church that we should have just taken advantage of the fact that there was already a wedding happening and gotten married, too. Everyone laughed.

We danced and danced, and my thighs hurt the next day, which meant I needed to dance more. I was also terrified that the ball would drop at any minute. That was my experience thus far.

CHAPTER 67
BALL DROPS

I swear I didn't set up to fail. I was still going at this when all odds thus far gave me every possible reason and excuse to give up. I surrendered to God, remember? Now, this was in Source's Universal hands. It was not up to me anymore, so I trusted that the energy of the Universe would break what was not meant to be and make work what was. I had relinquished my type-A control freakiness.

Four days after the wedding, Jim wanted to meet me in Boston at a work event I attended. I had saved him a seat. The row I sat in had several seats open, and he chose to sit one seat from me, leaving an empty one between us. Ms. Diva's bright green eyes rounded up like two shiny marbles, ready to pop out of her skull.

That was very strange. Why didn't he want to sit next to me? This didn't make sense to me after we had connected so much the last time we had seen each other.

The Jokester was taking a nap and wouldn't get up for this. He was getting tired, and sloth was taking over. He was tired of the endless stream of pitiful men I had been privy to meet. He deemed none of them worthy. I tended to agree. Ms. Diva wanted to slither into her sexy ninja outfit and get some moves on. Her patience faltered. I felt it on my skin. It was like a rash that never goes away.

After the event, Jim and I had a drink at the hotel where the event took place. He moved the chair to sit next to me, which seemed quite promising until I realized he did it so he could face the TV and follow the basketball game on the large screen. I was livid. The conversation was not fun anymore. It was borderline boring and too serious. I asked him what he was doing that weekend. He mentioned he would babysit his grandnephews on Friday or Saturday, but he didn't know which day. The kicker was that he reciprocated interest but did not mention us getting together again.

He asked me if the term Wellness Advocate was trademarked. That's the term we used in the company I was affiliated with. I replied that I didn't think so and that it meant that we were advocating for our own wellness with natural solutions and alternatives to synthetics. He responded that it was a good alternative to the word "caregiver," which he had been using for his new business of medical marijuana-food-grade products. This industry would be booming in New England very soon.

Imagine my surprise the next night when I was with our friend Sarah at my friend Lisa's house. Over wine and whiskey, we decided to use Lisa's fake Plenty of Sharks account to look up his profile, and I noticed he had amended his profession from Chef to Wellness Advocate! Our voices grew louder in outrage—I might have uttered some swear words after I saw the photo I had taken in my kitchen the day we went to the wedding. I was furious. I saw Ms. Diva fan herself profusely, and the Jokester changed positions on the couch while giving a one-finger salute. I knew it was not directed at me but at Jim. Still, I thought he would change his title on a business card or website, NOT his online dating profile.

"He's got something else in the works. He is still shopping around." Lisa took a sip of her drink.

I was livid and insulted, which explained why he had been so distant and why things felt off at the Boston event. It made sense now that he had a few pots on the stove and left me on the back burner.

When I finally thought I had met someone decent and normal, the greed for hunting women had to waltz in. These guys were always looking for the next best thing, where they thought the grass was greener. I was disappointed but not heartbroken, and very glad I hadn't taken things further with him. The attachment was minute. I saved myself from another impending disaster. God was watching.

Jim gave me some great moments and made my flicker of hope shine a little brighter. I still believed in possibilities and continued surrendering.

CHAPTER 68

LOCATION, LOCATION, LOCATION?

I dreamed of living by the beach, and maybe in the next stage of my life, I could have a small and clutter-free place near the ocean. It probably wouldn't be in New England, as I could not handle these winters. Ms. Diva was tired of wearing snow boots and big coats.

As I went through this process, I thought about location. I asked myself if, with online dating, location mattered. Was I limited by where I lived? If I lived in a big city, would my experience be different? Maybe the suburbs weren't better; perhaps the big city with more people was better. It was possible. It was a law of numbers.

Did IP address location matter in terms of which site to use? Actually, no. That was my empirical conclusion. After four and a half years of doing this on and off, I wondered if one site or app was better. I was on all major ones; no, there wasn't a better one. It was all advertising and the same crappy algorithms. I believe that the matches they sent you were non-matches. Why? Because they wanted you to upgrade. They sold you the illusion that by upgrading for a cost—sometimes very high, you'd get more hits, or they'd position your profile center-stage. Instead of being a prop on the stage of online dating, they convinced you that by paying for a membership, you would become a front runner and main belle of the ball. It was simply misrepresentation. If the system was designed to work, people wouldn't continue to be on the apps. So, it was designed to fail and keep you coming back for more. And they, the online dating developers, counted on the end user to remain hopeful.

The Jokester took a puff of his cigar and swirled his glass of maple-colored aged whisky. He lifted an eyebrow. Looking very unkempt these days, I wondered if he was even bathing. Maybe that was why Ms. Diva was on the opposite side of the house. The Jokester had lost hope. I knew it. I could feel it. Ms. Diva hadn't. My alter egos were diverging.

I turned to the Jokester and told him not to quit on me. "Get out of your funk! Take a shower, for God's sake! It's springtime, time to ditch the smoking and alcohol and do a 30-day cleanse. You need to refocus."

Ms. Diva backed me up on this. Since the weather was changing, she had fuchsia open-toe high heels that I could only stare at but not use. Perfect recipe for breaking an ankle, and I didn't need that at all.

I started talking to Ray, a high school teacher and father of two teenage boys. He was tall at 6'4—Ms. Diva purred for a second—blondish hair and blue eyes, extremely attractive, and our conversation was fantastic, even if we found each other on Plenty of Sharks, in that toxic pond of online dating.

We exchanged phone numbers, which was always a step that I didn't arrive at with most people I communicated with. We set up a Friday night date at the beginning of the week, which was a promising sign and not a last-minute-I-have-nothing-better-to-do date.

The day before, we agreed not to meet after all. Ray told me he was looking for a casual relationship and went on to explain that what he meant was a monogamous sexual relationship. In other words, I didn't even give Ms. Diva a chance to put on her lacey nightie, as Ray sought a sexual-benefits-only rapport.

We were both disappointed because we enjoyed talking to each other. I told him that type of relationship was too limiting for me. I wanted a connection encompassing all levels and not just the physical. I told him that what he was looking for was a risky thing. Most women could not separate the physical from the emotional, and someone was bound to get hurt. He reluctantly agreed, and I ended our exchange with, "My body is a sacred private temple, not a public church."

CHAPTER 69
PILOT UP

Against my better judgment, I renewed my Catch membership after a two-year hiatus. Yes, two years! I got one of those deals for three months and fell for it. The Jokester was dry-heaving in the corner and choking on his cigar. Ms. Diva left the house. She needed some air.

"I didn't do much on the first day. I just updated my dormant profile with new photos and a quick copy-and-paste process from the other apps. Even though that was never my intention, I was getting to be proficient at this. And I was not proud of that fact either. The place seemed the same. As I browsed, I saw familiar faces and thought: *Well, they're all still single too. Or maybe they're just using this as a meat market.*

On the second day, I browsed prospects again. I came across a profile of someone super active who sounded interesting. I was not the outdoorsy, super active type of girl, but some of Tony's words were semi-poetic and caught my eye. His occupation was listed as an arborist, but his background was in aviation. I was intrigued. I was not sure about him, so I didn't contact him. Then I noticed he added me as a favorite, which was something I got a warning about. Lo and behold, when I opened the chat option—I was excited to use live chat again instead of email—I saw him online, and since I was bored to tears that evening, I decided to make the first move.

The chat system itself was a little sluggish, but he was proving to be interesting indeed. He was British and could trace his family roots back 800 years. Very adventurous, he loved surfing, running, and mountain biking—I was certain I could keep up with him... NOT! He was also a pilot and was studying to become a flight instructor. Both my parents were pilots, so we connected on that level. He told me he wanted to call me, so we talked on the phone for almost three and a half hours. We decided to meet the following evening for a drink. He didn't have a British accent, as he had been in the United States since age five. We decided to meet closer to me.

He was better looking in his photos than in real life. That happened a few times. At fifty-two, he was in great shape, and despite telling me he didn't appear his age, my ex-husband, who was older than him, looked younger. We had a lovely time. And on the next date, we went to a nice, quiet Italian spot nearby for appetizers and drinks.

When we spoke on the phone earlier, I realized we were meeting quite late, as he worked 12-hour days. He implied getting together that evening but suggested I take him out or cook him dinner. I was a little taken aback, as I was old-fashioned with that stuff, and I knew that not only was I expecting the man to be a gentleman but also to pay at first. I also knew there were expectations of a particular order on date three, or was it five?

I made him a deal: I would cook him dinner if there was no dessert of any kind. He agreed. I was not okay with this, but I felt safe enough to have him over. I cooked a spectacular dinner. In addition, Ms. Diva had some handcuffs, and the Jokester hid a Glock under the table. I cooked a spectacular dinner. Ms. Diva was highly frustrated when he fell asleep on his bed before our date and only arrived at my doorstep at ten o'clock in the evening. This was way too late. I was usually either getting to bed at that time or already there, never mind eating late. I had occasionally been at a restaurant at that time, but I was not serving dinner at ten when I was the hostess. But I did! What was I thinking?

He brought a bottle of wine. We had a great dinner, and he ended up dozing on my couch, so I politely booted him out. This was not a hotel. Well, maybe for my cats, it was an all-inclusive five-star resort, but not for someone I was trying to get to know.

He texted me once or twice the next day when he got home, and I didn't hear from him again. I was not brokenhearted about it. I felt that as interesting and potentially promising as he seemed, he was not the one for me. And he never put the cloth napkin back in its holder, which slightly pissed me off. He had apologized for being late but didn't seem too worried about it.

He texted me a couple of days later, but in my book, that was way past the "I'm interested in you" phase, and I didn't respond. He then texted me a few hours later with 'Do you want to talk?" and he was met with absolute silence on my part. I was getting better at not settling. Finally. Ms. Diva and the Jokester popped a bottle of champagne open.

CHAPTER 70
CHOCOLATE SAMPLING

I talked to one of my besties, Karen—I have many besties, thank God!—a holistic chiropractor and healer who has been one of my mentors over the past eighteen years. She knew how frustrated I was in my search for a life partner, soulmate, significant other, or whatever you wanted to call the needle in this twilight zone of a haystack.

I told her I felt like lots of time had been wasted as I usually could only tackle one candidate at a time. I felt too loyal to one person, or it didn't feel right to multi-task men. I knew women who did this, but it was not the right approach for me. Not only did I have enough trouble keeping track of details, and thus why this whole book started in my log-in attempts, but I just inherently felt I was more old-fashioned in that respect and tried to put my energy into one person to see if that would work out. Time trickled away, and maybe it was not the fastest or most innovative approach to dating.

She told me to look at it like cake hunting. I informed her I was not a fan of cake. She then followed with, "What's your guilty pleasure?"

"Chocolate."

"Okay, what would you do to find the best-tasting chocolate in the world?"

"I would need to sample a lot," I concluded.

"Then look at this as chocolate sampling. You are looking for the best chocolate. You may try some that are too bitter, too sweet, or just not right. What do you think will happen when you find your favorite chocolate?"

"I wouldn't need to look anymore."

She encouraged me to chocolate sample, which became our code when she texted me how the chocolate sampling was going. I just laughed out loud.

Looking at chocolate may differ from looking at potential life partners, but the analogy is brilliant.

This was a sure way to stop beating myself up and trying to impose self-made rules, which only made things more challenging for me.

If I looked at this in this light fashion, the chocolate sampling idea could be fun. If a piece of chocolate doesn't taste that great, it might not be a great idea to keep it around for too long. It was only unnecessary empty calories.

Spring arrived, and the hot days of summer were right around the corner. Chocolate could melt at hot temperatures, so it needed to be discarded immediately if it was not great.

I glanced over at the Jokester channel-surfing, lounging on the recliner. He finally took a shower and looked halfway decent. His constant frown eased up a bit, maybe because he ate cleaner whole foods. Ms. Diva was reading a romance novel, sprawled on the couch, her hair flowing from the ceiling fan's breeze. She wore a black one-piece extra short nightie with white polka dots and white lace mid-thigh. She crossed her legs and leafed the book, hoping some chocolate would soon materialize.

When I looked up at the sky to communicate above that I was surrendering, I asked not only for the right person to come along but also to shorten things with the wrong people. I made it clear that I didn't want to waste time and asked that something be done to shorten the connection with the wrong guys. And since then, my wish came true. Even though the last three weren't horrible people, they were not the right fit. And I was secretly grateful that things were cut short with them because the right partner was still out there. I also knew that deep down, the Jokester and Ms. Diva supported me and wanted to see me in a happy, harmonious, and long-lasting relationship despite the fuss they sometimes put me through. Pass the chocolate.

CHAPTER 71
TIC TAC

F ive years had passed since my ex-husband and I went our separate ways. I never thought for a minute that, after all this time, I'd still be single and not have a child at this stage of my life.

Part of me wondered if there was a reason I missed the boat altogether. I looked around me; most of my friends had little versions of themselves, and I had longed for that for a long time. It was something I talked about with a few people. I felt like a failure in that respect. I also wondered if the Universe had different plans for me. I thought I would make an excellent mother, but with the biological clock ticking a thousand miles a second, I didn't feel I had that much time left. The tides were against me. So many factors indeed.

Out of the corner of my eye, Ms. Diva sat stone-faced. She could not fathom maternity clothes. "Honey, there is nothing sexy about that!" I reminded her of what it would mean to create a new life. "It would be fun trying and practicing." I wondered if I could even have a child at this stage. With the lack of a life partner thus far, would I be able to do it on my own?

Ms. Diva reminded me I could do anything I wanted. The Jokester got up to grab some carrot sticks from the fridge. "You would have lots of help," he mumbled between bites. Would I really? My family was abroad, my brother in NYC, and I had many friends who were my extended family, but would it even be fair and feasible to count on them for such an undertaking?

I didn't even know if I could carry a child. Maybe my eggs had gotten old. I only had one fallopian tube, and the risks were higher. I would have to go to a sperm bank and leaf through pages of donors, secretly suspecting that it was all from a handful of losers who needed the money in exchange for their loads. My child would be fatherless. I would be a mother and father. But then again, these are modern times. People were changing genders, medical advances progressed quickly with organ transplants, and you could find everything from anything after clicking once or twice on a laptop or phone.

I made an appointment to see my gynecologist in the spring, shortly before another European trip to my home country. I needed to find out what my options were.

I hadn't seen him since he inserted the IUD three years earlier, and I had almost fainted from the pain. He made it sound so simple after I asked him about my options to become a mother without a partner.

"I suggest you do this sooner than later. And the first thing we need to find out is if your tube is open."

I hadn't even thought about that. What if it wasn't, and what did it all entail?

"I have to inject a dye into your cervix, and then with a live x-ray, we will be able to determine if your tube is open or closed."

"But I have the IUD," I told him.

"That has to come out before the procedure."

I was mentally computing my schedule to create a timetable of when this would happen. He surprised me with, "We can remove it right now."

The Jokester looked at Ms. Diva, and both looked stupefied. What?

"Right now?" I parroted back.

"Yes, right now."

"Okay."

I had no idea this was going to happen so fast. I was not mentally prepared. My mind ran fast, wondering if I was jumping the gun with this. We adjourned to another room. I got naked from the waist down with just a sheet covering me, then waited. The doctor came in with his equipment and guided me through every move. It wasn't the most comfortable thing in the world, but there were many worse things in life.

He mentioned having trouble finding the string. I panicked. Ms. Diva whispered to me, "It's all the sex you had, darling." I wondered if I would have to go under the knife, but finally, he found it and removed the Internal Uterine Device.

"Now, don't get up too fast. Just relax. You might get dizzy and crampy. Take your time after I leave the room."

He shut the door, and I started bawling my eyes out. I was a woman again. Nothing impeded me from creating life—only the lack of a partner. I felt very emotional and free. In my mind, I thought, 'This could all be for nothing. Don't get your hopes up.'

CHAPTER 72
TIC TAC TOE

After getting off the table and dressed, I talked to the nurse about scheduling the dye procedure at the hospital. She informed me that it would depend on the start of my cycle. Luckily, I kept a log on the Notes section of my phone, so I had the start date. She looked at the computer screen at her calendar. This was on a Monday.

"We have to do it this Thursday." She glanced at me.

"Huh?"

"Can you be at the hospital at 7:15 a.m.? The doctor will do the procedure at 7:30 a.m."

She added, "You'll find out the results right away."

My mind spun. The world was changing. My world was changing. I didn't even consult Ms. Diva or the Jokester. There was no time.

"Okay," I nodded.

I stepped out of the doctor's office in a daze, a tad physically uncomfortable from what just happened and still digesting all the information.

I called Lara and told her what happened. She said, "You have my full support." Then I called another bestie, Sharon, and told her the news. I asked her if she would drive me on Thursday to the procedure. I had no idea what state I'd be in, but I suspected my nerves would be a mess, and it would probably be best not to be by myself. She agreed and said she'd take me.

The next day was a blur. My mind raced through the 'what if' scenarios. What if it was closed? I would have to accept a harsh reality I was unprepared to accept at this point in my life. I had flashbacks and regrets that I had allowed too much time to pass and that those years had been wasted for nothing. What if the tube was open?

Sharon picked me up at the crack of dawn. Ms. Diva and the Jokester still slept. There was no way they were coming with me on this one. They could very well be across the country. We arrived at the hospital before 7:15 a.m. I went to the Imaging Department, checked in, and waited. Then, the nurse came in and took us to another waiting room, where she instructed Sharon to wait for me. She said the procedure shouldn't be more than fifteen minutes.

That was comforting, but I returned to the waiting room where Sharon held on to my purse and dowsed myself with some calming essential oil blends, part of my natural remedy stash. My nerves were shot.

The friendly nurse took me to a bathroom to change, and I followed her into a vast room. She told me that the examining table didn't have stirrups, that I would lie down on it, and that she could get me a blanket if I were chilly. She warned me that the dye would also be cold when the doctor started the procedure.

The doctor came in. He had a kind aura about him, and he started prepping. I told him, "I didn't even ask you what happens if it's closed. We didn't discuss that part." He squeezed my arm and said, "Let's go through this first." I nodded. I noticed a giant X-ray machine above me. I tried to get my body to un-tense if there was such a thing. I felt some pain during the procedure, but nothing I could not handle. I was seeing the computer screen x-ray shots of my hip, and I couldn't understand what it was, but they obviously could. The doctor injected the dye and started taking photos. Lots of them. They had me move a few times. He came to my left side, squeezed my arm while looking at the screen, and said, "It's open."

I was in shock. I realized most of my nerves were not due to fear of the procedure itself but of the results. I feared that the answer would be the opposite and that I would have to dismiss this motherhood dream altogether.

I asked the doctor to say hello to Susan, who was still waiting for me in a separate waiting room. Before he left, he told me I needed to make an appointment across the hall from him to start a plan of action at the fertility center.

The good thing was that I had a trip scheduled to go home and had no plans to start a new life storm anytime soon. So that would buy me a month, give or take, jet lag and other adjustments upon my return.

Then, I would have to contact my health insurance company to ask them what would be covered with this new adventure and if they even covered anything at all.

I felt an avalanche looming.

CHAPTER 73
TIME CHALLENGES

Amid fertility checks, I continued my search. I met Gordon on Catch. I think Ms. Diva drove this one in for sure.

I swear I didn't look for guys with military history. They dropped on my lap. Some had been bold-faced lies and illusions; others had been disturbed by mental challenges. Gordon was six feet tall with blue eyes and a forty-five-year-old U.S. Marine. He was clean-cut, wore glasses, and had a military haircut. For the past years, he worked as an assistant to an oral surgeon and lived about an hour from me. He also went to school at night twice weekly to get his master's in chemical engineering.

On our first date, we ended up having lunch outside in a restaurant, and we hit it off. He told me a lot about his family, and I shared with him about mine. He was the middle son of three. His older brother was super lazy, and his younger brother, who used to be the same way, turned his life around and moved to Colorado.

His father passed away two years earlier; he became the executor and had been dealing with that for a while.

Our chemistry was great, and I was frightfully overjoyed. The problem was that I had a trip overseas coming up, and the timing couldn't be worse. I would be gone for three weeks—not on vacation. Three weeks was a long time, and I could not expect that Gordon would place his dating life on hold to wait for me.

We only saw each other twice before I left, and he texted me daily while I was overseas. Not a long communication, but always present. I was hopeful.

When I got back, he didn't communicate as often. I went on Catch, which I had avoided for weeks, and noticed he was online. I knew that didn't mean anything, but I was secretly disappointed.

He told me he got a cold that first week back, and we only saw each other on Sunday. After that, his communication was sparser. I got hopeful again as he shared more of himself with me and told me about his childhood. He started working as a dishwasher for an Italian restaurant in Rhode Island at age eleven. He soon realized it was mob-owned, but he made more money than his mother at that time, and they treated him very well, as he was a hard worker. He said he would go to work after school and stay until midnight. A few years later, he was promoted to valet, parking cars, and before he was sixteen, he bought his first car. By the time he got his license, he already had wheels. As admirable as this was, his long hours had not changed much since age eleven. He is hard-working and dedicated; I wondered if he could be that diligent with relationships.

After one week, he texted me to tell me that he hadn't forgotten about me and that he was working twelve-hour days and the heat was getting to him. I said I didn't think he had enough time to fit me into his schedule, and he replied that he was busy. In my mind, I thought, 'but not too busy to go on Catch.'

Ms. Diva stripped naked and threw her lace nightie on the ground. She then picked it up out of guilt and hung it. She got into workout casual clothes and rain boots and declared, "I'm mowing the lawn today." The Jokester glanced at her out of the corner of his eye with some admiration and respect. Deflated, I followed her outside. Another one bit the dust.

Chapter 74
TURKISH FLAIR

I was not wasting time. I concluded that time was of the essence, and I needed to either close the door to online dating or scrap this book endeavor. I needed to focus on baby-making because that was my long-term project.

I returned to the crazy ocean of POS and met Firat, a Turkish single dad who had been in the United States for sixteen years.

We met for lunch on a Saturday. I found out he owned a transportation business with his best friend and that his son was with him half the time. He didn't want any more kids, as he hinted at his son being a handful. Wasn't every child a handful?

He was 6'2. Ms. Diva liked them tall. He had a beard, even though most of his photos didn't reflect that.

I also learned that he was one of three. One of his brothers also immigrated to the States. He seemed close to his mom and wasn't on speaking terms with his other brother. He didn't elaborate.

We talked about the unsettlement in Turkey, and he said he didn't feel like Turkey was his country anymore because things had changed so much. In the 1980s, it was very similar to the Western depiction of women in magazines with big hairdos and shimmery makeup. Now, a printed ad shows a woman with her hair and body covered.

I nodded. I saw that when I was in Istanbul a couple of years earlier. Repression wasn't a positive thing in my book, and I silently thanked the higher powers for granting me opportunities and not having any of those restrictions. I had lived in two countries where such things weren't felt. At least overtly.

He also told me about his mandatory military experience of eighteen months in Turkey when he was in his early twenties and that there were 86,400 seconds in one day. I had never counted or even thought about that. Perspective is everything.

We enjoyed lunch and said goodbye. As much as Firat was intriguing, I suspected there was no love connection on either part. He texted me later that day, but it stopped, and I was okay with it.

I switched sites briefly and went to Cinder, a dating app. Everyone had warned me that it was a hook-up place, but then I had a couple of friends who knew of people who met through there and were happy. A sucker for happy endings, I started to swipe left if I didn't like their photos and swipe right if I did. Ms. Diva had a ball with this. She was very visual and picky, and if someone didn't look right or the photo looked like a mug shot or a crime in progress, like a shirtless selfie, her fingers swiped left at the speed of light. If it was a mutual match, meaning that both people swiped right, you could communicate.

It was too visual of a medium for my taste, and most people didn't write much. Another pet peeve of mine on that app was that you didn't know how tall they were, and that seemed to be the first thing I looked at. I shared this trait with many women. You also didn't know what type of relationship they were looking for. It was rare to find one stating the intent. But many said their height, which was a good thing. You also came across couples who wanted to add a third person to their relationship or their sex life. Out of the corner of my eye, I saw the Jokester rolling on my Persian rug, laughing hysterically.

I hadn't met anyone on Cinder until then, but Drew messaged me. He was a mortgage loan officer in Warwick, Rhode Island, and we quickly exchanged phone numbers. He seemed promising. He told me he wasn't looking for something casual either, but I started seeing another side of him as the texts progressed. He said the right things but then asked me for photos. He didn't want any normal photos but sexy ones. And he said I should trust him. He told me I sounded jaded and must have been burned in the past. He was right, but that didn't mean I would send sexy photos to a stranger. He laid off for a while, dangled some walk on the beach for the first date, and when I suggested we spoke on the phone, he started accusing me of being too jaded again and not trusting anyone. I nipped the whole thing in the bud. I didn't have time for someone who wouldn't even respect my wishes or understand that it was not customary to ask for or receive sexy photos from anyone and then pretend they were looking for something serious.

Ms. Diva screamed at the top of her lungs. "What a douchebag! You are not seeing the goods yet, asshole."

Our interaction ended with "your nuts."

I texted back, "It's 'you're nuts' and 'thank you.'" And I blocked his number.

What a nut bag! Cinder left a sour taste in my mouth. Maybe it was just a hookup app, after all.

I thanked him at the end because I was grateful that he showed me his true colors, and I didn't have to waste more time. The Angels were listening. The Jokester turned to me and said, "Duh!" But I knew he was still laughing at Drew's inappropriate request.

CHAPTER 75

CONSIDERING ALTRUISM

Since I was gifted the task of bringing my Mr. Perfect-for-Me Guy to the Infinite Wisdom of the Angels above, I felt a sense of freedom. I got the message from the ethers that my soulmate might not come in the form I expected. I tried hard to pay attention to my intuition and understand the messages from my gut and my companions, Ms. Diva and the Jokester. I felt like I had neglected my gut's opinion; even if sometimes, it sensed red flags, my mind bypassed my inner knowing like a giant bulldozer.

I started talking to Josh on Plenty of Sharks. Right away, he asked for my number and called me. It was always refreshing when someone wanted to hear my voice. Maybe they wanted to make sure I was a woman. Who knew these days? He had a nice voice; you could tell he was not from New England. He was three and a half years younger than me, my brother's age, to be exact. A minor difference like that was not a big deal. Josh was from Florida and had been in Massachusetts for two years. He had never been married and had no kids. He was a behavior analyst with a master's degree working for a company, helping autistic adults in their living arrangements and daily lives. He managed teams and analyzed data. He might have been secretly in love with graphs. Maybe not so secretly. I sensed he had tremendous patience, not one of my fortes.

We hit it off on the phone and even talked about past relationships—a topic that should not be covered right away—and what we were looking for in a future relationship. He sounded promising. I could tell he was educated, had manners, and wanted to find a long-term relationship. He didn't strike me as another disappointment. The Jokester and Ms. Diva rolled their eyes.

What was the catch? In our second conversation, I playfully asked him to share something I didn't know about him. Josh took it to an extreme. He told me he needed to share something very serious with me because that information might change my mind about dating him. I gulped in anticipation.

He said that he needed a kidney when he was in his early twenties and that his brother had been a match. He received his brother's kidney, and I could tell that this man, who already idolized his older brother, was now eternally grateful and viewed him as his hero. Understandably so. Giving up one of your organs to save someone's life is not only brave and heroic, but it also shows a sense of pure altruism and high regard for human life. I could tell this man had a genuine appreciation for life in general, as he had to endure that challenge when he was younger.

Josh told me he had a tough road ahead. He told me that the kidney had behaved well until recently. That he hadn't been feeling well and that he needed another kidney. I felt compassion and wanted to help as he expanded on that story. I could not donate any organs, not only because I was not a blood match but because doctors told me in my teens that I wouldn't even be able to donate blood due to food-borne hepatitis at sixteen. I was silent for a few seconds. He asked me if I needed time to process all that. I told him I just wanted him to be healthy. In the back of my mind, I was already making a list of what I needed to Google: kidney transplant, kidney transplant waiting time, and kidney transplant surgery recovery time.

Part of me was a fixer and a healer; I just wanted everyone to be healthy all the time. This very utopic vision of the world allowed me to continue my pink or purple-colored glass view of my reality. I wanted peace, love, and health for everyone, including this stranger on the phone.

He shared that he had lost twenty-five pounds in the past few months because he was in kidney failure. I was highly concerned as much as I was jealous of his weight loss. He also shared that certain friends of his were being tested to see if they could be matched. Otherwise, he had to wait his turn. He was more of a priority on that list due to his age. I later found out that the waiting time was three to five years, which meant he would need dialysis very soon, three times a week, and it would start in the next month or two.

What if Josh was the man I had been waiting for? What if this was the man I was expecting, and he came with this gigantic health hurdle? What was I to do? Was I willing to initiate a relationship now and be there? Would I be willing to put all my dreams and desires aside for someone else if he was the right person for me?

I could not have decided on this without meeting him first. For one week, Josh and I talked on the phone daily. I liked him more and more. I liked his sense of humor, his nerdiness, the way he shared his dreams, and the way he said "Goodbye, beautiful" before he hung up.

The truth was that an in-person meeting was crucial. If I were to consider a future with him, I needed to treat him like any other man I met for the first time. Would there be chemistry, or was it just a friend connection vibe?

We met on a Thursday night for dinner not too far from me. He arrived first at the restaurant, and I immediately saw him in the back. The three pictures I had seen of him did not do him justice. Josh looked extremely sick, sicker than I could ever have imagined. He must have felt self-conscious about the way he looked. He had mentioned it briefly on the phone before.

Nevertheless, we had a nice dinner together, and I felt like I talked too much. I was enjoying myself and realizing that many of his dreams were the same as mine. I noticed he was getting tired, and as we left, we said goodbye with a hug. Later that night, he texted me that he got home safely, and I thanked him for dinner.

Then he asked me, "What are you thinking?" I told him what I thought: I had fun, talked too much, and shouldn't have had that second glass of wine.

With my response, he interpreted that I didn't feel any chemistry, and even though he had told me that he had wanted me in his life in any capacity, he said goodbye by text. I called and left a message explaining that he had misinterpreted my message and asked him to call me back. I remained open-minded and did not assume that physical chemistry had to be there immediately, especially when someone was not looking their best. He never returned my call, and I had a feeling either he didn't feel the chemistry himself, or he was rejecting me first, so I didn't have to.

Ms. Diva got teary-eyed because she felt sorry for the whole situation. I never heard from him again. And the page turned once more.

CHAPTER 76

I DON'T KNOW ANYTHING ANYMORE

My friends were probably tired of hearing my failing attempts in the online dating pool, and sometimes, they uttered clichés that enticed borderline murderous tendencies I had suppressed deep down. Occasionally, I asked myself why I was so stubborn. Why was I still in pursuit of a life partner?

Both Ms. Diva and the Jokester argued with me. They abhorred clichés with every fiber of their being. One popular saying was "when you least expect it." I got frustrated because I was not the "when I least expect it" kind of gal. I was always prepared. I was always anticipating. Maybe it was the hopeful romantic in me or the obsessive-compulsive drive that created this situation in my life.

I was never "least expecting it," so how could I eliminate this expectation? How did I let go of an outcome? Was it even possible for me?

It was evident that my intuitive guidance system malfunctioned countless times. It was equally obvious that my exercise in tolerance far exceeded self-preservation and, at times, caused me endless wastes of time and emotionally painful experiences.

My brother told me the other day that it might arrive when I least expected it. The friends I had lunch with yesterday said it would happen when I least expected it. Everyone was using those words! God wanted to teach me patience because I lacked that quality.

I visited New York City that weekend. I hadn't seen my brother since Christmas, eight months earlier. It was a whopping 95 degrees every day, with humidity over 79%. I always chose summer to go to New York when it was extra steamy. Not on purpose. My brother was an amazing man, and I greatly admired him. I valued his input and advice. I chatted with him about all this, and he told me that the two things I wanted—a life partner and a child, might not come simultaneously, and I needed to decide which needed to come first. I always thought the life partner would come first, then the child, but it had been short of five years on my own, and my clock was ticking until it could tick no more. As I pondered his words, despite my wish for things to happen more conventionally, I had to think outside the box and tackle them separately.

I started talking to Jerome, a French guy who had been in the United States for ten years. He lived in California for a while, where his two kids were, and now he resided not far from me. In our conversation, he asked me if I wanted children. The conversation got very serious about that topic, and he told me I didn't have much time and that I should get pregnant as soon as possible. Duh. He told me to forget about going to the sperm bank and that he could get me pregnant!

I have said this numerous times before; I couldn't make this shit up! As nutty as his proposal was, not only did it sound preposterous, but he had no desire to have a relationship—he would be sticking around only for as many attempts as required until I conceived and had no plans to stay after that. I didn't know if I should laugh or cry. Ms. Diva and the Jokester couldn't stop laughing. Should I even consider such a proposal? It sounded insane. I immediately bushed it aside simply because I would most likely harbor resentment if I knew the "donor" willingly planned to abandon his child. There was no way I could even plausibly look at this. There was no other way to look at this except with mere laughter. I had a sperm donor if I needed one. He was French and European, just like me, but that was as far as it went. I could say that my online dating adventures not only presented me with a lot of sexual opportunities but also some sperm, ready to woo my eggs along the way.

Then, of course, there were the married men. Remember Steve earlier on Cherub's Arrow? That site included a bounty of married men and young guys looking for older women. António was a Brazilian IT guy and MMA fighter stuck in a sexless marriage. His first wife had passed away, and he married her best friend because he had a small son who still needed a mother. He didn't think things through because he could never be physically happy with her. His current wife had massive psychological trauma due to her uncle raping her when she was young, and sex had become taboo and painful. She hadn't sought help, leaving her husband sexually frustrated. Apparently, I moonlighted as a psychotherapist, but all I attained were men wanting me so badly that I almost drove them to madness.

They were playing with fire. The truth was that these guys should not be on these sites for single people like me, but they were. I started talking to them because they didn't immediately divulge their marital status. Through some digging, I eventually found out. I became heartless because I thought they should work on their marriage instead of seeking other women. Part of me wanted them to suffer. At the same time, I felt sorry for António. He felt comfortable talking to me about everything. I told him that if she didn't seek help, he had some hard decisions to make. He told me that his parents divorced when he was little and that he didn't want his son to go through the same.

He should have thought of that before he married her. António wanted me to find a life partner, but he was also willing to have sex with me while I searched. He wanted me to be his special friend. Ms. Diva and the Jokester shook their heads in what seemed like a music video dance routine. I agreed with them. This had all the ingredients of a bad soap opera, and I hated soap operas.

CHAPTER 77

PORTUGUESE-AMERICAN STYLE
Round 2

I always told myself I would not go Portuguese, maybe because of the stereotypes or because I was not your typical Portuguese girl. It became complicated when I tried to explain this to people, and I had to set the stage for a whole life flashback. However, this validated once again the fact that I should have stopped listening to my logical mind and listened to my intuition.

Ms. Diva and the Jokester constantly reminded me of this, and I knew I wasn't the best listener. As I spoke on the phone for the first time with Paulo, a first-generation Portuguese son of Azorean parents, I knew in the depths of my stomach I should have said, "Thank you, but no, thank you."

Instead, I agreed to meet him in Lowell, where he lived. Ms. Diva was appalled that I was the one to drive for an hour while Paulo remained in the comfort of his home. That should have been a red flag. But he had given me a plausible excuse, that he was waiting for maintenance men to work on his bathroom in his very chic loft and didn't have a timetable for when all the work would be done, so he suggested I came up for the first date and that for our second date, he could drive down to me.

Fair enough. He took me to a Thai restaurant. I love Thai food, but this place was underwhelming, and they didn't even serve alcohol. How important could that be? It could have helped me relax. After all this time, I still felt nervous and cautious about first dates. I thought it was normal. The Jokester shrugged because he couldn't care less now. He had checked out long ago and was now more concerned with his health and appearance. I was proud of him.

Paulo was a clinical therapist. I tended to give people the benefit of the doubt, but I remembered how the story with the therapist ex-boyfriend from Maine turned out and was apprehensive. I felt like Paulo was psycho-analyzing me, but I played it cool. After all, I didn't think I was imbalanced. The Jokester raised an eyebrow Ms. Diva-style, and I didn't appreciate it.

Paulo seemed very open and considered himself Portuguese even though he was born in the US, and he claimed his Portuguese was fluent. It could be fluent in his eyes, but it was full of oral mistakes, and I found myself correcting him on our second date. He did drive down because I deemed our first date okay. He wanted to eat Portuguese food, so we went to Sagres in Fall River, a more upscale restaurant. We also discussed who paid the bill, and I agreed with him that it could be my treat this time. I had gone back and forth on this issue over the years. The bill came to the table, and it was four times as much as the Thai place, which I didn't think amounted to twenty bucks, but then again, I said I would pay, so I refused his offer to pitch in out of pride. Portuguese pride or being a bull-headed Taurus might be to blame.

As we exited the restaurant, you could hear music in the distance. When we got into my car, he asked what that was, and I told him it was the Portuguese feast. He wanted to go. My face made it obvious that it was not my cup of tea, and I told him as much. I might have sounded a tad snobbish without meaning to. Plus, I couldn't go out partying until the wee hours of the night, and he knew I had to return to Fall River the following morning for a Sunday business breakfast. Lots of driving and life was busy.

The ride back proved excruciating, as silence left palpable shards of awkwardness. He told me how insulted he was and how his parents did so much for him when they immigrated to the States. He also told me for the fourth or fifth time how hard he worked to get two master's degrees from Boston University. He grew up with the feasts and how much he loved them, and it was typical of someone like me, a continental, to look down on the islanders because we thought we were better. He could not be more wrong, of course. The ride back continued to be torturous. I wished he had driven his car and left of his own accord, but no such luck.

Ms. Diva and the Jokester ate popcorn in my recliners and watched this train wreck unfold.

I wondered if what they said about certain people who picked psychology as a profession was true since we were talking about stereotypes and generalizations.

After this second date, all I knew was that Paulo and I weren't a good fit, and I knew I would never see him again.

He called me a few days later, but I didn't pick up. Then he used his office line, which I didn't have the number to, and I answered. Shoot, I knew what he wanted. He had boasted about how he was always the one who broke up with the girls, and he probably didn't want to break his record. As far as I was concerned, I didn't need to rehash or process anything, but I knew he wanted to keep the I-always-break-up-with-girls momentum for his peace of mind. So, after a few words and listening to him, I said, "I totally agree," and wished him a good night. I was the first one to hang up. He could think he broke up with me all he wanted, but that phone call was totally unnecessary.

CHAPTER 78
ON MY OWN

I needed to make an appointment with the fertility clinic. I timed things in my life. Without my iPhone calendar, I'd probably be lost. I needed to move full speed ahead and make this happen independently. It seemed entirely impersonal to have to pick sperm from an anonymous donor list. I read that all they let you do aside from a very general background was to see a baby/toddler photo so you could estimate what they looked like as a kid.

I was not fond of this idea. I thought the only one on board with this was the Jokester. He was friggin' tired of all these guys, and he had been very clear that if I wanted a baby, I needed to do this by myself. Take matters into my own hands and navigate parenthood as a single mother. Ms. Diva and I, on the other hand, resisted this idea because we were still holding on to the elusive Soulmate, who was lost and couldn't ask for directions to arrive at my doorstep. It was preposterous!

But there was no dull moment in my life. The crossroads were here, and life could change forever. I got a call from my doctor's office with the results of my routine mammogram, informing me that they found a 2.2 cm mass in my right breast. My heart dropped, and panic set in. I sat down, and they asked me if I wanted them to make the appointment at the hospital for an ultrasound or if I would like to do that myself. The timing of this was not convenient. It never was convenient nor pleasant to receive this news. I had some things scheduled, so I mumbled to the Nurse's Assistant which days were more convenient in a week. I knew that with this stuff, ultrasounds were urgently scheduled, and I got a call back with an appointment in three days.

I had to rethink my life. Instead of a pregnancy, I might be looking at chemo, radiation, lumpectomy, and mastectomy, and my health and survival were at the forefront of my concerns. Forget babies and forget dating and searching for Mr. Right. Cancer was no joke, and I knew so many people who were no longer here due to this devastating illness.

I didn't sleep much at all in the next three days. My mind could not compute this. I did not hear a peep from either Ms. Diva or the Jokester. They were probably just as shocked and fearful as I was. I didn't even want to Google what breast tumors looked like. I researched which essential oils could best support tumors and immediately made a concoction to be religiously applied every day.

I called Sharon, my emergency contact, and told her about the news amidst tears. She told me she would drive me there. I thanked her. I had the most amazing friends. I thought that was what I was most proud of: I was lucky to have these amazing people who loved and supported me.

We went into the hospital and tried to have a meaningful conversation in the waiting room. They only called me one hour after my scheduled time. I recognized the male technician. I think he had already performed an ultrasound on me. I was in a numbed haze.

As I lay there with a gown, waiting for him to come in, I called in the Archangels to protect me and give me strength. I didn't feel emotionally strong enough to handle anything. I went from Super Woman to Weak Woman in 0.2 nanoseconds. It was pathetic.

The technician began the examination, always looking at the screen with a poker face. I glanced several times at the screen and saw the round mass in black. It looked huge to me. There was an eerie calmness, and I thought fear might be suspended. I looked at the ceiling where a couple of paper origami birds were floating in the air. The ultrasound was complete, and he told me he had to show it to the radiologist.

Before he left, he gently touched my arm and whispered, "Nothing scary." I replied, "Thank you."

He returned confirming this, telling me the radiologist said it was a cyst with fluid and nothing to worry about. It may increase or decrease in size, but it was best to leave it alone. I thanked him again, and when he left the room, I started crying in gratitude to God and the Archangels. I knew Sharon was outside waiting for me, so I quickly dressed and told her the news.

That night, Sharon and I went to a friend's house who had launched a new business. In the middle of a lot of wine drinking, I shared my story. I had a new lease on life.

The following two days were spent in a daze, in a fog where the tension slowly lifted, bit by bit. I was the lucky one. Lucky indeed.

CHAPTER 79

THE LAW OF MANIFESTATION

I had always been fascinated by the law of attraction, vision boards, and the power of manifestation. With my lovely memory, I sometimes neglected to use these powers, but they were ever present in my life.

I had a printed version of my vision board on my refrigerator, and sometimes, I jotted down words on an assigned notebook of dreams and desires and pretended I already had everything I desired. One should always use the present tense when writing in this manner, and it was the same concept as an affirmation: you faked it until you made it. The key to manifesting, however, was believing and feeling deep down in your core with intense certainty that you already possessed what you wished for. It was absolutely within your reach.

One needed to be mindful of it, and my scattered brain conveniently forgot about using this method. Especially when it pertained to the man of my dreams. Frogs had come and gone, and the elusive One remained the needle in the haystack. I had believed that I was the Holy Grail—the ultimate catch—and that someOne just needed to find me. God knew I had been proactively searching, so the failure could not be attributed to a lack of trying. I sometimes whispered that I didn't expect the One to come knocking at my door, primarily when I worked alone most of the time.

One of my little notebooks was solely dedicated to a life partner. My old list had requirements of what I ideally wanted in a mate, for example, over six feet tall, honest, stable, etc. In that list, I also noted that he must prioritize and love me with a passion only known in romance novels. Well, maybe those weren't my exact words, but something along those lines. That list had been found by Larry, who, when invading my privacy by picking up that list and reading it, had said to me: "I am everything on that list." I snorted with laughter. "No, you're not." He had probably just filled the height requisite. Since then, I had placed that list aside and then found it again but felt like he had tainted it with his touch, so I ended up burning the list in an almost transmutative ceremony in my vegetable sink.

This notebook was different. It was very specific about the life I wanted with The One, written in prose with feelings oozing out of the page. I included details of our lives together and how we were each other's priorities. It was a work in progress, even though it sounded super repetitive. I should have set a reminder to write in it daily, but my disorganization skills needed improvement.

Ms. Diva was very focused on the carnal side of things with this right mate, and the Jokester tended to be a tad more practical, with things such as strengths and how we complemented one another as human beings. He focused more on personality matching than Ms. Diva's bedroom schedule.

As I sporadically wrote in this notebook, I jumped from site to site searching. I went on Cherub's Arrow and started talking to Eric, a 25-year-old. Yes, yes—way too young, of course. I replied to his message because I wanted to get rid of him. Surprisingly so, I found myself connecting with him on an intellectual level. He had a graduate degree, spoke five languages, and spelled words perfectly. We exchanged phone numbers, even though I knew this was not relationship material. However, since Eric had just moved to the Providence area, I thought he might need friends, and there was nothing wrong with having friends.

We ended up meeting, but Eric was highly disappointed that I would not go forward with a romantic connection, and truthfully, I couldn't get past the fact that we were sixteen years apart. It was inconceivable, and I found myself flashing back to when I met my ex-husband. I had been shy of twenty-four, and he was forty, so we were those same sixteen years apart. But now, when I looked at Eric, it did not make sense, and I could not imagine having anything else with him other than a friendship. He suggested some arrangement. Even Ms. Diva wasn't on board and was revolted by the idea. I found myself rejecting him. It was never a pleasant experience, and I knew it from having received rejection in the past; it was certainly not enjoyable, and it felt horrible. Not only did it hurt, but it was also something that could be traumatic.

I understood Eric's search did not encompass age that much; he often found himself connecting to older women, as they were more mature and emotionally more prepared to deal with him, not to mention his intellect, but this was not what I wanted. And he was not looking for someone to settle down with either. He was only twenty-five!

I was sick of the dating process. I had been feeling like this for a while now, and I knew my drive and determination propelled me to continue this.

I saw most of my friends coupled in some great relationships, and I wanted that for myself. That was always at the forefront of my dreams. Home was where the heart was, and my heart, despite not needing anyone else to pump and thrive on its own, wanted a companion by its side. And even though I had decided to pursue other dreams on my own, even if I was not in the ideal situation I had in mind, I still yearned for that.

And the ship continued to sail.

CHAPTER 80

BEING CATFISHED NEVER FELT SO GOOD

My skeptical brain could not be stopped. Part of me thought I was being catfished again, and if that was so, I had to say that this might have been the mother-load of catfish. I might get heartbroken again, but the light at the end of the tunnel was too bright, and I wanted the end to be near so badly.

Would a catfish send me flowers? Would a catfish send me a giant basket of fruit, cookies, and wine? Even if he used a stolen credit card, I asked myself: what was the end game?

Were all his pictures fake, including a passport? I tried to Skype, and of course, his camera did not work. This was a classic telltale of a catfish when one could not video chat. Many people have a smartphone, and it would not make sense to take photos with a cell phone but not use it for a live feed. I knew that much.

But I had gone through this so many times that I wondered if I was just too suspicious and that I could not even give someone the benefit of the doubt. I had been accused several times of having trust issues and didn't think I set out to be that way. It was possible that this catfish was just so smart and had such an incredible story woven that I just got suckered into it once again.

He was an Italian who immigrated to the United States five years prior, after the death of his wife. Both his parents had passed, and he was an only child. Before he was married, he was engaged to a woman who ended up cheating on him with his best friend as he caught them both in his own bed.

That right there would be reason enough never to trust another soul again. But no, not this Italian catfish. With his heavy accent—and now I regret that I never learned Italian to test this theory—he had told me pretty much everything I wanted to hear on the phone. My skeptical heart said that if it was too good to be true, it probably was.

I wished, at times like this, that I owned unlimited access to FBI-CIA resources so I could look up his information with a swift click and check whether his story was true.

We were supposed to meet a couple of weeks earlier, but it never happened, as Mr. Italian Catfish had to leave for Houston for a final presentation for a contract bid he was trying to get. Apparently, I brought him good luck. He won the bid and was now on the island of Cyprus for a month, working on this project.

I called the flower company, which pointed me to another flower company in New Jersey that got the online request from Teleflora. They managed to tell me that the beautiful bouquet was paid for by someone named Jose from California. This made no sense to me. Then, I called the fruit company located in Massachusetts to see if I could obtain the same information. The lady was so lovely but told me she couldn't confirm the exact address of the person who made the purchase. She told me it wasn't from Massachusetts. She was able to tell me his first name but didn't know if the credit card had the same name, except that it was from out of state. Could this person be using stolen credit cards? I wondered.

Mr. Italian Catfish professed his love to me without ever meeting me, which was another gigantic red flag. However, I, too, had fallen for his story and for this person he had created for me, real or fake. He had successfully sold it to me, and I was waiting for him to call me when he got to Larnaca with some crazy story about being mugged and requesting that I wire him some cash. But that never happened. Or should I say: it hadn't yet.

He kept talking about our future as if it was going to happen. My brain turned to soup because even though this whole thing screamed deception, I held on to the question, "What if it's not?" What if this man truly was legitimate, and I could be throwing away something extraordinary because of what happened in my past? What was the end game for sending me all these gifts and wanting to spoil me? I had yet to find out the answer. Maybe it was in a message in a bottle lost in the Mediterranean Sea, and there was no way I could decode it now. Patience was not one of my virtues, and neither was twiddling my thumbs.

I went to Rhode Island to see Gabby's new office. She was still super happy in her relationship. I told him about Bruno. I also told her I had plenty of reasons to doubt this, but applying logic and past experiences to present ones was always a double-edged sword.

We reminisced about my surrendering to God and the Angels, and we laughed about getting all those not-to-par, short-lived experiences. Gabby told me that I was still trying to control things too much when I surrendered to the heavens because I qualified it and put a condition that if it wasn't the right guy, for things not to last too long, and that was precisely what I had gotten. So, I had taken that back. I had another conversation with God and the Angels and removed the condition. I truly surrendered and asked for the right person for me to show up. Period. No limitations. No conditions. There was no need for me to try and control things any longer. None of that had worked.

When I burned the list that Larry had tainted a few months before, I might have unleashed the right energy to bring me the right person. When

I burned that piece of paper, its energy and content transformed in the ether. I still wanted all that, and now it was no longer up to me.

Gabby and I understood how powerful manifestation could be.

CHAPTER 81

CYPRUS BOUND

My Italian catfish, Bruno, had been in Cyprus for a month. How did I know this? Well, I didn't. Not for sure. I had become such a cynical human when it came to people being honest with me because I had caught some really nasty catfish.

I even contemplated calling Nev and Max from MTV's show Catfish to help me catch an international catfish. They had done it before when they followed someone's trail to the United Kingdom. Those two taught me so much, and I was grateful to them. I learned to search for an image online using Google Images, look up phone numbers on Spokeo and other search sites, and identify some classic catfish MOs. I might have graduated from Catfish University with a PhD in Catfish Investigation and Unveiling, but it hadn't been smooth sailing the whole time.

However, something stopped me from emailing the show. I questioned Bruno about Jose from California, and he told me his credit card had been stolen three years before and that his information was kept private. I had never heard of this. He said he had a Master's in Information Technology. I couldn't compete with that. I brushed it aside even though it was another major red flag. I needed to trust my intuition.

I brushed all this aside because Bruno told me that apart from the gifts he sent me, he wanted to get some clothing and shoes for himself and wanted me to receive those packages, as he was not home. It wouldn't be wise to leave a bunch of packages on his front doorstep for over a month.

I came home one day, and six packages of miscellaneous sizes were on my front steps. I called him flabbergasted and asked him if he had a shopping addiction. He laughed and said this was all the stuff he was buying for the coming winter, even work boots.

Now, it would make no sense for a catfish to send me packages of men's clothes to my house. He told me he would have all this by the time he got home from Cyprus. There was one more thing I expected from a catfish shortly after he arrived in Cyprus: a phone call about being mugged and needing some money wired.

However, Bruno sent me more gifts and talked to me on the phone for hours about our future together. As the eternal hopeful I was, I realized the impossible had happened. I had bought his story. Fully. I have fallen for someone I had not met in person. With all my fears and doubts about him being a catfish, I was nit-picking at every possible detail; I allowed myself to ride this out. I chose to stay positive and not give fuel to the red flags. The Jokester wore a rather alarming face.

Bruno talked about merging our lives as we both wanted the same things out of life. He loved traveling. He also wanted to have a house by or near the beach. He didn't care where we lived as long as we had a swimming pool. He wanted children and wanted to start as soon as possible. His parents had passed, and I knew my family would become his family. He was smart and kind. He wanted to make me the priority. He wanted to spoil me. He was funny, even with an accent, and I never thought I would end up with an equally strong-tempered Southern European, let alone an Italian man!

The stars had aligned. Finally. Each minute that went by, I knew in my heart that the Universe had brought Bruno to me because, despite the stream of catfish and other men who were not up to par during the past four years, the cosmos arranged things to bring him to me.

As I reminisced about the list I had written down of the perfect man for me, Bruno was everything on that list. There was not one iota missing. He had been designed for that list. The divine was at work, and I could not deny that fact. Ms. Diva wore bright pink lipstick and matching heels. She had the sexiest bra and panty set she could find, and she was wearing a white lace nightie from Nordstrom that arrived in the mail and fit perfectly. Her eyes were bright and shiny, and she couldn't contain the giddiness in her little heart.

A bathed, shaved, and nice-smelling Jokester sat at my desk, sporting a grin on his face, and was typing away. He seemed finally at peace and knew my story had unfolded like a beautifully wrapped present with a giant red bow on top. I could not have predicted my happy beginning would start after a four-year obstacle course.

Chapter 82
CYPRUS DISASTER

My cynicism had no frontiers. I had been told time and time again that I had trust issues, and it became true. I didn't set out to have those. I didn't want to have those and lose faith in people, but part of me had. It hadn't been more apparent than now. Men had told me this repeatedly.

Throughout this online dating process, I thought I would quickly find a gentleman who would perhaps sweep me off my feet. I secretly wished no one had told me about fairytales and happy endings as a young girl. All of those set you up for failure with very high expectations and with standards of human decency one would hope to get from another human being. The reality was harsh. Not everyone was decent, and not everyone spoke the truth. I should have never even read one romance novel, but I had read many throughout my teenage years.

The Italian catfish I had fallen in love with gave me the news that he had been mugged in Cyprus by four men in hoodies, his wallet stolen, one of them punched him in the face, and another one even stabbed his leg. He called me from the hospital, where he got stitches, and I was only able to get the full story later in the day. My heart dropped in fear and powerlessness. Fear for his safety and fear for my belief system. Powerlessness because I was unable to help and powerlessness of this hope paralysis spell I was under. Ms. Diva and the Jokester were reclining on my double couch and eating popcorn.

When I woke up from a disturbed sleep the following day, I wondered if this was all real. I obsessively clicked on Google and searched for romance scams in Cyprus. I found similar stories, and I knew what the end game was: money.

And guess what? I fell for it. Naturally, my Italian Catfish's credit card, which was in his wallet, was stolen along with the 10,000 euros he was carrying to buy materials for his contract job. Why anyone would have that amount of money on his person was beyond me, and part of me thought he was begging to be mugged. The other part of me felt that if this happened, I would be the most heartless person on the face of this earth and have no compassion whatsoever. And this was all due to my trust issues.

Ms. Trust Issues here did what she was asked and wired money to Cyprus via MoneyGram to the Hotel Manager, and I was still not even sure that was the hotel manager. If I had asked any of my friends, they would have all done a massive intervention and had me shackled and thrown into a mental institution for some severe mental disorder. It was only money, after all. I didn't even tell anyone the details of Bruno's story because I felt ashamed.

I beat myself up for all this silly behavior, and Mr. Italian Catfish kept dangling the bait at the end of the fishing pole, which was his return home to Boston and me. I was either the stupidest person on the face of this earth, the most gullible, or the most hopeful despite all the odds of my online dating adventures.

I told myself that all would be revealed in the next five days. Because that was the timeline I was looking at. I took a nice deep breath, looked around at the yellow and orange leaves of a perfect New England Fall day outside, and prayed.

Chapter 83

FISHING FOR GOLD

The following five days had come and gone. Bruno's project was completed, but the company he worked for had to send a supervisor to inspect the whole thing.

I felt divided. Part of me still doubted the validity of everything I was being told, while the other part was ready for this person to come into my life IRL (in real life). At the end of the day, this was what it was all about. A new lease on my romantic life needed to materialize.

I never expected to gain a male best friend from all this. I had never really had that experience with a male counterpart. In a way, talking to someone on the phone for at least an hour a day had been very positive. The duration varied as he was seven hours ahead in Cyprus. I could not even believe all this, and I did not expect to laugh so much with a man. I laughed a ton with my girlfriends and was proud of my friendships with my tribe of soul sisters. I never imagined I could add a man to that same type of energy along with a romantic companion. I guess I had never been lucky enough to have that before.

The countdown was on, and in one more day, Mr. Italian Catfish would land in Boston. Did I mention he was Sicilian? He might be just as feisty and stubborn as me. I guess I should stop calling him that. If he only knew.

He knew I had doubts and suspicions about him being a catfish, and I had given him a long list of why I had this opinion. Whenever I brought anything up, he got furious and didn't understand why I didn't trust him. Naturally, I did not explain to him that I had an entire manuscript illustrating the countless reasons why. I didn't think I needed to share that information, which laid the foundation for my trust issues because I did not want to scare him away. It could be intimidating enough to deal with my tribe interrogating him.

I pictured Ms. Diva and the Jokester running from room to room, monitoring the interrogations, where each of my friends made sure Bruno was good enough for me. That might be the concept of hell personified for a guy who had just started dating me. The Jokester wore a business suit and transformed. I wouldn't have recognized him if I didn't know it was him. He looked like someone who took care of himself.

Wearing a fancy black jumpsuit, leopard print heels, perfect hair, make-up, and nails, Ms. Diva went from room to room and checked her phone for engagement rings with lots of diamonds. I saw a smirk from the corner of her bright red lips, and her eyes glittered like stars in a perfect night sky.

Two friends would ask Bruno, "Do you know what you are getting?"

He'd look at me, not understanding what they meant by that question. I'd tell him, "They mean if you know you are getting a precious and priceless treasure as your life partner." He would be the only one confused by all this and probably wondering if he'd be signing his life away. This was all in my hypothetical mind because my reality was different now.

The problem with this whole situation—because things could never be easy—was that the countdown kept getting postponed for various reasons. My heart was so sure about him that I was blind to my cynical mind and every obstacle that seemed to occur, which Bruno always had the perfect and ready-made explanation for generating conflict in my core. I accused him of being a scammer and told him countless times that I was not sending money to MoneyGram to pay his hotel bills.

But there came a point where the well dried up. My cash supply ran out, and I was not borrowing money or touching my credit cards, let alone my bank accounts. So, I told Bruno that I was not sending another dime. He told me that he didn't want me to. He planned to sell his laptop and wire me back part of the money he owed me.

At this point, I was a few days away from leaving for Europe to visit family. He told me it made much more sense for him to meet me in Europe as he was already there. I was highly skeptical and told him he would have to do this alone. I informed him I was not changing my flight or trip plans. I was spending time with family and had some work commitments scheduled. The suspense continued.

Both the Jokester and Ms. Diva broke out in hives.

CHAPTER 84

RED FLAGS

Of course, Bruno didn't meet me in Europe. Something about his project again. With him being mugged, he made some mistakes, and the company he contracted with was not happy. He had to stay behind to do damage control.

I felt deflated like a balloon losing some air and then getting slightly refilled. It was the flicker of hope in me which never died. He dangled plans for our future like bait, and I wanted to believe him so much.

Our daily phone calls, usually full of laughter, turned into monstrous arguments, with me accusing him of lying to me and making promises he could not keep. If only he were real. If only he would show up, we could begin our lives together.

I asked the skies above what the meaning of all this was. What was I supposed to learn? Or was I supposed to finally abandon hope that the great love of books and movies was not my fate and was just for others?

Our fights escalated out of my frustration and patience dwindling, and they showed a side of me I didn't like. As a self-defense mechanism, I used words like daggers—verbal abuse at its most fundamental core. I didn't like that I was doing this. I was frustrated and disappointed. Three months of this had come and gone, and my patience faltered. My sleep turned into choppy ocean waves, and I was emotionally drained during the day. I could not continue like this. I needed to cut the cord. It was not healthy for my state of mind, and I knew that despite time being a healer of all things, my heart was full of scars. What was the lesson? What did I need to extrapolate from this? Was this me being stubborn because I wanted Bruno to be real so badly that I ignored all the red flags? Was this wishful thinking or plain denial?

I felt alone, like I was the only one fighting this battle. Ms. Diva and the Jokester were done. They were also in disbelief that I kept putting myself in these hopeless situations or that these situations and people had a strange way of finding me.

I knew I was learning a lot about myself. I knew this would be a deep dive into my beliefs and behavior. I was at a loss as to why. I had surrendered to the powers above but still didn't get it.

Maybe this was all a huge lesson in letting go, and I found myself asking what I was letting go of. Was it me? Was I letting go of hope and accepting that it was not my fate to have the life partner I longed for? I was left with a hollow inside and more questions than answers, and I thought age and time were supposed to bring wisdom. The jury was out. Reality had become warped with not only my life but the state of society in general. The mime-like disbelief that maybe the world was changing around me, and I was not.

If this was a lesson in patience, I passed it. If this was a message that I was not supposed to have the life partner I yearned for, then I guess I didn't want to accept that lesson. Accepting it meant that I admitted defeat. I was not okay with that.

The wireless connection was faulty. Before I showered, I'd bring my tiny little iPod to the bathroom, where I had a wireless speaker. Sometimes, when I turned on the speaker, the iPod didn't connect. The Bluetooth connection was turned on on both devices, but for some reason, the connection wouldn't happen in Bluetooth land. Maybe that's what I was. I was the iPod looking to connect with a speaker, and the connection was faulty. It had been defective for the past five years, and I didn't know when it would be fixed.

It was time for me to reboot the system once more, and instead of trying to find a new connection, I had to clear my head, let my heart heal again, and enjoy the upcoming holidays. The following year was approaching, and I had to decide about single motherhood. Next year was going to be different. The love of my life was yet to come, and I felt it was unconventional. After all, there was nothing conventional about me, the Jokester, or Ms. Diva. The Jokester had gone from a drunken slob to a healthy, decent being. But my immediate future might not be as glamorous as Ms. Diva wished. I didn't think it involved sexy lingerie, sequence, or leopard print high heels. She might be looking at diapers and sleepless nights instead.

CHAPTER 85
DISTRACTION

I decided I needed a distraction to get my mind off the Bruno debacle and returned to Plenty of Sharks. The ocean landscape hadn't changed much. I always saw the usual suspects, familiar faces, year after year. I recognized that those people also saw my face year after year and probably thought the same, 'Oh, there she is. Still single. Still on the prowl.'

It was very depressing. I got a lot of messages, and most went unanswered for the usual reasons: too short, obviously not reading my profile, and the relationship intent being mismatched, couldn't spell, write a generic long email, or forward propositions of having drinks at their place before even setting eyes on each other. None of these deserved a reply. Ms. Diva and the Jokester snorted at the same time.

FootballCarl started emailing me. I checked out his profile, and he seemed normal. He was not that tall but not bad to look at. He had a bachelor's degree and claimed to be in the car insurance business. Okay, that was employment.

He asked me what I was looking for. I told him: a relationship. He concurred. He asked me out. We discussed potential dates on the calendar and settled on Wednesday night before I left for Europe for Christmas. It was only a drink, and I needed the distraction.

He picked a Mexican restaurant about twenty minutes away from me. Not bad at all. He asked for my number through the site at the last minute, and I obliged. I also asked for his but never got a reply and brushed it off as a 'he must be driving' excuse. I got a no-caller ID call and did not answer. Probably telemarketer.

I backed into my parking spot in a plaza where the Mexican restaurant was. After I locked my car, I noticed two cars from where I parked, there was a man on the phone in a dark Toyota sedan. I quickly dismissed it as I did not recognize him from the photos.

FootballCarl had instructed me to meet him at the bar, so I walked in about four minutes late, headed to the bar area, and immediately realized I was the first one there. Two women were chatting in a corner, and two others were at the other end of the bar. I sat about two seats from the corner, even if my back was to the door, and casually glanced over every so often.

I ordered a glass of wine and looked at my phone, wondering if I was being stood up. A few minutes later, the man who had been in the Toyota walked in, still talking on the phone, and sat a few seats perpendicular to me. I stared at my phone and glanced at the three TVs playing different college basketball games.

I noticed the man had a dark complexion and a white discoloration around his left eye and some parts of his face and neck. He wore an oversized, ill-fitting coat. He asked me what kind of phone I had and then introduced himself as Charlie after some small talk. I was polite but not overly talkative, but I noticed him treating our interaction as a date. "Do you like sports? Do you like football? What do you like to do for fun?"

Something in the back of my mind had me on alert. He never once asked me if I was waiting for anyone. And I got the feeling he knew no one was showing up. I thought of the username FootballCarl. Carl was close to Charlie. I already told Charlie I was not into sports. Still, he focused the conversation on football, how he went to Florida in the summer to see the New England Patriots play the Miami Dolphins, and even showed me pictures of him tailgating with his friends. I didn't care about football and even less about his friends. He told me he was thirty-seven years old—online FootballCarl was listed as thirty-five and 5'10—Charlie was about 5'10. He told me he was a security firm supervisor and dreamed of becoming a State Trooper. That he was studying to get into a program. For some reason, I did not picture him in law enforcement at all, but who was I to judge?

I realized after a while that he probably was FootballCarl, and the fact that I had this weird feeling made me want to bolt. I asked the bartender for the check and paid with my debit card. Charlie did the same. He had two beers while he was there. Then, before I left, he told me he enjoyed talking to me and would love to hang out, and he asked for my number. I tried to decline politely. I told him I must go as I traveled the next day, and he probably didn't like that answer. After all, I rejected him. I hated doing that, but I felt lied to. Again. What if I was wrong? I still didn't want him to have my number. And he probably already had it through the website.

Within an hour, I was home.

My cell phone rang the following morning shortly after 7 a.m.—no caller ID. I was not very alert but already awake, and against my better judgment and thinking it could be an international call, I picked up. It was a male voice I didn't recognize.

"Did you remember to put on your perfume this morning?"

I think this was a very clever telemarketing strategy, and I laughed it off.

"Who is this?" I murmured, half asleep.

And a list of similarly weird questions ensued.

"Who is this? Is this a robot?"

"Did you know that you are a snobby c^*t?"

I hung up. I was in shock. It all clicked and confirmed my suspicions. Charlie was FootballCarl, and I rejected him, so this anonymous call was his way of insulting me. I had never been called such a profane name in my life. I felt my heart jump out of my chest. I'm not sure if it was adrenaline or anxiety, but whatever it was, I didn't like it.

CHAPTER 86
CHRISTMAS BREAK

I admitted that the call shook me up, but I needed to get ready. I had some last-minute computer work but decided to start packing first. I heard some noise outside. The guy who was supposed to install a pair of iron railings had arrived almost a month late. I sighed. Well, at least that work would be done before I left.

I went out to quickly say hello and told him to ring the bell once he was done so I could give him a check.

He did just that about an hour later. He left, and I went back to my office to finish work. When I was done, I decided to take a photo of the new railings.

I opened my side door, the one I usually used, and went to take a photo of the railings installed at the other entrance. When I walked back, I glanced at my car in the driveway, and my heart stopped. I noticed a flat tire, but when I looked closely, the other tire was flat too. I got closer: all four tires had been slashed, and the sharp object was also used to carve the entire left side of the car. It had been brutally vandalized on the day that I was flying out.

I went back inside the house and called 911. For some reason, it was not going through. I used my home phone to do it and was finally successful.

Crying, I told the dispatcher what happened, and he told me they'd send an officer right over.

I waited, dumbfounded.

The officer arrived. Of course, he was super good-looking and naturally had a wedding band on his left ring finger. I cried as he inspected the car.

He was appalled at the amount of damage and said he had never seen anything like it in his twenty years of service. He asked me if I had any road rage episodes to warrant such vindictive action. I told him, "No, of course not."

"Has anything out of the ordinary happened recently?"

The previous evening's episode and the anonymous phone call popped into my mind. I had to tell him. Afterward, he asked for my written statement. We walked into my house, and I invited him to sit at my dining room table, which he politely declined due to his weapon and accessories around his waist. My cat Rocky approached the officer, looked up at him, and meowed for what seemed to be the whole time he stood there. I wrote down what I could remember. I managed to halt my tears but was trying to understand what I was writing. I had limited space, and he urged me to disclose everything I had told him.

It might have taken twenty minutes. My concept of time had left the building. All I knew was that I needed to finish packing. I had packed all the Christmas gifts but none of my clothes. Even if I only stayed for four days, I still needed a change of clothes, underwear, socks, and toiletries.

The officer gave me his email address, scribbled on a piece of paper, and apologized for not having any business cards on him. I confessed I was not expecting a colossal investigation since no witnesses existed. He asked me to follow up with the railing guy in case he saw something. Then he left. The reason why I was not counting on much follow-up was that I had had a break-in a couple of years earlier, and even though the police allegedly caught the guys and told me I was going to be called to court and could have sued for restitution, it never materialized.

The rest of the day was spent multi-tasking between packing, calling the insurance company to file a claim, and figuring out my next steps. One of my friends was picking me up to take me to the airport, and I needed to be ready. Even though my emotions were frazzled, I panicked, thinking I would forget something important. I just needed to remember my passport.

Miraculously, I did not forget anything, and because I was traveling business class, I went to the Air France lounge at the airport and started drinking. I had doused myself in essential oils, a liquid calm of sorts, and now I needed alcohol. I felt like the whole world was against me in many ways, and I did not feel deserving of all the calamity. I drank a small red wine and then made myself a Bloody Mary. Yes, the Air France lounge had all of that, and if I had more time, I would have made more. No matter. I would ask for more wine on board. The Jokester approved of my binging. The occasion called for it, after all.

I arrived in Europe the following day after a two-hour layover in the Azores Islands, and a few hours later, I noticed a voicemail from the police officer who had been at my house. Ms. Diva's eyebrow lifted with a jolt of excitement. I called the station through WI-FI, but he was not there. He eventually called me from the road and told me he wanted to update me. He was planning on going to the Mexican restaurant. I was pleasantly surprised that he was following up. He also asked me to get in touch with the railing guy. I called and emailed the guy, who eventually called me back.

I was appalled to find out that the iron railing guy did notice one flat tire in my car when he arrived. When he left, he saw all four tires were down. I asked him why he didn't tell me. He replied that he was focused on his work and assumed I knew. An ocean away, I wanted to strangle this guy. However, with this new information, it dawned on me that the crime might have happened much earlier than I thought. Maybe Charlie followed me home. I could not be sure. My head spun a little. I realized after all this time that this whole online dating thing had become dangerous, and even though I was very secure in my own skin, I needed to accept the fact that if I googled my first name with my phone number, my home address popped up and that was a security issue. The officer had told me that little tidbit. The Jokester and Ms. Diva looked for weapons on the internet.

I was a woman living by myself with two cats—it sounded pathetic when I put it that way, but my home was my sacred space. I could not put it at risk, which meant I could not use my actual phone number. If I were to continue this journey, I needed to devise an alternate solution where I got a secondary number or something similar.

I researched alternatives and realized many apps enabled me to get a duplicate number not associated with my name or address. They were free to download, and I could use my cell phone—the app allowed you to obtain a local phone number, which you could use to text and make phone calls through your current cell phone while using the app, and the other person would only see that secondary number. If one used it for the long haul, a small monthly fee could be associated with it, but in my mind, it could be worth it.

I secretly wished I had found this a few years earlier. It would have avoided this whole vandalism episode.

That same afternoon, the day before Christmas Eve, the police officer called me again. "Too bad he is taken," said Ms. Diva while filing her nails. I agreed with her. He had more news, though. He was at the restaurant going through the camera footage. He had pinpointed the time and was trying to identify me and the alleged perpetrator. He was also looking at the credit card receipts from that night. He found mine and Charlie's, except he said that for his, he could only see the last four digits of the credit card number with no name. I later realized that he probably had a prepaid credit card. He was a criminal, after all. This must have not been his first rodeo.

The officer told me he had more news. Charlie had struck again. The night after I was there, the same thing happened to another woman from the same town. In her case, however, the criminal threw a brick at her house, shattering a window. I silently thanked the heavens that my car was the recipient of the violence and not my house. That would have been a pain to get squared away on the day I had to fly overseas.

But he told me it was the same MO, the same username, and the same guy approaching her. He called himself Charlie, also drank two beers, and struck up a conversation. Practically identical to my story. I forgot to ask him if she also received an anonymous phone call, but I hoped to touch base with him once I got back to the States and find out then.

I only told a handful of people about what happened, and I forgot which one told me, "I thought you were done with your book and didn't need any more content." To which I replied, "I didn't." They suggested, "Maybe a sequel?" My answer was blunt: "Hell NO!"

CHAPTER 87

CRIME AND PUNISHMENT

I found out I was one of at least three victims, and now several police departments were involved, trying to build a solid case to bring this guy in. It was a waiting game, just like the online dating process.

Sometime later, my car vandalism episode appeared on major news outlets and newspapers. One newscaster called it "the online date from hell." I was told I might still have to testify at a future trial when I first wrote about this.

I got close to Kerry, the woman with the same story as me, who lived not even a mile away. In her case, Charlie—yes, that was a variation of Carlos and not Charles—had thrown a brick through her living room window. The State was charging him with stalking, property, and vehicular damage; between the three of us, there were five more cases, possibly more, popping up left and right due to the media coverage.

Anne, our victim advocate, called me after the arraignment and told me that he had been released with a GPS monitoring device, with instructions to stay away from our towns. She also told me to be vigilant. I was out and about and did not have the habit of checking my surroundings or observing who was watching me. I had not anticipated that fear would crawl back into my life, and I noticed that my breathing became shallow because of her phone call. My muscles tensed, and reality hit me like a silent alarm.

I had to go to the police station to pick him out from a photo lineup for identification purposes, and then I was formally interviewed by a detective. The police filmed and recorded my interviews. I didn't feel in control of my story, and this was not how I wanted to end my online dating journey.

More information was being released to the media. I discovered that Charlie was a Special Police Officer at some point but had been fired for similar allegations, and his license to carry revoked. So, his story that he was going to try out for the State Police might have been bogus due to his history or his wishful thinking.

To think that I'd have to testify at a trial was not really what I wanted, but I would if it came to that. Thinking of myself as a victim gave me a feeling of unease. I felt vulnerable and not in control of my own safety. Those were fundamental human rights: to feel safe. To think that online dating could be this dangerous and that I was very lucky was mindboggling, but I also knew that most people would not have to go through anything like this.

My hope for love had not diminished, and I still believed online dating could be good. As I had countless times, one only needed to be extremely savvy and never doubt the red flags. It would have saved me a ton of heartache, aggravation, and money.

Seven years later, the trial got rescheduled three times within six months, forcing me to put my life and travels on hold. By then, I had moved from Massachusetts to Florida, where I had lived for five years.

Anne and Helen, the Assistant District Attorney, told us we must prep for trial. I had to reacquaint myself with the police report and my initial statement. The prosecutor asked me to watch my interview at the police station several times. The idea was to refresh my memory.

I had forgotten I had even given an interview. As I was prepping, I began having insomnia. I was expected to fly up and had yet to learn how long this would last. Charlie remained in control, even seven years later. The court system enabled him. The victims were the last priority. Charlie's rights and choices trumped everything else. We weren't even a thought in judges' minds whenever they allowed his delaying tactics with firing lawyers, reneging on a plea deal, suppressing evidence, making outlandish motions, his lawyer having the flu, and every excuse under the sun. And the various judges mostly accommodated his shenanigans. Never a fleeting thought about how any of it would affect our lives.

In the weeks before the trial, anxiety crept in. I couldn't think of anything else. Kerry and I texted and called each other to find solace and mentally prepare for what would come. We were angry and appalled that we still had no rights. The third victim that we never got to meet would fly up as well for trial. We had no idea how she had fared. All we knew was that she now had a baby. I hoped she wasn't alone and someone could care for her child during her absence.

As victims, we have no choice but to be present. Even though the torture and trauma are continuous, the law would come after us if we didn't participate. After all, we weren't the ones suing him; the State was.

In the years that passed, we would hear from Anne periodically in our three-way group text, informing us of motions, pre-trials, etc. Every time a text buzzed through, my heart jolted uncomfortably. It was never good news.

As there had been a fourth victim around the same time as us but in a different county, in that case, Charlie pled guilty quickly. Between being deemed a danger to the community and his plea deal with that case, he ended up getting shy of two and a half years of time served.

We couldn't believe it had been seven years. Our case had still not been resolved. And we knew there would be a twist to it every time. Charlie held the reins all along, just like he liked it—power over women. Ms. Diva and the Jokester didn't like it when someone else was in control, plus both were hardcore feminists. They wanted Charlie to rot in hell, perhaps torture him slowly, but the truth was that he had been living his best life, free, for the past five years. We suspected he was still practicing his hate of women. He just hadn't gotten caught.

On the day of the trial, I flew up to Massachusetts for nothing, which enraged me further against the justice system. Charlie had decided to plead guilty again. The court and the defendant heard my wrath and opinions when I read my impact statement. The third victim got to stay home and read hers via Zoom. As a result of his plea deal, Charlie or Carlos got two and half years behind bars, where time was considered served, five years' probation, and restitution. If the crime had been committed at the same time as the others from a different county in Massachusetts, you could double-dip on time served, so he didn't have to spend any more time in prison. It was a slap on the wrist, in my opinion.

And to make matters worse, we would have to be reminded every single month about this when we got a miserly amount of restitution in the mail that would take him to pay in full in the next three years. The payments didn't come on time and sometimes took two or three months. Charlie was still in control. And the victims would continue to be haunted. Justice hadn't been served. Out of the corner of my eye, I saw Ms. Diva clean her Glock, and the Jokester methodically sharpened his hunting knife.

CHAPTER 88

CATCHING THE ONE

I could have given up many times, even with this latest incident. Some might think it was irresponsible even to consider getting out there again after this. I could not live in fear or allow it to rule my life. I still believed that online dating could work. I never thought I would be subjected to so much havoc in the process. Other friends had great luck with it, and despite all the craziness, the lies, the scams, the broken hearts, and the disappointments, I never lost hope. That was the greatest lesson I discovered. Maybe it was my stubbornness—Ms. Diva lifted her left eyebrow an inch or two, and the Jokester forgot he was now respectable but made a loud snorting noise. Or maybe it was my inner little girl's wish that I, too, could have the happy ending I wished for, or perhaps it was blind, wishful, delusional thinking, and I should have known better.

But the bottom line was that I was the eternal hopeful. I still believed that I deserved the amazing man and the amazing relationship. I had so much love to give and was still excited about the future, even if I had no idea what it held for me. I didn't need anyone to complete me. That was not a discovery but an assertion. What I realized throughout my journey was that I was the ultimate catch. The right person for me would be a partner in this ride called life. That's all I ever wanted.

There were some new online dating apps out there. They could be an alternative. I had been talking to Adam on Plenty of Sharks a few weeks before the vandalism incident, but his profile kept disappearing. I saw his picture one night and sent him a message, asking him what had happened to him. He replied that he had dealt with a woman stalker on the site, and she kept finding him, so he constantly deleted his profile. At least he didn't get his property destroyed.

Part of me felt relieved to know that it was not only women who got nutcracker people in the online dating pond. I had always felt good about Adam, so when he asked me out that night, I asked if he was serious about meeting up. He replied, "Yes," and I agreed.

Adam was casual in his attire compared to my typical European fanciness, almost polar opposites. Still, I later realized he was one of the kindest and most laid-back people I had ever met. At 6'3 (almost 6'4), he was good-looking and unaware of it. He had his own computer business and dreamed of moving to a warm place by the beach one day, just like me. He loved to surf. Maybe I could let him surf while I relaxed on a tropical beach.

We took things slowly as he didn't want to rush. He said he didn't want to ruin anything because he liked me so much, so I was cautiously optimistic. I called him "rushaphobic," and we laughed about it.

If a woman were considering online dating, I would never tell her not to go for it. However, I would point out that she could experience a lot through my adventures and learn from them because even though it was never my intent, the learning curve of this journey was exponential for me, not only about this process, but I also learned about myself, and there had been many surprises. Yes, I would do it all over again for those reasons alone. In this priceless unveiling, I never lost hope.

After that one night, Adam would drive nearly an hour and a half to see me, and for the first time, I felt like I was the priority and someone's number one most important person. He was a cat lover, which was a massive bonus for me, and I knew he was a keeper because both my cats fell in love with him, too.

I happily deleted all my apps and accounts after I met him.

Two and half years into the healthiest, easiest, and most enjoyable relationship I had ever had, we did the unthinkable. We put all our stuff into two giant containers, which remained stored in a climate-controlled facility, packed our cars, and drove south toward a warmer climate. We rented a beachfront condo for six months while we house-hunted, then bought a house on Florida's Treasure Coast. A treasure in more ways than one.

The Jokester sobered up and retired. Ms. Diva changed her sequence gowns for skimpy bikinis. She casually picked up the letter I had written my future soulmate years earlier, smirked, and nodded, blissfully satisfied.

Over seven years have passed, and it seems Adam and I have been together forever. We laugh daily and enjoy each other's company, and I couldn't ask for anything more.

Life is an adventure, and I finally found my perfect catch.

ACKNOWLEDGMENTS

I want to thank two very special groups: my Nomad Writers, who have kept me writing weekly for the past two decades, and the Florida Writers Association's Treasure Coast Writers Group, whose members have been listening and critiquing "Catching the One" for the past three years. I am grateful to Sofia Cruz Diniz for her feedback on my first draft and to Lisa Glass for helping me restructure the ending, which I must have rewritten three or four times. Thank you to Lisa Djahed for helping me tweak the back cover content. Finally, I would like to extend a heartfelt thanks to the brilliant Karen Howard for her precious feedback.

ALSO BY
Mónica Fernandes

"Freefall — Poems, Essays and Stories"

Get "Freefall" here. https://amzn.to/4cBwFEd
Please leave your reviews for my books anywhere you can think of.
Thank you so much!

Buy on Amazon

www.monicawriter.com

 **@monicawriter**

facebook.com/MonicaWriter

ABOUT THE AUTHOR

Raised in Lisbon, Portugal, Mónica Fernandes discovered her passion for writing at the age of nine. Her literary journey spans poetry, prose, fiction, and non-fiction. She holds a master's degree in marketing communications from Emerson College. Mónica founded the Nomad Writers Group in 2004 and is an active member of the Florida Writers Association's Treasure Coast Writers Group.

Mónica has won multiple poetry awards, has been featured at the Massachusetts Poetry Festival, was first published in the anthology "Finding Water: Poems and Stories," and is the author of "Freefall: Poems, Essays and Stories." She splits her work as a marketing consultant and life transition coach, empowering women post-divorce. As a passionate animal advocate and cat mom, Mónica serves on the board of directors of the local Humane Society. Residing on the Treasure Coast in South Florida, she indulges in her love for chocolate and enjoys cooking savory dishes for her loved ones. She is currently working on her second literary collection, a poetry book, and two novels.

www.ingramcontent.com/pod-product-compliance
Lightning Source LLC
Chambersburg PA
CBHW060855120626
46553CB00001B/98